CopTales 2000

Compiled and edited by
Liz Martínez DeFranco
Marilyn Olsen
Keith Bettinger

Copyright © 2000 by .38 Special Press
This book may not be reproduced or transmitted
in any form without permission in writing from the publisher.
Copyrights of the individual stories in CopTales 2000
reside with the individual authors

.38 Special Press
6251 Winthrop Avenue, Suite 2
Indianapolis, IN 46220
(317) 254-1221

Printed in the United States of America

Cover designed by Lucas Patterson

Library of Congress Catalog Card Number: 99-75884

DEDICATION

To all police writers, famous and not yet famous and to
the Police Writers Club that brought us all together.

Acknowledgements

A special acknowledgement to Ernie Dorling who keeps the books
and keeps us all on schedule, to Roger Fulton who got us together
in the first place and to George Cockburn for his encouragement and backing.

INTRODUCTION
By Liz Martínez DeFranco

There's no denying that cops all have great stories. Regardless of what department they work for or at what level, all law enforcement officers tell terrific tales. When I was a child, my parents had a friend who was an FBI agent. I always enjoyed listening to his stories. Partly because of his influence, I decided I wanted to become a police officer. I majored in criminal justice and took the tests for several departments, only to turn down the offers at the last minute.

It wasn't until I gave up my last chance to become a cop that I finally figured out why I was so resistant, even though the attraction to police work was strong. Simply put, I'm lazy. In my lifelong quest for the easy way, I don't really want to put in the work on the street to get to the goodies. I want to skip right to the rewards – which for me are the stories.

For a time I worked inside a jail, recognizing that it's much more pleasant to deal with the bad guys once someone else has taken the time to chase them down and lock them up. I managed to drag myself out on the street in an NYPD Auxiliary Police Officer's uniform long enough to figure out that unless the department was willing to provide the auxiliaries with adequate training and support, I was not going to stand out there as a target for criminals.

Today I satisfy my desire to be involved in police work by writing about law enforcement and cops. I have no interest in getting up early, putting myself in danger or taking orders on a regular basis. But I have the utmost respect and appreciation for those who put themselves on the line each day and do those things without complaint. I recognize that although most of them are unsung, they are heroes. They regularly take risks that the rest of us would never dream of in order to protect our wellbeing and our property. In the process, they come across a cross-section of society: some nice people, some scum of the earth types. But throughout it all, they do the job that they swore to do. And in doing that, they live the stories that the rest of us only read about.

I was thrilled to have the opportunity to read everything that the Police Writers Club members penned for this anthology. Some are true accounts of life on the street, some are lighthearted looks at crime, others are sheer fantasy – but all of them are genuine cop tales. Among the writers are current and former police officers whose names you will find on jackets in any bookstore. Paul Bishop, Ed Dee and Jim DeFilippi all took time away from their other duties as novelists to write stories for this anthology. Writers whose names you will see on book covers in the near future – Ernie Dorling, Gina Gallo, Laurick Ingram and Penny James – fell in love with the idea of a collection of police tales and sat down at their keyboards to produce short stories for this collection. Other extremely talented writers, whose work is celebrated in the police community, also made tremendous contributions including Stormy Barton Apgar, Philip Bulone, Robert Cohen, Will Cordes, Marlene Loos, Charles Padias, Louis Savelli and Robert Shaw.

Among the other award recipients whose work is showcased here, almost one-third of the stories in this book – were winners of the Police Writers Club's annual non-fiction and fiction writing contests. These include those by William Bell, Keith Bettinger, John Eller, Arthur James Farrar, Marilyn Olsen, Pamelia Stratton, Joseph Truncale and James Weiss.

Dan Mahoney, who as a rule doesn't write short stories, tore himself away from his latest novel-in-progress long enough to provide this volume with a foreword.

Credit must be given to the founder of the Police Writers Club, Roger Fulton, who conceived of the idea of the organization, then plunged an incredible amount of time, effort and financial support into it to ensure its success. Although Roger is prolific, working through the night on books and articles that appear in all the best law enforcement publications, he did manage to sit down at his keyboard long enough to share a segment of his career with us through his non-fiction short story Special Delivery.

The stories in this collection are as diverse as the writers themselves. The authors include current, former, retired and auxiliary city, county, state and military police; federal investigators, transit police; chiefs of police; customs inspectors; LEOs who have held the ranks of sergeant, lieutenant, captain and above; law enforcement instructors, professional LE writers and editors; and at least one arson photographer.

Putting together this volume has been an unprecedented opportunity to immerse myself in the best part of police work: cop tales. I hope that you have as much fun reading them as I did.

Liz Martínez DeFranco

FOREWORD
By Dan Mahoney

The stories contained in this anthology don't describe the police work that grabs headlines. There are no diabolical murderers, greedy kidnappers, cruel rapists, clever robbers nor fanatical terrorists running amok through these pages. Also absent are the savvy wise cracking detectives who somehow succeed in fighting the system and their corrupt bosses as they match wits and trade shots with the latest absolute menace to society and civilization as we know it. If those types of cops and villains are the desired fare, the reader is advised to pass on this book and pick through the entertaining pulp police fiction lining the shelves in any airport bookstore.

However, if the reader has already had enough of that for the moment and would enjoy sharing the lives, humor, attitudes and perceptions of ordinary, real-life cops and detectives as they perform their day-to-day duties to the best of their abilities, this is a good book to read. The majority of the short stories within are by cops who candidly describe the trials and tribulations of their job, the daily grind without meaningful end in sight. As part of their occupation, some of them were condemned to witness the dark side of human nature and handle crimes of emotion that senselessly damaged or destroyed lives and they write about the experience. It will become apparent to the reader that these crimes also profoundly affected the lives of the officers, people trained and paid to always think clearly, supposedly immune to emotion. The heroes of these stories – sometimes the writer and sometimes not – aren't pulp cops lacking empathy and routine emotions. They're real, quite ordinary people-the guy or gal next door with that cushy civil-service job who gets paid every two weeks, no matter what and never seems to have a problem in the world.

Other stories, also by cops, are light tales of minor crimes told with understated, tongue-in-cheek humor of the type that only cops seem capable of mastering. Readers of police fiction will instantly get the point, but those new to the genre may have to read the piece again to get the giggle and wonder how it was missed the first time.

Also inside are cop tales by civilians, but these writers are obviously perceptive people with an eye for detail. They also possess the ability to see the world as cops see it, and describe the unusual or the absurd and make the circumstances seem routine and natural. Their stories show that these writers know, love, respect and maybe even understand cops and their peculiar ways.

They successfully walk the walk and talk the talk throughout their pieces, sometimes getting closer to what's real than a few well-paid fakers who occasionally pop up on police fiction best seller lists.

Learn, understand and have fun reading.

CONTENTS

 POLICE WRITERS CLUB WRITING CONTEST AWARD WINNERS

1997 NONFICTION

Grown Up Kids in Hot Cars	Marilyn Olsen	12
Murder at Foxcatcher Mansion	John Eller	15
Knight of the Living Dead	William Bell	20

1997 FICTION

Tom Threepersons & the Cudahay Ranch	William Bell	22
The Hardest Thing He Would Ever Have to Do	Marilyn Olsen	25
The Final Assignment	Joseph Truncale	27

1998 NONFICTION

Unknown Warrior Contemplation	Pamelia Stratton	30
Harvest Time for the ISP	Marilyn Olsen	33
JDLR-10-49 One Dead, One Dying	Arthur James Farrar	36
Paid in Full	Keith Bettinger	39
Dispatch to Eternity	John Eller	41

1998 FICTION

Follow the North Wind	Keith Bettinger	44
The First Performance	Pamelia Stratton	47
The Great Church Robbery of Hermannstadt	James Weiss	50

FAMOUS (& SOON TO BE FAMOUS) POLICE WRITERS

COMMENTARY
The Healing Game	Marlene Loos	54
The Last Dirty Word	Gina Gallo	57
But For the Grace	Marlene Loos	60
Where's the Crime?	Ernie Dorling	66

SOUTH OF THE BORDER
The Feast of St. Cecilia	Liz Martínez DeFranco	74

CRIME IN THE CITY
Babes in Gangland	Gina Gallo	80
Vertical Patrol	Gina Gallo	83
Water Tower Hill	Jim DeFilippi	86
Going to Manhattan	Robert Cohen	94
The Spectacle Case	Liz Martínez DeFranco	101

LEARNING THE JOB
Training Ride	Charles Padias	115
Special Delivery	Roger Fulton	125
On the Job	Lou Savelli	130
Lunch Encounter	Robert Shaw	140
Yet Another Crime Foiled	Stormy Barton Apgar	144

LEAVING THE JOB
The Tailman	Ed Dee	149
Blue is the Color of Death	Philip Bulone	154
Iron Will	Will Cordes	157

OFF THE BEATEN PATH
It Wasn't Perjury, It Was Only a Little White Lie	Keith Bettinger	163
Café Midnight	Penny James	166

HUMOR
A Heinous Crime on Staten Island	Keith Bettinger	180

NOVELLAS
The Grinch Who E-Stole Christmas	Laurick Ingram	182
Derringer	Paul Bishop	199

POLICE WRITERS CLUB WRITING CONTEST

AWARD WINNERS

PWC 1997 AWARD WINNER

GROWN UP KIDS IN HOT CARS
First Place, nonfiction, 1997
by Marilyn Olsen

It's a swell day. The road up ahead is clear. The sun sparkles off the metallic purple paint of the hot new Camaro with the Corvette engine under the hood. In a shower of dust and gravel, this speed machine roars off the shoulder, across two lanes of traffic and whips into the left lane. Zero to 65 mph in under 10 seconds. It's a rush every time.

Most drivers notice this car. An elderly lady in a large beige Buick turns, shakes her head and frowns. A middle-aged guy in a light blue Honda Accord smiles wanly, wishing, no doubt, he still had such a fine ride. He wonders who the lucky kid behind the wheel of that road monster might be.

The guy in the Mercedes already knows. His feet hit the brakes, his turn signal flashes. He executes a quick and hopefully inconspicuous dodge in front of the old guy in the '83 Pontiac going exactly 55. He stares straight ahead, intently studying the road. Concentrating on obeying the law.

But it's too late. The lucky kid in the road monster hasn't been a teen-ager for a long time. For more than 15 years, in fact, he's worn the blue uniform of an Indiana State Police officer.

You may own a Mercedes, but you can't fool him.

Without taking his eyes from the road, he flips on the red and blue lights and slips in behind the Mercedes. Brake lights shine in every direction. For a few minutes at least, on one small section of Interstate 65 in Indianapolis, drivers are actually all going 55.

Which, of course, is the point.

According to a recent study conducted by USA Today, nearly one-fourth of the 2.3 million tickets written to speeders on interstates in 1996 were to drivers going faster than 80 mph.

"Those folks are a danger to themselves and everyone else on the road," says Trooper Jeff Kellogg, who drives the snazzy purple Camaro. "Those are the folks we are here to stop."

While some police officers can't wait to get off road patrol, Kellogg couldn't wait to get on.

He made a special effort to get assigned to this duty.

In order to qualify he had to have been on the department for three years, have driven accident-free for 50,000 miles, be certified in the use of radar and vascar, have received above satisfactory personnel evaluations and attended high performance vehicle driving school.

To keep his Camaro, he must keep writing tickets.

That's just fine with him.

"We stop the people who really need it," says Kellogg. "We don't give warnings. We give tickets. We have one of the few opportunities in law enforcement to prevent accidents from happening."

Trooper Kevin Fisher is also a confirmed Camaro cop. Assigned to the program since its inception, Fisher has driven two Mustangs and is on his fourth Camaro. This one is shiny red with a red and gray interior. It gets him no end of grief from his fellow officers. "They refer to it as the 'Pimpmobile,'" he says. "I believe they are simply extremely jealous."

As a veteran of the program, Fisher has all the gadgets. In addition to the traditional radar and vascar, he also has a Dual Stalker radar system and a video camera.

To illustrate their use, Fisher pulls into the middle lane on a busy traffic day on I465 where he cruises at just around 60 in a 55 mph zone.

"Watch this," he says, pointing to the digital display mounted on the steering wheel. The number 74 flashes as a late model sedan flies by in the left lane.

"Gotcha!" says Fisher, as he simultaneously turns on the red and blue lights and the vascar mounted in the console between the seats.

The guy in the sedan can't believe what he's now seeing in his rear view mirror.

Once pulled over, he tries a lame excuse. Fisher politely gives him the veteran police officer's deadpan stare.

In case there's any doubt later, both the conversation and the pursuit have been preserved on videotape. No contest.

Kellogg and Fisher are two of 22 Indiana State Troopers who comprise the state's Camaro detail. Their cars are every color of the metallic paint rainbow and equipped with the latest speed detection equipment.

During most of the year, they are assigned to one of the state's 18 districts where they work singly or in pairs. But up to 10 times a year, depending on the availability of grant funding, they spend a week working together in one area.

It's an understatement to say they make an impact.

"The first day or so, it's no problem to write five or six tickets an hour," says Kellogg. By the fifth day or so, the word is out. Truckers from hundreds of miles around talk about us on their CB radios. Only cars with out-of-state plates continue to blast through the area, unaware.

"Then, for the next couple of months any time anyone sees a Camaro, one of ours or one driven by some kid, they assume there are 21 more around somewhere. Everyone just slows down for awhile," says Fisher.

Although Indiana wasn't one of the states to increase its speed limits last year – it's still 65 on rural interstates, 55 on most other roads – people act like it did. Last year the average ticket was for 74.7. In most cases that means 10-20 mph over the limit.

Of the 323,767 speeding tickets written in the state, the 22 Camaro drivers wrote 41,579 – 13% of all tickets written by the Indiana State Police. Of the 204,367 moving violations, the Camaro drivers wrote 33,412 – 16%. Kellogg often writes 100 or more a week.

"It's what we do," he says.

Although most motorists are surprised to see the flashing lights of a Camaro in the rear view mirror, few decide to try to flee.

"People often try to outrun me in my stripe (so called because Indiana State Police cars have a blue and gold stripe on the side)," says veteran Camaro driver Joe Dixon. "Most people who see my Camaro know there's no chance."

But there are always some who, due to an alcohol or drug induced lapse in common sense, give it a try anyway.

Trooper Mike Nufer distinctly recalls a guy on a stolen racing motorcycle who thought he was faster than the law. When Nufer's Camaro finally caught up with him, he calmly pulled the motorcycle onto the shoulder. "I looked in the rear view mirror and saw you bouncing up and down right on my tail," said the guy. "I just couldn't believe it."

With all the recent controversy about pursuits, do Camaros pose a risk?

"I'd say quite the opposite," says Sergeant Neil Beck, who, along with Sergeant Steve Whitaker, coordinates the Camaro program. "With a very few exceptions, people don't run from us. They see us. They stop. The pursuit never gets started."

Although the Camaros would obviously be just as effective at night, at least when they work as a team, they work in the daytime.

"The idea is not to scare people," says Beck. "It's to blend in. When we stop people we want them to see the uniform, to know who we are. They already know what they did wrong."

"With a few exceptions most people are pretty cooperative," says Whitaker. "In fact, you'd be surprised how many times they actually compliment us on the car."

"That's usually before they find out their speeding ticket will cost $165," says Beck.

Speaking of costs, just what does one of these speed machines run?

"People are always surprised at this part," says Whitaker.

A basic police package 1997 Camaro is $18,162 –about $1000 less than the department's standard Crown Victoria. $9565.30 worth of equipment later, it's still about the cost of an average sport utility vehicle.

For the citizens of Indiana, that's quite a bargain.

"When the whole idea of community policing got started back in the early '80s," says Whitaker, "the people we talked to in town meetings across the state said their main concern was speeding. The people I talk to today still see speeders as a major problem. In the 13 years we've had the Camaro program our 22 guys have regularly written at least 15% of all the tickets. We've gone after the most dangerous drivers on the road, stopped a fair number of criminals and generated tens of millions of dollars in fines."

That's not bad for a bunch of grown up kids in hot cars. ★

MURDER AT FOXCATCHER MANSION
Second Place, nonfiction, 1997
by John Eller

On the afternoon of January 26, 1996, gunshots broke the silence of the serene countryside at Foxcatcher Farm.
Within a few seconds the lives of many people were impacted.
Gold Medal Olympic Wrestling Champion, David Schultz lay dying in the driveway of his home. Multimillionaire John E. DuPont, Schultz's friend and confidant, who fired the three deadly shots, would end up in prison after being found guilty but mentally ill. Nancy Schultz, who witnessed the shooting, became a widow with the responsibility of raising their two children without a loving and caring father.
The following story depicts the forty-eight hours following the fatal shooting and the actions of some of those individuals who had to deal with a standoff between the suspect and over three hundred police officers.

At approximately 2:50 PM, on a quiet Friday afternoon in January 1996, David Schultz was working on his car in the driveway of his home on Foxcatcher Estate. Schultz was a 1984 Gold Medal Olympic wrestling champion and was working at the John E. DuPont Estate, the home of "Team Foxcatcher," the largest Olympic Wrestling Training Facility east of the Mississippi.

While Schultz was working on the car, John DuPont drove up, accompanied by security officer Pat Goodale. DuPont left his car and walked over to Schultz and mumbled something. He pulled out a .44 calibre magnum and fired twice at Schultz, striking him in the chest.

Nancy Schultz, hearing the sound of gunfire, ran to the door of the house only to see DuPont shoot her husband again while he lay in the driveway. DuPont pointed the gun toward her and told her to get back into the house. He ordered Goodale to get out of the way, got back into his Lincoln and drove away.

Goodale rushed to the aid of Schultz, who lay dying in the driveway. Nancy Schultz dialed 9-1-1, to report the shooting.

Delaware County Police Radio dispatched the call to a Newtown Square officer, indicating a shooting had occurred at the Foxcatcher Estate.

Foxcatcher is a sprawling 800-acre estate. There are numerous cottages and outbuildings occupied by members of the staff and wrestlers training at the Olympic Facility. The first responding officer notified the dispatcher that he had an unconscious male with multiple gunshot wounds, requesting the paramedics be expedited and that his superior officers be contacted.

Shortly thereafter, Chief Michael Mallon and Lt. Lee Hunter, along with other members of the department, arrived. Chief Mallon, realizing the severity of the incident and knowing that his small department of 13 officers would be overwhelmed, called for the assistance of Springfield Township's Tactical Response Team to assist in securing the area. He also requested the District Attorney's Delaware County detectives.

Flash information indicated that John DuPont had left the scene and possibly was inside a large three-story mansion which resembled Thomas Jefferson's Monticello.

Calls went out all over Delaware County. Since Springfield Township staffed their tactical team with 10 officers, an additional 15 officers were assigned to the team from eight other police departments. The four separate tactical teams within the county were eventually called for the Foxcatcher standoff.

The operational commander for the tactical team was Lt. Jack Francis, second in command of Springfield Township, and a practicing attorney. This assured that decisions were made from both a police and legal perspective. The tactical response team leader, Detective Paul Andy Trautmann, was known as a no-nonsense kind of cop, who knew weapons and tactical response. The chief hostage negotiator was Detective John Ryan who specialized in investigations and hostage negotiations.

The tactical team members were on location at the Newtown Square Police Department within 45 minutes for a briefing. A Newtown officer spotted DuPont on the second floor of his mansion. There were at least two employees inside the mansion. It was not known if they were being held hostage.

More critical information: a tunnel beneath the mansion led to the outside; DuPont was an expert marksman and had his own firearms range on the estate; he had an armored personnel carrier in the garage and was an accomplished helicopter pilot.

The tactical unit secured the exterior of the premises by 5:00 PM. Problems began to arise. There was no phone system in the mansion. A fire had burned the phone wires in October and DuPont never had them repaired. It would be necessary to operate with cellular phones. Communications problems arose between the tactical unit and the command post four miles away. A decision was made to move the command post to the fire department one mile away from the scene.

One female left the residence at approximately 5:40 PM.

She was picked up and escorted back to the command post. Two mobile communications vans were requested to assist the tactical team in communicating with the command post.

Phone contact was made with a second female employee at approximately 6:35 PM. Shortly thereafter she walked away from the mansion unharmed.

The containment team moved to secure DuPont's vehicle by disabling the right side tires of the Lincoln. Driveways to the estate also were blocked by police vehicles.

At approximately 7:10 PM two windows were opened on the second floor. AT 8:35 PM the telephone crew arrived to repair the telephone lines in the tunnel area beneath the mansion. A tactical decision was made at that time to turn off the heat in the mansion.

Tactical units were warned that DuPont might be carrying a 9 MM semi-automatic behind his back and a .357 revolver in a shoulder holster.

Media reporters began to arrive in numbers at the outer perimeter. They were contained by police, constables, state troopers, fire and ambulance personnel. Supplies began to arrive. A communications administrator was assigned to handle radio communications. Support personnel were dispatched to the Olympic Training Facility to handle the needs of the tactical teams.

At 11:50 PM a PA system was used to try to communicate with DuPont inside the Mansion. No success! Finally the telephone lines were repaired but attempts to call the Mansion were futile. A second mobile communications van arrived on location.

At 1:07 AM the Haverford Township Tactical Unit arrived on location for backup. At 2:46 AM a third police helicopter was placed into service.

Six cellular telephone calls were met with no success. A decision was made to allow Pat Goodale to contact John DuPont by phone. At 3:36 AM successful contact was made by Goodale. DuPont sounded calm at first, then he became irritable. He demanded to see Valentine, wrestler Mario Seletnick from the Olympic Committee and his attorney Terry Wochok. Contact was broken. In a second contact with DuPont, he demanded that Goodale do whatever it took to reach his people. DuPont claimed he was the American President who negotiated nuclear arms. He refused to come out.

At 5:18 AM another telephone contact was made with DuPont. He demanded to see Seletnick and Valentine. Another six calls were made but not answered. At 8:00 AM Goodale phoned DuPont and told him that Valentine was sick and would not come out. DuPont responded by asking for his attorney and Seletnick again. He insisted he was not afraid and asked that Val be told he loved him. He protested being held a prisoner and requested that Goodale meet in front of the house.

"Valentine says he loves you," Goodale said. DuPont replied he thought Valentine was being used as bait. In the ensuing conversations DuPont disclaimed any knowledge of the previous day's activities. DuPont continued his delirium with such statements as "We're in charge, you have federal authority. The local police have to obey us. Leave one of your people in charge."

DuPont called and asked for Valentine. He wanted to be connected to the outside world and said he would not talk to the police. He made another request for an attorney. Goodale told DuPont the police wanted him to come to the kitchen door. He inferred that if DuPont would not obey he might have to turn the phone over to a police negotiator. DuPont refused to talk to the police. He added that he might start to play with some of his "toys."

Meanwhile DuPont's attorney had been located. DuPont immediately requested that he be sent to him. He requested Mario also. The phone contact was terminated.

Several hours later Goodale called DuPont and told him that he was turning the phone over to police negotiator Bob O'Donnell, a detective sergeant with the Lansdowne Police Department. O'Donnell began by asking him if he could call him John. DuPont replied "I am his holiness the Dali Lama."

O'Donnell told DuPont that he hoped to resolve the situation. The response was, "The ball is in my court." DuPont said he would not talk further until his attorney arrived. O'Donnell asked why. DuPont replied that "His holiness is under siege. I need to get this resolved. I want the lights removed."

Next O'Donnell called DuPont to tell him that his attorney had arrived. DuPont became irritated when he could not speak with the attorney immediately.

After some time Chief Michael Mallon, the Incident Commander, authorized Tarus Wochok to speak to DuPont over the negotiator's phone with no recording and no direct monitoring, stipulating that the negotiators must be in the room with the attorney. Wochok told DuPont that the house was surrounded and that DuPont's safety was of the utmost importance. He told DuPont that the police were not going to leave and that no one would be allowed in. He informed DuPont that the incident had attracted worldwide press and the incident had to end.

Another six phone contacts by negotiator Detective Barry Williams of Marple Township resulted in no progress. At 7:30 PM Williams called and told DuPont that he needed to talk about the shooting. DuPont replied, "We are in a war with the Soviet Union and you have no right to tell me as a head of state what I can and cannot do." He suggested Williams call the president of the United States.

Former FBI Hostage Negotiator Tom Cupples and psychiatrist Dr. Gary Glass arrived. They discussed DuPont's demeanor and state of mind. Glass advised that DuPont should be told that he was a very important person, but was not the Dali Lama, not the president, or the president of Russia. It was suggested that he was important because he was John DuPont. Dr. Glass recommended that his ego be stroked.

At 7:50 PM DuPont called and stated that he was working on his missiles. He said the missiles were not aimed at police at present but might be later on. Williams tried to calm him to no avail. Tarus Wochok told DuPont that he had contacted the Bulgarian government and they agreed to not interfere in a U.S. Government domestic matter. He told DuPont that there was a warrant for his arrest and that no visitors would be allowed in the house. DuPont replied that he did not want to come out and he would sleep on it. The call ended. Approximately 30 telephone calls were made between 9:40 PM and 8:00 AM. At 1:50 AM the tactical unit reported seeing a glow in the bedroom that possibly could have been a lighter. At 4:15 AM the tactical unit disabled the left tires on DuPont's vehicle.

Early that morning Wochok advised negotiators that DuPont telephoned him at home on a cell phone and told Wochok that he was Jesus Christ and if Christ died it would be the end of the world. He said that he was low on food, water and cigarettes. He wanted to go outside to exercise. He repeated that he was not coming out and that he could create chaos.

Wochok again phoned DuPont from the command center, to tell him the place was surrounded and that police would not let a maid and a butler in the house. Wochok cautioned him to be careful. DuPont replied that he was coming out through the tunnel. Wochok told DuPont that the police controlled the tunnel. He told DuPont if he fired the first salvo it would be returned.

Wochok advised the police that DuPont wanted to come out to fix the heat and remove the lights from the grass. He wanted to come out to visit the Buddha on the property, his usual Sunday routine. He said that he wanted to talk again at 4:00 PM and wanted to know if the Bulgarian government had been contacted. He expressed the belief that the tunnel beneath the mansion was private property and that the police could not touch him in the tunnel.

At 10:00 AM DuPont's cell phone was cut off by the cellular phone company.

DuPont was observed looking out the window and walking inside the mansion. At 2:30 PM DuPont contacted Negotiator Detective Sergeant Anthony Paparo of the Upper Darby Police Department and requested that he be allowed to leave the house to fix his heater. Permission was granted.

At 3:10 PM DuPont opened the rear door of his residence and walked into the yard. Team Leader Andy Trautmann and tactical team members were waiting. When DuPont, who was unarmed, saw them, he turned to run back into the mansion and Trautmann pursued him and took him to the ground. He was quickly joined by other tactical team members who subdued DuPont and placed him in custody for transport to Newtown Square Police Headquarters.

The 48-hour siege that had the world watching was over without a shot being fired and no one being injured. John E. DuPont was charged with the murder of David Schultz and later convicted. More than 300 police officers, fire fighters, paramedics, communications personnel, fire police and members of the news media participated in an event that will be talked about for generations to come. ★

KNIGHT OF THE LIVING DEAD
Third Place, nonfiction, 1997
By William Bell

    The heater was not working very well in our "pre-worn out" patrol unit, as Bobby and I cruised the East Side public housing complexes on a cold winter night. Befitting our second-class status as "Blue Knights of the Projects," we had recently acquired some used patrol units from a large department, a couple hundred miles north of us. Most everything on the cars worked except for the heating and air conditioning! The chief's answer to our dilemma was "Roll up (or down) the windows" and "Whadda ya think we issued you the heavy leather jackets for?"

    As housing authority cops, we had many additional duties that the city police would never dream of doing. A lot of these tasks earned us the undeserved taunt of "Rent-A-Cops" from project residents. The least favorite duty was abandoned apartment checks. Tenants would depart without notice and immediately the apartment would be stripped of everything that wasn't welded or bolted down. Windows and doors would be broken and at night these apartments would become the homes of vagrants or "shooting galleries" for junkies. The fixtures in the bathrooms would be filled with excrement and the roaches and mice would have a field day. Danger was always present and we entered these apartments with guns drawn.

    One of the most onerous and belittling chores was checking out emergency medical service calls at Dosker Manor, a multi-building high-rise complex for low-income old folks. During the nighttime hours, different able-bodied residents acted as door monitors, letting people in the buildings. However, after midnight, the monitors left and only those with keys could get inside the building. That's where we came in. If the EMTs got a call to Dosker, we had get there pronto to check things out and let them in, if needed. Often times calls there were unfounded, which is how we got this "duty."

    The apartments at Dosker were set up like hospital rooms. There were alarm pullcords in the bedroom and bath of each residence which could be activated in case of an emergency. A glowing red light came on over the apartment door and an alarm monitor was activated in the manager's apartment that showed the location of the alarm.

    This particular night we responded to a Dosker alarm, let ourselves in and made our way to the apartment in question. A manager was usually there to let us in, but that night the regular manager was on vacation and the substitute had not yet arrived. Bobby and I knocked loudly on the door, but no one answered. We proceeded to let ourselves in courtesy of a knife blade inserted between the door and the frame, defeating the cheap spring lock.

Inside the apartment was dark and quiet. I went to check out the bathroom while Bobby made his way to the bedroom. A quick look indicated nobody was in the "can," so I moved back to the bedroom. A small night-light illuminated this room, which was modestly furnished with a double bed, stuffed chair and a chest of drawers. In the bed, tucked beneath heavy covers was an old lady. Her face was the picture of death in the dim glow of the night-light. The near-transparent skin was etched with wrinkles and she had thin, ivory colored hair. Her head angled back on the pillow, with her chin pointed up and her mouth was open, in what looked like a final gasp. There was no movement of the covers to indicate breathing.

What had not occurred to Bobby or me at this point was who had pulled the emergency cord. We stood there seemingly mesmerized at the old lady's bedside, when the acting manager came into the room, moving up behind me. Bobby asked in a whisper, "Whadda ya think, Bill?" I replied that, as he was not wearing gloves, perhaps he should check for a carotid pulse. We both moved forward on opposite sides of the bed and I leaned over as Bobby's fingers probed for the appropriate spot, just to the side of the old lady's throat.

The instant Bobby's cold digits made contact with parchment-like skin of the old lady's neck, she sat up in bed, arms flailing, and let out the most blood curdling shriek I'd ever heard! This instantly prompted a horrified scream from the woman manager behind me. The next thing I knew, I was down behind the stuffed chair, looking over the high back. In the slow motion world of high stress events, I noted Bobby was trying to press himself into the sheet rock wall on the opposite side of the room.

In moments that seemed much longer, calm finally prevailed and the overhead light was turned on. The old lady actually seemed to recover quicker than any of us. As my breathing and pulse returned to normal, I started to question the lady as to what was going on. She preempted me by raising a bony hand and exclaiming, "Hold on sonny, I gotta turn my hearin' aids on." During the shaky conversation that followed, we found out that the old lady was almost stone deaf when her hearing aids were off.

We quickly notified dispatch to cancel the EMTs and as we looked around the room, the mystery of who had pulled the alarm was solved. Just above the headboard of the bed, there had hung a large picture of the crucifixion, in a heavy, filigreed brass frame. The picture now swung slowly, suspended by the alarm cord which the old lady had wrapped around a part of the frame. The small wire nail which once held the picture was bent downward at a sharp angle, having finally lost the battle with gravity.

I'll never forget that night as long as I live. ★

TOM THREEPERSONS AND THE CUDAHAY RANCH
First Place, fiction, 1997
By William Bell

Tom Threepersons lowered the Stetson shading his eyes from the hot summer sun. It was mid-July, 1923, and the temperature had stayed in the upper 90s for the past two weeks. In stark contrast, the Great Sonoran Desert, through which he was now riding, could experience a temperature drop of more than 30 degrees come nightfall. The heat made Threepersons a touch lightheaded and he found himself daydreaming. Not a very smart move when you're trailing rustlers who could be watching their back track, ready to ambush anyone that looked like they may be in pursuit.

From Threepersons' experience as a tracker and scout, he could see by the tracks that there were three rustlers, or perhaps banditos, herding along a couple of dozen steers. He had been on their trail for about a day and a half, as they moved eastward, across the huge expanse of the Cudahay Ranch. The Cudahay spread was one of the largest in Mexico and was almost as big as the state of New Jersey. It stretched from the Arizona border, south toward Nacozari. Although managed by a "Gringo," it was technically still a part of Mexico. Foreigners couldn't be landowners, but could only lease the land from El Gobierno de Sonora, a sometimes touchy proposition.

Still alert, but with his mind wandering, Tom Threepersons wondered how a full-blooded Cherokee Indian from Oklahoma could be down in Old Mexico, risking his life, for the second time in less than a decade. He thought back to his first trip to Mexico back in 1916. He'd hired on as a scout for Blackjack Pershing, as U.S. troopers chased the Villistas into the Mexican state of Chihuahua after Villa's raid on Columbus, New Mexico. Threepersons had been captured and was to face a firing squad as a spy, but had managed to hack a hole in the wall of the adobe "carcel" and he and several other Americanos had escaped. They'd eventually made their way on foot back across the U.S. Border.

Now, here he was in Mexico again, this time as a foreman for Cudahay, but as it actually worked out, he was a "Regulator." When this position came up, Threepersons was between jobs. After the Great War, he had mustered out of the army at Ft. Bliss in El Paso. He'd stayed on in El Paso and worked alternately for the city police department as a patrolman and detective and for the county sheriff. An early proponent of veterans preference, Threepersons had sent a letter to the civil service in Washington, stating that the veterans of the World War should get special treatment when it came to being hired for federal jobs.

When the Volstead Act passed, creating national prohibition, Threepersons was offered a job as a Prohibition Agent. The job at first was interesting and full of action. Waiting in the shadows by the Rio Grande for some rumrunners to cross over with a load of "hooch" offered plenty of opportunity for gunplay. Threepersons, however, would wait until the group of "Contrabandistas" passed his position before he sprang out for the capture. During the short time he worked in this position, he foiled eighteen smuggling attempts without a shot fired. With a "speakeasy" on every corner, the hypocrisy of this crazy law finally convinced him to give the job up. Threepersons wasn't idle long.

As he continued on the trail he thought of that day, just a couple of months ago, when he was breakfasting on steak and eggs in a favorite café on Texas Street. A familiar figure strolled through the front door and spied Threepersons. "Buenos dias, hombre," called Emilio Esquiveros, an old friend and partner from the El Paso PD. "Hey, hermano, I heard you are out of a job, no?" Threepersons, never a man for a lot of words, grunted in the affirmative.

"You know, compadre, mi primo over in Deming was telling me that the Big Jefe at the Cudahay Ranch over in Sonora was looking for a man with your abilities."

Threepersons looked up, but continued to munch his last mouthful of beefsteak. He knew the abilities his amigo referred to were his speed and accuracy with a six-gun. Threepersons had killed his first man while still no more than boy after rustlers killed his father and the father of his best friend. The two young men had tracked the rustlers and finally found them in a saloon. The wild shoot-out that ensued left the rustlers dead. Since then, Threepersons was rarely without his specially built Colt "Peacemaker" that he carried in a radical fast-draw holster he himself had designed.

The holster was fashioned in "Tio" Sam Meyers' saddle shop in El Paso. The design was so popular that old Sam had asked Threepersons if he could copy it for others. He promised Threepersons a nickel for every holster he sold and put a mason jar on a shelf top into which "Tio" Sam dropped a nickel periodically.

That Colt and the floral carved holster rode on Threepersons' belt, within easy reach, as the shadows cast by the greasewood and mesquite bushes began to grow long in the late afternoon. The owner of the Cudahay had some real pull, or perhaps enough pesos to get the local commandante to issue him a special permiso so he could carry his Colt in Mexico. This alone had clued Threepersons in on just what his job as ranch foreman was to be in reality.

As the sun began to set and the temperature dropped, the rustler's trail became warmer. Threepersons didn't know if he would be facing more local banditos, Indians off the reservation desperate for meat, or north-of-the-border rustlers, who crossed the imaginary line from Arizona into Mexico to have at the thousands of heads of beef wandering loose on the Cudahay spread. In his short stint as "foreman," Threepersons had already sent several cattle thieves to meet their maker and corralled a number more. Tonight, he hoped these desperados would give up and not choose to die over a few lousy steers.

The tracks entered an arroyo and as the evening star began to shine, Threepersons knew that his quarry would soon stop for the night. The steep-sided arroyo was the perfect place to contain the stolen stock, offering a natural corral. As deep as it was, it would also hide the small fire the rustlers were likely to build.

Threepersons dismounted and secured his horse to a nearby salt cedar. He made his way quietly up the arroyo, careful not to kick a rock or fall over a root exposed by the last rain. His Indian upbringing allowed him to pass though the darkness like a spirit, and after less than a mile he detected the faint smell of mesquite smoke from the rustlers' fire. As he eased up behind a large salt cedar, he spied the small fire and two banditos crouched around it. Both wore large sombreros and had bandoliers of cartridges slung from their shoulders. Heavy revolvers hung from the holsters on their ornate concho belts.

Threepersons stood stock-still and watched to see where the third bandito was located. After several minutes of watching, he concluded the other man was keeping an eye on the cattle, while the other two cooked a meal and got some rest. They apparently thought they were safe from any pursuers and began to spread out their serapes on the sandy ground to catch a little sleep.

Now was the time to act. Threepersons stepped from the behind the salt cedar, his hand on the ivory stocked Colt at his side. "Buenas noches, muchachos," Threepersons growled. The sound of his voice caused a reaction much as if he'd thrown gasoline on their campfire. The two banditos instantly sprang to their feet, their faces turning toward the sound of his voice, hands clawing for the "pistolas" at their sides.

Threepersons' Colt leaped into his hand and he eared back the hammer without any conscious thought. He had just commanded "No se mueve," when the bandito nearest him cleared leather and sent a slug whining by a little too close for comfort. With the events out of his control, Threepersons raised his gun to eye level, triggering off a shot. The big .45 slug instantly crumpled the first "mal hombre" and his second shot, which followed almost instantly, ended the career of the second desperado.

The cattle began to bawl off in the distance, but Threepersons could plainly hear the hoof beats of the third bandito as he left his compadres to their fate. A quick check of the two rustlers on the ground confirmed their departure to the Great Beyond. Threepersons relieved the dead banditos of their weapons. He knelt by the fire and warmed himself, then slowly made his way back down the arroyo to his horse.

"Hell of a way to make a living," thought Threepersons. One of the ranch hands mentioned the other day that he'd heard U.S. Customs was looking for some help. "Maybe it's time to head back to El Paso." ★

THE HARDEST THING HE WOULD EVER HAVE TO DO
Second Place, fiction, 1997
By Marilyn Olsen

He knew some day he would have to do this. And that it would be the hardest thing he would ever have to do.
   So he braced himself as he stepped out of the car. He gave a tug to the back of his dress uniform, straightened his tie and put his sunglasses in his pocket.
   He took a deep breath, then started up the dusty sidewalk to the door of the brand new brick house with the two spindly maple trees in the front yard.
   She opened the door, cradling the four-month-old child in her arms and smiled. It was her husband's lieutenant. She always looked forward to seeing him. In fact, he had been at their house just the weekend before. He had insisted on cooking the burgers on the grill and good naturedly lost the free throw contest at the hoop above the garage.
   She had only been a cop's wife for two years. No one had yet told her what a visit like this in the middle of the day meant.
   He couldn't smile back. He stood stiffly – almost at attention, holding his breath as he slowly turned the gold wedding ring on the finger of his left hand.
   Her smile faded then, almost as quickly as it had appeared. He knew that although he had not said anything, she had somehow figured it out.
   Without a word, she turned her back on him and walked slowly through her house and into her sunny kitchen.
   He followed, going over in his mind once more the little speech he had hastily written at the post and rehearsed in his car on the way over. But now the words seemed all wrong.
   Not knowing what else to do, he went to the sink and poured her a glass of water, even though she had not asked for one.
   As the water ran, he looked out the window at the field behind the house. He had a wild, irrational urge to run out the back door and into the rows of corn.
   But he didn't do that.
   He wiped the bottom of the glass with a towel and set it down in front of her next to an empty jar of pureed carrots.
   She looked up at him then and the tears began to run down her cheeks and

drop silently onto the hand knitted afghan covering her little girl.

Then he began to tell her. As he spoke, he could see that she could picture what had happened. The car stopped by the side of the road. The smiling face of her high school sweetheart who had become her husband. The blue uniform and shiny silver badge he was so proud of. Him, joking with the woman as he helped her change the tire. Neither of them noticing the truck coming up over the hill or the driver taking his eyes off the road as he reached down on the floor for his cigarettes. The horrible sound as the truck slammed into the car, the woman and the trooper at more than 70 miles per hour.

The blood everywhere.

He didn't tell her that part, of course. But still she knew. Just as she knew she would not see the face she loved so much even one more time.

She stood up then. And he walked over to her. Wordlessly, he put his arms gently around her – careful not to wake the child. They stood like that for a long time, his tears dampening her hair.

Both of them knew that there was much more to be said. A large and formal funeral to be planned. Papers to be signed. Forms to be filled out.

But there would be plenty of time for that later.

Right now all he could do was hold this young woman and her child who would never have a chance to know her daddy. And weep silently with them both.

It was the hardest thing he would ever have to do. ★

THE FINAL ASSIGNMENT
Third Place, fiction, 1997
By Joseph J. Truncale

This was Mike's last day on the job. After 25 years he would finally retire from police work. He looked forward to spending more time with his family and building his hobby into a part-time business. Few officers on the department knew that Mike loved to paint. He had even sold a few of his paintings to people interested in his work. He especially loved doing landscapes and sea scenes. He used to enjoy the challenge of working nights, as this was where the most action is in police work. However, the last few years he had grown to love working the hours that the average person takes for granted.

As Mike drove his squad car down the sleepy side street on the east end of town, he reminisced about his first day on the job. He had been assigned to ride with a crusty, old weather beaten lieutenant, who could barely read and write. The tall, beefy lieutenant was quick to give advice to young rookie officers like Mike.

"You know, boy, (he called everyone boy), the most important part of this job is being able to kick ass," he barked in his gravely voice. Even though Mike had been new to the job at the time, he knew there was a lot more to police work than just fighting, but he made no comment at the time.

"You has to show 'em who's boss and don't take any shit from peoples."

Mike recalled, wondering to himself how this man could have passed the patrol entrance examination, much less the sergeant and lieutenant's promotional tests. Later, Mike discovered that he had been promoted because he had friends on the police and fire board.

A call blurted out over the police radio, wiping out Mike's daydreaming.

"Car 902, handle a vandalism to lawn complaint at 1504 Wagner Road."

As Mike pulled up to the house he saw an elderly couple standing on the lawn to meet him. Apparently, a large off-road vehicle ran over their lawn breaking a small tree the couple had been cultivating. Mike felt compassion for the old couple. Their gardening was the only thing they had left in life and that little tree meant a lot to them. Perhaps the tree symbolized a new life, a renewed purpose for the couple who were in the winter of their lives.

Mike resumed his patrol and began to laugh to himself. He recalled handling an intoxicated woman complaint with Sergeant Bower. Mike was still a rookie and this was one of the first complaints he responded to after graduating from the police academy. Unbeknownst to Mike at the time, Sergeant Bower had been to the house several times in the past and he knew the woman. She was about 45 years old and had only a pair of pink panties and a bra on when they arrived at the house. Sergeant Bower told the woman to quiet down or she would be arrested.

"I'm lonely," she slurred looking directly at Mike.

Mike recalled being nervous, as the woman walked directly up to him and rubbed herself like a cat in heat against his body.

"Why don't you arrest me, officer?"

The woman sensed Mike's inexperience as he gently pushed the intoxicated woman away from him. Sergeant Bower laughed, as he told the woman to settle down and that he would stop over after he got off work to check up on her to make sure she was all right. Mike knew it was more than a concern for the woman's well being that the sergeant was interested in at the time.

Mike opened his briefcase to place his last report in when he noticed a switch blade knife. The image of the knife provided thoughts of how he had obtained the weapon. He had taken the knife away from a youth who had been high on drugs. The young man was planning to kill his father with the knife. Even after many drug-related incidents involving their son, the parents would always beg Mike not to charge their son. Since the youth was a juvenile, he was constantly let off by the judge who heard the cases. The youth eventually made the big time by committing an armed robbery and was now in jail for the crime. It had always amused Mike when the parents constantly accused the police of harassing their son. They protected him right up to the day he was sentenced to five years for the armed robbery.

Despite the thousands of complaints Mike handed over the years, he never ceased to be amazed at the lack of common sense people exhibited in society. He remembered a couple who were continually fighting. The police had been at their house more than 20 times. They were both alcoholics and would end up beating up on each other with anything they had in their hands. The police would persuade the woman to sign a complaint against her abusive husband, but when they came to court, she would always drop the charges.

Mike had responded to such a wide variety of complaints over the years that he had become cynical. Nevertheless, he still held the belief in the natural dignity of humanity and the basic goodness of most people. He realized his part was small in the drama of life. Yet, he believed his role was essential to keep the savages of society from destroying the weak and helpless.

He felt the criminal was nothing but a parasite feeding off the producers in society. He looked at himself as a social surgeon, whose job was to remove the cancerous tumors from society to preserve a healthy culture. In spite of public criticism and citizen brutality toward law enforcement, he knew philosophically that police work fulfilled a noble purpose in society. He had no ivory tower illusions about life, as he had seen too much of reality. He would, however, always hold the conviction that good is more powerful than evil.

It was 2:15 pm and Mike would kiss this job good bye in 45 minutes. It had been an average day up to this point. The police radio again came alive calling his squad number.

"Car 902, handle a disturbance at 1042 Forest Drive. A husband is threatening his wife. Unknown whether any weapons are involved because the wife hung up the phone."

Mike recognized the address. He had been to the house numerous times over the years. The subject had serious psychological problems and had been committed to a mental institution for a few years. The backup units were on the way, but Mike knew he would arrive at the house first.

Mike turned down Forest Drive and parked two houses away. He advised the dispatcher of his arrival. As Mike cautiously walked toward the house, he noticed a man standing at the front door outside the house. Mike recognized the man as the person he had handled in the past for beating up his wife.

At this point, the man saw Mike approaching and immediately raised his right hand. A nickel-plated, four-inch revolved glittered in the sun. Mike's reflexes were still sharp because he made it his business to keep himself in shape and never get sloppy on the job. Mike dove behind a parked car, drawing his own Smith & Wesson .45 caliber semi-automatic at the same time.

Mike felt a burning sensation in his left thigh and realized he had been hit. But he was not incapacitated. Mike always wore body armor, but not on his legs.

Mike immediately called on his radio, "902 to base. The subject has a gun and I have been shot."

With dispatch and the backup units aware of the situation, Mike now focused on the job at hand. He had always practiced good officer survival procedures, never letting complacency creep into his personality.

The assailant fired at Mike again, both bullets striking the hood of the car. The subject never changed his position, and that was a mistake. Mike peered over the hood and fired three quick rounds at the assailant. Two of the three rounds struck their target, one in the chest and one in the head of the gun-wielding assailant.

The man fell forward, dropping his gun as he hit the ground. Mike's leg began to hurt as he pulled himself up to cautiously approach the subject. The beautiful sight of squad cars pulled up before Mike was able to reach the downed assailant. The ambulance pulled up at the same time.

Sergeant Jones grabbed Mike and guided him into the ambulance. Mike took a deep breath and smiled.

"I got hit in the left thigh."

Jones smiled back. "You're going to be all right. I bet you're glad this is your last day."

Mike never felt more alive and relieved in his entire career as a police officer. He grinned at the sergeant as he answered: "This is definitely my final assignment." ★

UNKNOWN WARRIOR CONTEMPLATION
First Place, nonfiction, 1998
By Pamelia Stratton

Experts advise not to take your work home with you. A home should be a refuge from the stress of work. Sometimes, however, home is the only safe haven where you can contemplate the full implications of your job.

Tonight is such a time for me. I am a sniper on the Special Weapons and Tactics (SWAT) team. Tomorrow we will conduct an operation that could be quite violent. We will undertake the arrest of three bank robbers known to carry high-powered assault weapons like M-16 rifles, AK-47 Russian-made rifles, and MAC-10 automatic pistols that spray bullets like a machine gun. These subjects have committed numerous armed "takeover" bank robberies and have sworn they won't be taken alive. And, they are known to wear protective body armor, just like the police. They brag about being the Pennsylvania version of the bank robbery duo who staged a bloody shootout on the streets of Los Angeles. If they have to go down, nothing would please them more than to orchestrate a war that would take as many police officers as possible with them. We have been working this group for months now and have made several failed attempts to arrest them due to changes in their plans. Finally, tomorrow is the day it will really happen.

Today has been hectic. It began with another briefing on the subjects and the anticipated arrest scenario. Next came several staged practices of the arrest. Since it was not possible to run through the plan in the location of the arrest, it was important to discuss the adaptations that might be necessary tomorrow.

As roof snipers, the potential for our visibility by the subjects was great because there was no plausible reason for anyone to be up there. We were instructed to stay out of sight. Our only form of communication and warning will be through radio transmissions by members who have a visual advantage and will detail subject progression. The radio signal word "execute" means that the arrest plan will start. A countdown will occur and at five seconds the snipers will move into a visibility position. Unless, of course, we hear a screech of tires which means the plan has gone awry and we must react immediately.

The day was culminated by my partner and me going to the firearms range to practice shooting our .308 Winchester rifles with Leopold 10 Power Scopes.

This exercise was vital for several reasons. First of all, in this situation we are carrying a fully loaded magazine of five bullets due to various contingencies that could develop in the arrest. Normally, we insert one round into the rifle at a time because we are trained to shoot to the head and kill with one shot. Snipers usually only get one shot and it must be accurate. Secondly, we are using a different bullet than usual, because we need a round that will pierce the glass of the vehicle and still have the velocity to do its job on the people inside.

And last, we are going to be shooting from a mere 25-yard distance while most sniper activity is usually further away. We are also going to be shooting down onto the subjects from above. We need to be aware of how the bullets might react when they hit objects other than glass since they can ricochet and continue moving.

After firearms practice I came home. My first order of business was to clean my weapon so that it would be ready for action. Then I laid out all my gear and tried to decide which equipment I wanted to take. Unlike most SWAT operations where all team members would be dressed in uniforms, we are to be dressed in casual attire to match the people expected to be at a rest area on the turnpike, so I had to decide what clothes to wear. Now that I have made these decisions, I am free to enjoy the evening with my family.

Right. Fat chance.

My mind is consumed with thoughts. Tomorrow I may have to kill someone. Can I actually pull the trigger and take someone's life? This was a question I contemplated before I took the sniper position but now it is no longer hypothetical. If I'm not positive, I can't do the job. I can't go up on the roof because my failure to complete my mission could result in the death of someone else. Yes, I tell myself. To save the life of one of my team members or an innocent person, I can take the life of a criminal.

I am fully confident in my ability to handle my weapon with skill. But will I be able to observe the activity below and adequately determine whether or not to shoot? What if I interpret the actions of the subjects as surrender when they appear to be dropping their weapons, but, in reality, are faking submission to gain a shoot advantage? Or, what if I believe that they are acting aggressively, when they are actually raising their guns to drop them out the window and surrender? I will have a millisecond to make life and death decisions. If I fail to make the right decision to shoot, one of the good guys might not go home tomorrow night. But if I make the wrong decision to shoot when one of the bad guys is trying to surrender, he won't get a second chance to turn his life around and I'll have to live with that decision the rest of my life. So both the good guys and the bad guys are depending on me to make the right decision. I realize that what happens tomorrow could change my life forever.

And then there are the legal implications of shooting. I have microseconds to make my decision whether or not to shoot. Regardless of what I do, lawyers, other law enforcement officials and most likely the press will spend days, months and possibly years, analyzing the decision I made. And every one of them will have 20/20 hindsight and will clearly know what choice I should have made at that moment.

Thoughts of Lon Horiuchi hover in my brain. Horiuchi is the FBI Hostage

Rescue Team member at Ruby Ridge, Idaho who, in 1992, accidentally shot and killed Vicki Weaver, the wife of white extremist Randy Weaver who killed a US Marshal. The bullet that killed Vicki Weaver went through Randy (the actual target), one of his accomplices and a door prior to reaching her. But in 1997, Horiuchi was charged with involuntary manslaughter in Idaho and these charges were not dropped until 1998. Horiuchi went through hell because he did the job he was instructed to do.

Not only is my mind racing but my body is reacting, as well. I feel pumped up. Blood is coursing through my veins and my heart is beating loudly. Every one of my senses is working in overdrive. The temperature is hot. The sun is extra bright. I smell and hear things I never noticed before. My body tingles as if a current of electricity were flowing through it. I can't imagine how I will get to sleep tonight.

I try to carry on as usual by emptying the trash, walking the dog and watching TV, but nothing quiets my mind or body. I try to pay some bills but I can't concentrate long enough to fill out a check. My wife puts a nice dinner on the table. I have no appetite. My 13-year-old son acts up as usual, but tonight I can't deal with his childish behavior and I yell at him to stop chasing the dog and go to his room. Instantly, I feel bad, but I can't take the extra noise and distraction.

My wife senses my apprehension and we discuss the situation. I am really lucky here because my wife is also a law enforcement officer and can understand what I'm feeling. Otherwise, I would not talk to her about such matters because I would not want to burden her unnecessarily.

Finally, I am exhausted and I go to bed. The next thing I know, the alarm goes off and I pop out of bed immediately. Every sense in my body goes into full alert. I dress quickly. While looking at my wife still sleeping soundly, I take in a long slow breath and pray silently to God to guide me in doing the right thing and to take care of all of us today. Slowly, I lean down to kiss my wife so that I don't wake her. I turn and walk out of the room.

This is it, I tell myself, as I get in my car and start down the road.

I am a warrior heading off to battle. ★

HARVEST TIME FOR THE ISP
Second place, nonfiction, 1998
By Marilyn Olsen

On a crisp fall day a young man in a shiny red Camaro drives slowly down a county road in rural Marion County. He pauses, does a double take, speeds up, goes up the road, turns around and cruises by again. He can't believe what he's seeing.

Two Indiana State Troopers are standing next to a cornfield. They're dressed in coveralls. They're carrying machetes. And they appear to be headed to the spot where the State Police helicopter is now hovering, along with a helicopter from a local TV station.

If the pained expression on this young man's face has anything to do with the marijuana that's growing between the rows of corn in this field, he can say goodbye to his next car payment. What may have been his big cash crop is about to be hacked and stacked and made into a story for the nightly news.

He makes another pass by the scene.

He frowns.

That's just fine with Trooper Ed Rohrman. He's spent a good part of the last three months in the heat and the dust making a lot of marijuana growers frown.

It makes him smile.

It's been a bumper year for marijuana in Indiana. And Rohrman is just one of hundreds of Indiana officers from 60 agencies who have been toiling in the fields all summer. They've already harvested 19,000 cultivated and 7 million "ditch weed" plants, confiscated 700 pounds of processed marijuana and made 431 arrests – and there are still six weeks or so to go before the first frost puts an end to the growing season.

"It's not the job for everyone," admits Rohrman. "If you don't like to get your shoes dirty or get bugs in your hair, you should just stay in your nice clean police car and chase tail lights up and down the Interstate. Personally, I get a lot of satisfaction out of it. There's nothing quite like the expression on the face of a guy when you knock on his door and show him what used to be a nice tax-free income."

The marijuana in this cornfield is growing pretty much out in the middle of nowhere next to a cluster of double-wide trailers with Confederate flags out front. Rohrman probably won't be able to nab a suspect this time – although he did jot down the number of the Camaro's license plate.

But, still, he has a job to do.

Opening the battered back door of the Army surplus ambulance they use to transport the marijuana they eradicate, Rohrman and Trooper Lou Perras retrieve sturdy work gloves, portable radios and bottles of water. Even on a fall day, this job is a hot and dusty one.

The TV station van pulls up, a reporter bounds out and checks out his hair in the rearview mirror. He's wearing pressed khaki pants, a starched blue oxford cloth shirt and a colorful tie. He's followed by a cameraman in jeans and a short-sleeved T-shirt lugging a tripod, a camera and a canvas bag full of microphones, cords and extra tapes.

The TV station helicopter circles around the state police helicopter taking wide angle shots of the field and close ups of ISP helicopter pilot Sergeant John Kelley and Lieutenant Chris Hall of the Indiana National Guard pointing at the ground. Then it swoops down to get a shot of the reporter next to the road and the station's colorful logo painted on the side of the van.

All of this helicopter activity creates a huge, swirling cloud of dust and flying corn tassels. The TV reporter recombs his hair.

Then, Rorhman's hand held radio crackles to life signifying that the TV station has all the footage it needs. The ISP helicopter moves back into position over the marijuana plants and the whole entourage heads into the rows of tall, dry corn.

Within minutes everyone is covered with burrs and tangled up in morning glory vines. The cameraman, who announces that he is allergic to dust, starts to break out in a rash.

"City boys," mutters Rohrman.

It's supposed to look like a breaking news story. Actually, Kelley and Hall had spotted the marijuana the day before, but since the station couldn't schedule a news team until morning, they'd had to send three shifts of troopers out to sit on the field to make sure the cultivator hadn't chosen that night to go in for the crop. Perras had drawn the midnight shift and had now been up for more than 24 hours. But he's been a trooper for a long time and lack of sleep is nothing new to him.

Since it's remarkably easy to get lost in a field of eight-foot tall stalks, the troopers, the reporter and the cameraman keep each other in sight as they move to the spot just under the helicopter.

And there they are. Bright green, healthy marijuana plants, swaying gently in the breeze. There's little doubt about how they got there. A tidy pile of potting soil is still visible at the base of each plant. The soil around the corn is dry and cracked but there's a little puddle of water around most of the marijuana stalks. Someone has been taking very good care of them.

Alas for the grower, all that effort is about to be in vain. Rohrman and Perras methodically bend each waist-high plant over on the ground and give it a whack with the machete. Then they pile them into bundles and hoist them up on their shoulders.

The TV cameraman dodges in and out of the corn, taking artsy shots of the sun sparkling on the blade of the machete, Perras in his refelcto sunglasses and hat embroidered with distinctive pointed leaves, the helicopter hovering over the action and the reporter looking solemn as he asks Perras all about the operation.

When the only thing left standing is the ripened corn, the group files back out of the field and onto the road. The plants are counted and piled into the back of the ambulance. There are sixty of them with a street value of around $800 per plant. It's been a good day.

The cameraman does one more shot of the reporter looking serious as he studies the pile of marijuana.

The helicopter banks sharply over the field to make sure the troopers didn't miss anything, then clatters back toward the hangar.

The doors of the ambulance slam shut.

The TV van speeds off in a cloud of dust.

The red Camaro slowly cruises by one more time.

Trooper Ed Rohrman smiles.

He hasn't been able to arrest the kid in the shiny new car.

But chances are, he sure has been able to ruin his day. ★

JDLR: 10-49: ONE DEAD, ONE DYING
Third Place, nonfiction, 1998
By Arthur James Farrar

It had been a long, dull swing shift and the drive home was a welcome breath of cool, fresh air. As I pulled out of the department's parking lot and onto the city streets after work, my thoughts drifted to the activities that were planned for the next workday.

As a patrol lieutenant/watch commander, my duties included monitoring the ebb and flow of calls for service on a daily basis. Traffic accidents were a common occurrence in my city of 90,000 people, but fatalities were still rare. Driving up the freeway on ramp to start the drive home, I focused on merging with the flow of traffic. The furthest thought from my mind was the possibility of a fatal accident ahead of me.

As I headed eastbound from the city into the rural surroundings outside the city limits, I noticed that the pavement was wet from a rain shower and the ground fog was unusually thick and obscured the freeway lanes. I slowed my truck as other driver's raced by oblivious to the danger in the wet pavement and reduced visibility.

Before long, I was alone on the freeway and approaching my off ramp. As I braked to leave the freeway and drive up the ramp, my attention was attracted to a single beam of light coming at my passenger window. Since I was tired and ready for bed, I ignored my initial instinct and drove on.

At the top of the ramp, I turned left and drove over the freeway to the adjacent residential neighborhood. As I crossed the overpass, I looked over my left shoulder and again considered the shaft of light directed across the freeway lane at my passing truck.

As is common in police work, especially after several years of patrol assignments, officers come to rely upon intuitive responses to unexpected occurrences. JDLR or "just doesn't look right" is the description given to incidents that defy definition and clarity until investigated. I had had one of those JDLR responses, but had rationalized the observation away.

I reasoned that the light I had seen from the side was probably from a farm tractor working late at night cultivating the nearby fields. My rationale was satisfactory until I reached the top of the overpass and slowed to study the light again. I rolled down my window and peered out into the rain and fog.

This time, I noted that the light did not move and was not accompanied by the sounds of mechanical apparatus customary for that type of operation. As I sat at the top of the overpass considering my thoughts, I began to break out in a sweat. Perhaps my rationalization was wrong – dead wrong. I slammed the truck into gear and made an illegal U-turn to enter the freeway again.

As I raced down the on ramp, my heart was in my throat. I slowed the truck to a stop in the center divider. As I jumped from the truck to peer through the brush that divided the lanes, I still could not see clearly across the lanes into the orchard because of the fog. Since I was in civilian clothes without my duty gear and in my personal truck, I had no spotlight or flashlight to illuminate the orchard.

A few seconds passed as I evaluated my options. If I radioed for help now, with my newly-issued department portable radio and this was an unfounded call, I would be subject to ridicule and the source of locker room gossip for many days. Nevertheless, my instincts told me to investigate further and disregard the possible negative outcomes. I jumped back into my truck and roared down the freeway to the next off ramp to turn around and return to the orchard.

As I slowed opposite the site on my second pass, I realized that it wasn't a farm tractor that I saw, but the single headlight of a passenger car, approximately 200 feet from the freeway lanes, jammed between avocado trees. The car had come to rest on its wheels, facing out onto the freeway. I was able to walk down the side of the freeway following the path that the car had taken through the barrier fence. It had spun out of control after striking the first of several large trees. All but the one headlight had been extinguished in the collision with the trees.

It was an eerie sight on a foggy night. As I walked up to the driver's door, I could see a young female driver, obviously fatally injured and could hear moans from the passenger seat. The driver's eyes were open and fixed and she seemed strangely rigid in her seat. I'm sure she saw the accident coming and tried to steer a safe course.

The female passenger was almost hidden among the debris on the passenger side. I offered words of encouragement and then ran to my truck to radio in my location and details of the accident. Our dispatcher was shocked by my radio call – 10-49 the code for an injury accident – one dead, one dying.

Our swing shift had ended almost an hour before and the sound of my voice frightened her. She told me later that she was speechless for a few seconds after she received the details of my radio call. She said that she thought, at first, that it might have been a practical joke sometimes played by the midnight shift to keep everyone on their toes, but that she had never heard the tone of voice that I used that night. She quickly sensed that I was serious and alerted the California Highway Patrol (CHP) office that had jurisdiction for that section of the Ventura Freeway.

I had often heard citizens complain of long response times to serious calls, but had dismissed many of those complaints as unfounded. I was in for a lesson that night. As I returned to the car and continued to monitor the passenger, I glanced at my watch and saw that it was almost 3 a.m. I knew that the closest rescue fire station was less than two miles away, but that the CHP office was closed at night and only minimal staffing was on the road to cover the entire county.

It seemed like an eternity, but was actually only minutes, before I began to hear the wail of the sirens in the distance and by then the passenger's breathing was labored and shallow. As I waited, I studied her features and realized that she was barely out of her teens. My thoughts rushed to my young daughter, our first child, and I shuddered to think of the officer that would have to contact her family that night and deliver the news of the driver fatality and the passenger injuries.

As the army of rescue crews arrived, I stepped to the side and watched them go to work. Since I was in civilian clothes, I was soon asked to clear the scene. As I walked back to my truck, I gave thanks to those who perform these life-saving services. When I got home, I quietly walked down the hall to my daughter's room, opened the door, and looked in on her. She was sleeping peacefully and safely in her room. I stroked her forehead and whispered to her that I loved her.

In the days that followed, I received a commendation letter from the local CHP commander who filled in the blanks in my knowledge about the accident. He reported that the vehicle had left the roadway and in all probability wouldn't have been found until early the next morning except for my observation. He said the timely reporting of the accident prolonged the life of the passenger whose condition was critical when removed from the vehicle.

Although, ultimately, this was a double fatal accident, I never forgot the power of the JDLR response and shared that with many of my supervisors, peers and subordinates and, later, students in our local criminal justice program. I reminded them that JDLR is a powerful response – Trust your instincts. You just might prolong your own life or that of another human being. ★

PAID IN FULL
Honorable Mention, nonfiction, 1998
By Keith J. Bettinger

I am sitting at my desk, but what I should be doing is cleaning the house. Since we need to paint the room and we are thinking of moving eventually, I have packed away almost all my police memorabilia. This includes all but one of my law enforcement uniform patches. Right now, there are over a thousand patches in a box waiting to be mounted or placed in an album so they can be displayed. However, there is one patch in a frame, all by itself. It sits on my desk because it is special to me.

The patch is not a fancy emblem. It is just black and gold. All it has on it is the name of the community, the word "POLICE" and a gold star embroidered at the bottom. It is not a new patch. In fact, it is kind of battered and worn. It is not the type of patch over which most collectors would make a fuss. You might be wondering what is so special about this patch. It has a history and a story all its own.

In January 1991, I was assigned to work investigations in my precinct's plainclothes unit. One afternoon, while sitting at my desk, shuffling through my cases, the telephone rang. It was a police officer from the Midwest calling to speak specifically to me. He had read one of my articles about living through the effects of post shooting trauma. He said he enjoyed it and it was informative. Now he needed more information. His brother, also a police officer, had been in a shooting. The officer was not only concerned about his brother's personal safety, but also his physical and emotional well being. He asked if I had any more information on post shooting trauma. He wanted to know more about what to do for his brother. He also wanted to know if I would speak to his brother if he needed to talk to someone.

I told him that I had written a few more articles on post shooting trauma and would be more than happy to send him copies. We discussed the symptoms of post shooting trauma, what to look for, and what to do to help his brother if any problems arose. I told him I would be more than happy to speak to his brother, and was available any time his brother needed me. I also told him I had a friend who was a police officer and a peer support person. This friend lived only a couple miles from the officer and his brother. This friend would be someone nearby if they needed immediate help.

The officer thanked me and wanted to know what he could do to repay me.

I told him I appreciated his thinking so highly of my work, and that was enough. I did add that I was a patch collector, and said if he could send me a couple of patches from his area, it would be appreciated.

A while later, I heard from the officer. His brother was working his way through the shooting aftermath and the struggles that came with it. He thanked me for my help and told me he would keep me informed of his brother's progress. He also said he was working on obtaining some patches for my collection. That was the last I heard from him.

One day a few years later I was on one of the on-line services on my computer. Lo and behold, while in one of the law enforcement areas, I found the name and e-mail address of the officer who contacted me. I sent a quick note. I asked how his brother was, and included a little dig, "By the way, where are those patches?"

I received an e-mail reply telling me his brother was doing well and the patches would be coming soon.

A few days later a large envelope arrived. I opened it up and found it full of patches. Inside were patches from his department, his former department, and patches from neighboring departments. There also was a patch from the department his brother had transferred to since the shooting.

His brother had become a high ranking supervisor in the new department. The last patch I took out was the old beaten up one. It had a note on it. The note said, "I know this doesn't look like much, but this patch was on the uniform my brother was wearing the day of his shooting. When he left the department he kept that shirt. He took one patch off and kept it for himself. I took the other one for you. It belongs to you. Without your help I don't know if my brother would be here today. Your help made a difference. If there is anything I can do for you, give me a call. If you want some other patches, just let me know."

I sat down and wrote a note. I wanted to let the officer know he did not owe me a thing.

I was paid in full. ★

DISPATCH TO ETERNITY
Honorable Mention, nonfiction, 1998
By John Eller

July 1, 1993 was another busy night on the Chester City Police console. Chester is a city of 40,000, with the highest crime rate in the state and the police were understaffed, as usual. Six patrol officers worked to cover almost five square miles of crime, problems and people. Thirty-nine-year-old Connie Hawkins, a three-year veteran of the force, was one of those officers.

Several miles away, behind the Chester City Console at the 9-1-1 Center in Lima, was 22-year-old Kevin Smith, with four years experience in the communications field.

Dispatchers who work day in and day out have one major fear-to lose an officer. The words "officer down" are a dispatcher's nightmare.

At 11pm, it was a typically busy night. All six officers were involved in calls. Smith received a 9-1-1- hang-up call at 206 West Fifth Street. He attempted to call the phone number back and received no answer. Policy dictates that an officer must respond to all 9-1-1- hang-up calls to ascertain that everything is all right.

Two of the street officers were involved in making an arrest and another was at the hospital with an assault. Hawkins had finished assisting other officers and cleared a call.

Smith tried again to call the number back and again there was no response. He transmitted the 9-1-1 call to an available Chester car. Hawkins acknowledged the call and responded, even though it was two blocks outside her beat.

Meanwhile Sherman Carver, an off-duty Philadelphia Housing Authority Police Officer, was having a stormy relationship with his 40-year-old girlfriend, Marie Bates. Carver was banging on the door at 206 W. 5th Street while Marie Bates and her eight-year-old son, Odel, were inside. When his mother hurried to answer the door, Odel was scared and was attempting to dial 9-1-1. Carver entered the house and took the phone away from the boy.

Within a few minutes, Hawkins arrived at the house and knocked on the door several times. There was no response. She knocked again. Inside, Odel saw Carver take a gun out of his pocket. Carver then opened the door and, with no warning, shot Hawkins in the neck. Still conscious, Hawkins staggered backward off the porch and fell into the street where she died from the fatal gunshot wound.

Carver turned inside and then shot Marie Bates four times, killing her. He then walked outside and down the street. Neighbors frantically dialed 9-1-1. A caller from 204 W. 5th Street dialed the 9-1-1 center, ten minutes after the initial dispatch and said, "Officer shot." Upon hearing those words, Smith immediately began to feel very cold. His mind was racing.

But, turmoil was breaking loose on the street and it was his job to deal with it. Within a minute another voice screamed over the radio, "It doesn't look good." In addition to all the confusion, there was a lot of radio interference. Supervisors and other personnel came to the Chester console to help Smith.

The word spread quickly and police from the entire county were responding. William Ronan was one of those officers and Hawkins was on his squad. While enroute to the "officer down" call, he encountered Carver, two blocks from the shooting scene. Carver fired once at Ronan and missed. Ronan returned fire, but both of his shots also missed. Carver entered a red Thunderbird and fled the scene. Ronan was able to provide a description of the suspect vehicle and it was broadcast over police radio.

It was Smith's job to get help as quickly as possible to the scene. Paramedics, an Emergency Response Team, the Delaware State Police helicopter and the District Attorney's Criminal Investigation Homicide Unit were all needed at the scene. The cold feeling did not leave Smith. He was acting on instinct and training and knew he couldn't let his personal feelings interfere.

Carver fled south on Interstate 95 and sped into Delaware. At 12:30 am, Sergeant Thomas Noonan of the Delaware State Police stopped Carver's vehicle for speeding. After stopping Carver, Noonan determined that Carver was under the influence of alcohol and placed him under arrest. He was unaware at the time of the initial stop that he had just apprehended a cop killer.

Carver was taken into custody on driving under the influence and held for extradition on homicide charges.

Meanwhile family and friends of both Hawkins and Bates were being directed to the hospital by the police authorities on the scene. Connie Hawkins, police officer, wife and the mother of a 17-year-old son was pronounced dead.

Marie Bates, mother of two, day care worker and sister of Chester Township Police Officer Bret McNair, was also pronounced dead of multiple gunshot wounds.

Kevin Smith was relieved from the console at 12:30 am, at approximately the same time Carver was being arrested in Delaware. He broke down both emotionally and physically and a member of the Critical Incident Stress Management Team debriefed him and provided support.

Smith questioned himself for a long, long time. What could he have done differently? Why did he send Hawkins on the call? Why didn't he wait for another unit? The questions haunted him.

The tragic incident ended with two innocent lives being taken needlessly. All because a fifty-year-old Philadelphia Housing Authority Officer became involved in a domestic quarrel because he was unhappy with his job.

The night of July 1, 1993 changed the lives of many. It was the kind of night that dispatchers dread. An officer was lost in the line of duty. It was truly a "dispatch to eternity."

Epilog

Connie Hawkins was buried with full departmental honors, July 7, 1993.

Marie Bates, an unfortunate victim of domestic violence, was put to rest by her friends and family.

Kevin Smith was recognized for his actions as a true professional in the face of tragedy. He was honored by the Delaware County Police Chiefs Association and designated as Dispatcher of the Year. Smith continues his duties as a police dispatcher at the Delaware County 9-1-1 Center in Lima, Pennsylvania. He entered the police academy in September, 1993 and after graduation began service as a police officer in training in Burough, Pennsylvania.

Sherman Carver was extradited from Delaware, tried and convicted in the deaths of Connie Hawkins and Marie Bates. He is currently sitting on Death Row in Pennsylvania, exhausting the appeal process. ★

FOLLOW THE NORTHWIND
First Place, fiction, 1998
By Keith J. Bettinger

Park ranger Dan Tarrington worked in the parks in the north country. He worked alone, and enjoyed living and working that way. However, he did have a partner – a big black Newfoundland named Northwind, Windy for short. Dan loved Newfies. He could not remember ever being without one. It started with the one his parents purchased to protect him when he was a child. Newfoundlands are a special breed of dog. They are loyal, hardworking, protective, devoted, and the best friend you could ever have.

That is why Dan had Windy with him at his desolate ranger station. They were partners and friends. Dan could have had a German Shepherd or a Labrador Retriever when he was assigned to the post, but he wanted a Newf, and bought the dog himself. A little unorthodox, but, most of the things Dan did were unorthodox. His bosses knew him and knew how well he worked when left alone. As with most other times, they just looked the other way. Dan trained Windy himself. Windy loved to be around people. He loved to patrol the park with Dan. Dan in his tan and green uniform, and Windy with his official Ranger bandana. He always wore it on patrol. He thought he too was in uniform but Dan had it there to keep Windy's face clean of Newfie drool.

Windy could not wait to visit with the tourists. Windy loved kids - especially kids who had been eating ice cream. He would waddle over and give them that special Newfie kiss, and clean their faces, when he could get away with it, or when Dan let him. Windy outperformed all the other dogs, except in pursuits. But, Windy did not have to be fast. When Dan and Windy were tracking and chasing someone involved in a crime, people usually gave up when they saw Windy coming after them. Most people never saw a Newf, and when they saw Windy tracking and chasing them, some thought they were about to be eaten by a large black bear.

Newfs are born water dogs. They love to work, swim, and rescue people. Windy was a big hit around the lakes where he had saved many a person floundering in the water. Newfs also have great noses. Whenever a person got lost in their forest, Windy and Dan were always successful in finding them and bringing them out to safety. Sometimes, Windy and Dan had the unpleasant task of being called to scenes after the fact. Dan and Windy always gave the grieving families a sense of peace. When asked why they were always successful, Dan would repy, "I go where the Northwind takes me."

Dan and Windy loved to patrol their forests on foot. It was their special place together. They would camp in the park's forests for days at a time while on fire patrols. Both had knapsacks that they carried on their backs. Dan had his green department issued rig, and Windy had his own bright red saddlebags. As soon as Windy saw Dan getting the packs down, he would start to bark, and carry on until he was dressed for work. A Newf is a working dog, and always wants to work.

Around the campfire, Dan would talk to Windy, and Windy would cuddle with him, barking and growling his own communication, keeping Dan company and being a friend. They had a special bond, not of owner and pet. They were something more than friends. Soul mates is the best way to describe their relationship.

Dan had done his time and was preparing to retire. Windy was nine years old, and also ready to retire. Dan figured once the spring came, they would pack the job in and open a kennel and raise Newfs on a large piece of rural property Dan owned. The spring thaw would bring about a new career for both of them.

As spring approached, a young man entered the park and went camping, – winter camping. The weather was mild and it looked like it would be a beautiful weekend. Late Saturday afternoon, a sudden drop in temperature came on. The wind started to blow, and an unforeseen blizzard fell upon the area.

Dan and Windy were in their four wheel drive, checking the parking areas for stranded tourists. They found the camper's car in a snowed over parking field. They radioed the main desk and found out where he intended to hike and camp, which was not too far from the parking field. The ranger at the main desk told Dan there was nothing that could be done that night. The weather was too severe. The rangers would have to wait until the storm broke the next morning and hopefully the camper was prepared for the elements. Dan was informed he and Windy would lead the other rangers the following morning.

Dan told the ranger at the desk he and Windy had never left anyone stranded before, and they were not about to start now. Dan told him that he and Windy would start a search, and the rangers could begin a helicopter and snowmobile search at first light if the weather broke. Dan got his and Windy's equipment and they started hiking through the blinding storm.

After a couple hours, nearly frozen themselves, they found the camper. He was in his tent, but barely alive. Hypothermia was setting in. He had to be warmed. Dan broke out all the blankets, shirts, and other clothing that they had in their packs. He got a small fire going, but it was so cold. Dan went out and cut a large branch and stuck it in the snow outside the camper's little tent. He took Windy's red saddlebags and hung it over the limb, like a red warning flag. He then went back into the tent. He knew what he and Windy had to do. He called Windy over and they huddled together and laid on top of the nearly frozen camper. They huddled for warmth. They huddled for life itself.

At first light, the rangers from the main station were on their way. Snowmobiles and helicopters traversed the area. One of the helicopters saw something red. When they set down, it was Windy's saddlebags that they saw. They searched the area and found the little tent under drifts of snow. When they went inside, they found Dan and Windy on top of the camper. Dan and Windy were gone. The wind chill and subzero temperatures had taken them. They had succumbed to the elements. Beneath them was the camper. He was barely alive, but he had been saved.

Dan and Windy were perfect to the end – they never lost a person they searched for. Since Dan was a bachelor, the rangers were planning his and Windy's funeral. They looked in Dan's personnel jacket and found an envelope. Inside was a letter he thought would be opened years in the future. He had never thought that he and Windy would go together. As with most humans, he expected to outlive his dog. In his letter, Dan wrote that Windy was the best dog and friend he ever had. He requested that he be cremated and both his and Windy's ashes be spread in the high country of the park they both loved to patrol together.

His ranger friends followed his wishes. After the funeral, they loaded containers into helicopters and flew over the forests, lakes and meadows of the park. In each helicopter they opened an urn containing mixed cremains, and let the winds scatter the ashes of the partners to the parklands below.

Even though it was Dan and Windy's area, it still had to be patrolled after they were gone. Someone had to cover the post.

There is a new park ranger and her canine partner. Ranger Sandra Carmichael and her golden Labrador retriever, Wellington, patrol the area that used to be patrolled by Dan and Windy. They too, love their work and make an excellent team. However, it seems Sandy and Wellington have an easier job than their predecessors did. In the year they have been at the post, no one has been lost in the forest. Oh, it isn't that people haven't been reported lost. It's just that after the report is taken, and Sandy and Wellington suit up to begin the search, the people do not remain lost. The person just seems to walk out of the forest.

When the lost soul is asked how they found their way back, no matter who the person is, the reply is almost always the same, "I was about to give up when this ranger, walking what looked like a big black bear, found me. They led me down the mountain and brought me to this ranger station and I knew I was safe.

"When I turned to thank them, I felt a north wind blow, and they were gone." ★

THE FIRST PERFORMANCE
Second Place, fiction, 1998
By Pamelia Stratton

"The house sits on the corner of 5th and Washington Streets with doors on both streets. We don't know which one she uses as the main entrance, so you may have to go to both doors to get an answer," Sid instructed as he drove toward the house.

Tammy sat beside Sid on the front seat. The brightly wrapped package was on her lap and three helium-filled balloons danced against the head liner of the vehicle. Fred sat in the back.

"Sure is a nice day for a birthday. What a celebration Linda will have," Sid remarked.

He seemed pleased that the party was finally going to take place. The guests were all enroute and would arrive on time.

"Man, this is gonna be a gas," Fred chirped from the back. "I haven't had this much excitement in a long time. I'm just itching to get going."

"Just hold your horses, Fred. You can't jump the gun or you'll spoil the whole thing. Tammy has to go to the door first and get inside so the rest of us can sneak up and really shock the shit out of her," Sid cautioned.

Although Sid and Fred appeared to be enjoying the anticipation of the event, Tammy was feeling a little queasy. In fact, she was downright nauseous. Her hands were shaking and her legs were trembling.

This is stage fright, Tammy told herself. Most people are scared when they have to perform, especially for the first time. This is normal. I'll be fine. I hope, I'll be fine, she wished internally.

"Now remember...," Sid began. "Tammy... Tammy."

Finally Tammy realized that Sid was talking to her.

"Uh, yeah? I mean, what?"

"Are you all right? You look a little peaked," Sid said as he stared over at Tammy.

"Yeah, I'm fine. I'm just going over everything in my mind."

"Well, don't be nervous. Your job is actually quite simple. All you have to do is get Linda to open the door so you can go in. Once you're inside, the rest of us will sneak up and come through the door and the show will begin. You don't have to worry about a thing. We have people on both streets so no matter which door you go through, someone will give the signal to the others, and we'll be right behind you.

"The only possible problem is that sometimes Linda is a little shy and might not want to open the door or let you in. If she opens the door, you have to make sure that she doesn't shut it before we can get there. And if she won't open the door, just give us a signal and we'll have to come out and convince her to let us in," Sid instructed.

"If all else fails, I'll send Fred and his buddy Sledge to change her mind. Fred and Sledge have quiet a history of putting on a good show."

Tammy turned around slightly to see Fred display a huge grin. His hands gripped tightly around an imaginary object that he swung back and forth several times and then he began to bow to his imaginary, appreciative audience.

As Sid rounded the corner, a loud thump was heard from the back seat.

"Damn, my instrument fell over," Fred said as he put it back between his knees.

Sid pulled the car over to the side of the street.

"This is 5th. Linda's house is the last one on the left. See the door on this side?"

"Uh huh," Tammy responded weakly.

"The other door is just around the corner on Washington. Go to this one first. If no one answers there, go to the other one."

"Well, we have a few minutes, wonder what's on the radio?" Sid turned the radio on and music spread softly through the car.

Tammy's nausea was building to a crescendo. She was afraid she was going to be sick. I can't believe I actually volunteered to be the lead act, she silently told herself. I've never done anything like this before. What if I trip and fall? What if I freeze up and not a sound comes from my mouth? I must have been a fool to think I could pull this off. What was I thinking? Why did it seem so exciting before and now I honestly don't know if I can do it? My budding career could die on the vine, right here, and I'll never be a star.

Some static came over the radio but with all the fighting Tammy was carrying on within, she didn't notice it.

"Are you ready, kid? It's show time! Fred and I will stay here until you get inside, then we'll be right behind you. OK?" Sid asked hesitantly.

Tammy took a deep breath, a heavy sigh burst from her lips. "Yeah, I guess. As Elvis would say, it's now or never, baby. Wish me luck."

"Break a leg, kid," Sid encouraged.

"Here's looking at you," Fred grinned as he picked up his instrument, ready to begin his own show.

Slowly Tammy got out of the car. She cradled the present on her left forearm. Her left hand held on tightly to the balloons that began to flutter in the slight breeze. Tammy's knees were weak as she walked. Her feet weighed a ton and her legs were like lead. Her heart was racing and her breathing was labored like she had just run several miles. There was a throbbing sensation in her temples. She had about a half a block to walk to reach the first door. Tammy felt like she was moving in slow motion and might never make it to that door. "Dear God, please help me do a good job," she prayed.

When she got there, she grabbed the handle on the storm door and turned it gently. It was locked. There was no way she could get it open. She began to knock loudly on the aluminum side of the door. She knocked and waited. No response. She banged a little harder on the glass. No response. Tammy hesitated slightly, contemplating whether or not she could move toward the other door.

Suddenly a small voice called out from down near the corner.

"Yes? Can I help you?" a pixie-sized woman called out to Tammy.

"Are you Linda?" Tammy called back.

"Yes," the woman replied.

"I have something for you," Tammy announced as she plastered a big grin on her face and proudly marched toward Linda.

The balloons bucked and darted in the air to the rhythm of her gait and she let the present sway back and forth in her arm. As she closed the distance between Linda and herself, she could see that Linda was in her sixties, was dressed in one of those short flowered lounge robes that are popular with older women and was wearing pink terrycloth slippers. As Linda saw the present and balloons, a smile lit up her face and she began to come toward Tammy.

"Happy Birthday, Linda!" Tammy announced jubilantly.

"Oh, thank you, thank you," Linda gleefully answered as she reached out for the present.

"No, no," Tammy cautioned, "there's more to it than this. We have to go inside first."

"Oh, sure," Linda said as she headed for the door on Washington Street. "Right this way."

Tammy followed Linda toward the door. She took her right hand, which had been holding the right side of the present and reached underneath to grasp the black leather case. Linda opened the door and Tammy followed her inside the house. Linda turned around to face Tammy, excitement glowing on her face.

At that moment, Tammy pulled the black case out from under the present. A gold flash was seen as she flipped the case open and announced, "Tammy Hodges, FBI. Stay right here. We have a search warrant for your residence."

Instantly the color drained from Linda's face. Her eyes widened and her jaw dropped. Suddenly the door burst open and twelve male FBI agents, led by Sid and Fred, came running inside and dispersed through the house.

Sid went directly to Linda. "You can tell Bobby Bellarosa that your days of taking gambling debts and laundering money for the mob are over, starting today."

With that, Sid turned to Tammy. "You did a great job, kid." ★

THE GREAT CHURCH ROBBERY OF HERMANNSTADT
Third Place, fiction, 1998
By James Weiss

A continental glacier moves slowly; little by little and inch by inch. On the surface, the woman didn't move, not a muscle. There it was again, a horse, men's low voices. Danger, her mind screamed and her thoughts ran, demon-driven, like ice chunks being smashed by hammers. Her skin surfaces grew as cold as an ice sheet.

"Don't go into the woods by yourself. Go with the townspeople. Be alert. Always be cautious. There are robbers. Wolves. Bears. And, creatures that bite in the shadows of the forest's trees. Don't trust men. Men are rotten and evil," Mutter had told her years ago, her long dead mother.

At age 37, she could still be characterized as a handsome woman; high cheekbones, clever eyes and honey colored hair, not yet gray. Fear and anxiety gnawed at her.

Bad weather the whole summer meant hard times. Farmers' hay wouldn't dry. Its quality would be dreadful, soft and not fit for horses. Horses would get sick and have to eat mostly straw. Bad for horses: good for chanterelles. Damp, cold August weather satisfied the dark forest floor's mushroom growing needs. Half a rough cloth sack of yellow colored chanterelles, with their earthy aroma, rode the woman's hips. Fresh picked mint and sweet wood twigs for teeth cleaning – she had defeated the Tooth Stealing Trolls – shared space with the valued chanterelles.

She wished now that the townswomen were mushroom hunting with her, but circumstances paid her a hard-hearted price. She had few friends, because she had a son but had never married. People tracked mud over her name. Now, even her son had left, off to study. Others had over picked those chanterelles closer to Saxon Hermannstadt's protective stone walls.

She'd made a fool's mistake and found herself further out than ever before. Her legs felt wobbly as soup noodles. She reached down inside to her inner steel. She steadied herself. Over there, rocks and bushes, she moved slowly with precision, a dancer's synchronization, no twig snapping. She made herself small and hid.

What are the facts? Lukas possessed an analytic mind and set out to decipher them. He stood at the doors heading to the altar of his father's church. His heart was tight with commitment. He pieced together what happened.

It had been a day of Hermannstadt's Great Fair. People filled the town's square to celebrate the festivities. Old Mattes' eyes must have bulged and his stomach done flips when he found the church's treasure stolen. Lukas saw what Mattes had seen. The doors to the altar had been pried. Lukas investigated further. Now standing open, the altar closet doors had also been pried and the holy cups gone. Lukas noted all of the forced doors had been pried from the inside. Father had been in the Town Square with the Royal Judge and Burgomaster when Mattes stood shaking before them saying, "The church treasure is robbed!"

People say Father "turned pale and trembled." Mattes had been questioned, probably harshly. People took the news with a form of madness. Hostile. Aggressive words and fingers targeted poor Mattes. He collapsed under this pressure. Lukas paid particular attention. His shrewd eyes worked the puzzle. A tile over the chancel (the space above the altar of the church usually enclosed for clergy and other important people) had been removed. This means a rope must have been used. Meaning, two or more men.

Next, he questioned the city's gatekeepers. Two red-haired men left the city with packhorses on the afternoon of the theft. One went north. One headed south.

Lukas traveled the south trail. Surprised, he found both red-haired men together in the town of Mediasch. Discreetly, he learned their names. "That's Strong Getz, the blacksmith. That's Black Hans, the cabinet maker."

"Still I don't have enough evidence to accuse them."

He watched. Both men left, but in different directions. Lukas trailed after Black Hans, all the way to Schassburg. Strong Getz just happened to be there, too.

Despite Lukas' efforts, they spotted him and fled south to Kronstadt, toward the border. Lukas pursued. In Geister Forest they ambushed him. It came without warning. Lukas tumbled from his horse, knocked by a thick pole's blow. Dumbfounded, he tried to straighten up. He re-focused. Strong Getz moved to slam the staff into Lukas again. Inside, Lukas' adrenal gland pipetted adrenaline into his bloodstream. His heart rate increased. His blood pressure fast-tracked. His eyes tunnel visioned all else out. Except a staff and the person holding it.

Devil's duppies squeezed more blood from Lukas' heart. Hell's imps shifted yet more blood from Lukas' digestive tract to his brain and muscles. His face paled. He hurt. His mouth dried, worse than desert sand.

Sugar fast charged into his blood. Modern civilization meant nothing, because skeletons swinging curvy swords and bone-webbed riders rode and danced just outside of his vision. Fear of death steel jacketed him. So sudden. Shock. He would fight. Lightening and thunder exploded alongside Lukas' head. He fell flat, as solid as meat falling off a butcher's block. Blood erupted in front of his eyes. It spread into a pool, thickening into a paste of blackness. They beat him and left him tied to a tree for the wolves – a highway robber's trick.

"They have got to be far enough away by now," Lukas thought after he came to. He screamed for help. Travelers released him. Back in Kronstadt he stood before the Burgomaster. Lukas' suspicions were believed. Now with 20 soldiers on his side, Lukas captured Black Hans and Strong Getz near the Wallachia border.

It is recorded that they didn't confess – at first. Investigative procedural tools were applied: the tools of the Hermannstadt torture chamber. Thumbs smashed and their bodies rolled over a board of nails, the two red-haired men held to their innocence. Harsher methods were employed. They confessed.

"Lukas, my favorite and only son," his mother, a presentable woman with honey-colored hair addressed him in the privacy of her room, "I am ready when you are. Be a good boy and grab my trunk." A wagon stood ready to take the two to Agnetheln. Her brother the goldsmith lived there. Lukas heavy-shouldered his mother's trunk. Being a good son, he never fit the final pieces into the puzzle. His analytic mind fumbled that one – the two still missing gold cups.

People praised Lukas, a hero, for the recovery of their church treasure. He became wealthy and studied in some of Medieval Europe's finest universities.

As for Black Hans and Strong Getz, it is written, "They were tortured seven more days, skinned alive and hung by their heels. Their skins were tanned. One skin was taken to Marien Church where it was sealed into a globe on the church steeple." ★

FAMOUS & SOON TO BE FAMOUS POLICE WRITERS

After the second Police Writers Club conference, several of the attendees asked that the contest winning stories be made available. We all thought that was a good idea and decided to publish them in time for the 1999 conference. The more we talked about it, however, the more interest began to grow in producing an anthology that would also include the work of our other police writer colleagues. And the manuscripts began to appear. Among the many manuscripts that were submitted, we selected the ones you find following. Our criteria for inclusion were adherence to the police genre, originality and writing excellence.

Some of the works included are those of authors who have been published many times. Some of the stories are by authors who are seeing their first work published here. We are certain that you will find them all an enjoyable read. ★

COMMENTARY

THE HEALING GAME
By Marlene Loos

    I met the devil at a Long Island gas station on a sunny day in December while on patrol. Although much of the event is cloudy, certain things are forever a part of me. My mind functions like a broken record replaying a couple of minutes of the encounter over and over again. His intention was clearly articulated. "I'm going to fuckin' kill you!" He tried. He really did. He pulled the trigger. He shot me. He hit me twice. He tried fifteen times. Lucky for me, the devil is a poor shot.

    Humor. That is an important rule to remember when playing the healing game. Unfortunately, the rules for this game are ambiguous at best. I struggle to figure them out as I go. It's been five months since I've begun the game. I'm getting tired, but I'm still playing.

    Month one. I learn the mind is a wonderful and amazing creation, sealing away memories that are too traumatic to remember. The physical wounds take up most of my time. Two gunshot wounds, one to the chest and one in the right arm. They are open wounds, so I change the bandages twice a day. There is nothing I can do for the head trauma, the fractured cheekbone, or the broken rib. These injuries heal by themselves and, unfortunately, at their own slow pace.

    Nightsweats wake me at four in the morning. I place a second pair of pajamas near my bedside so I can change into something dry and focus on trying to calm down. My body develops an all over body rash and I am informed I am allergic to penicillin for the first time in my life. I am readmitted into the hospital for three days after being released less than a week before. Why is my body betraying me? I learn a new phrase this month "post traumatic stress disorder." The lesson for month one is patience. Healing takes time and sometimes has setbacks.

    Month two of the healing game. For the first time I am alone in my apartment. I over react to everything and find myself to be irritable. I come home from the local 7-11 convenience store after getting my morning coffee and find five messages on my answering machine. Telephone calls are very stressful. It seems like every ex-boyfriend is trying to get back into my life. I should find solace in the fact that they didn't want me dead, but I prefer my solitude to their company. Interaction with people is stressful. I realize everyone is trying to help. I thank them for their concern, but I don't know what they can do for me. I have the bandage thing down to a science. I watch television, avoiding anything with violent content. I notice my television viewing drops to an all time low. A couple of officers tell me they too have been shot, and forewarn me of months five and six.

"What happens then?" I ask.

"Don't worry about it," I'm told.

The lesson for month two is be gentle to yourself.

Month three of the healing game. I have successfully created a cocoon for myself. Physically I'm getting better. The wounds have closed. Emotionally I feel weak and vulnerable. Now what do I do? Go back to work? Someone asks if I'm going to retire. Retire? The thought is foreign to me. I can't comprehend why I would retire. Wait, the game is not over yet. The lesson of month three, enjoy the calm before the storm.

Month four of the healing game. I find myself going back to work. Everyone is amazed at my quick recovery. Fellow police officers joke around saying that being shot once would be enough for them to have their disability pension forwarded to a golf course on Myrtle Beach. Others suggest making little bulls eye targets over the visible scars. Their light comments miss their mark. I'm getting nervous for unknown reasons. Dark shadows have found a home in my mind, entering into my dreams and creating nightmares. I'm tired. I try to focus at work and it is extremely difficult. I now have a partner. He is my security blanket. I can't focus on anything. My concentration is lost. I took pride in my mind. It was a good mind. Now it's tapioca pudding. I see my opportunity to study for the sergeant's test come and go. I am getting frustrated. I step out of the shower and see the scars. Pink and indented. Every day I am reminded of the devil. I watch as some friendships dissolve, not understanding why. I sit at the edge of my bed, I'm in pain. Why me? Why did the devil want to be so mean to me? Why am I so unappreciative that my life was spared? Why are these days so painful? Who has the rules to this damn game?!

Month four sucks. More pain and no answers. Can someone tell me when it gets better? Silence followed by more of the same. Lesson for month four is to learn to be comfortable in silence.

Month five of the healing game. Someone put this game in reverse! I'm on therapist number four and feel I'm free falling into a complete state of chaos. Anger and betrayal are the two most common emotions I have right now. It's all misdirected and I have no idea where to channel the emotions that I am experiencing. I sit on the therapist's couch, looking down at the red and sore fingernails I've bitten to the point of "what now?" I'm lonely and missing my old self. I liked her. How come the devil changed me? Every day I am reminded of him through my scars, award ceremonies, his court dates, and talk of an impending trial to begin in the fall. I want it all to go away. I throw out extra bandages and bottles of saline solution. I hide the newspapers and tuck away the video tapes of the news reports my aunt made for me. I push it away. I push everyone away, tired of dealing with it, trying to make it disappear. I'm very busy in month five. The word 'retire' has a new meaning to me. I now understand why someone would retire. I frantically search my mind for another occupation. If I quit, would the devil then win the healing game? Would I be admitting defeat? He has altered my life forever. I find a new inner strength. He cannot win. Lesson for month five is to learn to accept pain and live with it.

Who wins the healing game? I will. The devil had his chance to win on that sunny December day when he viciously beat and shot me. He blew it. I have learned many lessons since that fateful day and I'm sure as I enter into month six and beyond there are many more lessons to learn. I realize I can't hide from the devil and what he has done to me. I need to confront all of the new fears he has created within me and mourn the innocence that he has stripped away.

I don't know how to handle month six to the end of the game because I'm not there yet. I just hope my words will help others who, from some unfortunate roll of the dice, find themselves playing the healing game. ★

COMMENTARY

THE LAST DIRTY WORD
By Gina Gallo

No one ever said we were angels. And, if it's true that a person is judged by the company he keeps, no one can reasonably expect us to be. We spend long hours associating with the bottom feeders of our society – the "A" (for aberrant) list of criminals, psychopaths and various lowlifes that often populate a cop's working hours. By necessity, our demeanor is sometimes a little rough around the edges and we hear, and use, language that would make a longshoreman blush. It's all part of the job description, what comes with the turf when we swear to serve and protect. Our oath of office came with an unspoken clause, the one that stipulates that we are cops first, on duty 24/7, in a profession that guarantees us a first hand look at the entire spectrum of human – and inhuman- behavior. An endless parade of people and situations that keep cops closer to the sediment than the cream of society.

As officers, we witness enough heartbreak, anger, grief and pain to fill untold books, countless TV cop shows that serve as a chronicle for our profession. And because we're professionals, we learn to hide our own feelings, use a "game face" to mask those emotions that surface with each savaged victim, each damaged soul we encounter. We're the designated warriors assigned to defend the law, protect the innocent, preserve the peace. And, if in doing so, our manners more closely resemble Robocop than Officer Friendly, it's understandable. We've seen it all, witnessed on a regular basis what might qualify for the average person's worst nightmare. We're seasoned cops, the rough and tough gunslinging cowboys of the techno age…aren't we? So why then, with all our game-faced, blue-streak cussing, vinegar-pissing bravado, is there one word no cop will allow himself to utter?

It's the last dirty word, the forbidden "F" word that even the saltiest street vet won't say. To speak it would be to conjure up the demons, envision a parade of nightmarish scenes most of us prefer to keep buried. It's a word that chills our soul, an uncomfortable reminder of the mortality we push to the limits every time we hit the streets.

Fear, like our instincts, is a phenomenon that never leaves us through the whole of our careers. It lurks around us, in various forms and postures. In its least damaging form, fear serves as a cautionary tool that keeps us sharp and hopefully keeps us alive. A "heads up" emotion that protects us even as we shrink away from it. A little fear can be healthy. A lot can be debilitating.

Some types of fear can paralyze, might even, in field conditions, be the critical difference between police action and a department funeral. A powerful emotion ill-afforded by those of us who wear the badge, yet it remains our constant companion. The silent companion we refuse to acknowledge, and try to ignore.

Consider the police "hero's funerals" we attend to pay homage and respect to our fallen comrades. The official department color guard marches at the head of the funeral cortege bearing those emblems of valor – the Stars and Stripes, the city, state and departmental flags. Mournful bagpipes sob out Amazing Grace as the flag that draped the casket is removed, folded slowly in the ritual presentation to the victim's family. The sun glints off the gold casket handles as well as the badges of the uniformed men and women who stand at attention for this somber assembly.

A single piper in black tunic and Glengarry plaid steps up and begins to play. The song is Honor Our Fallen, the traditional hero's sendoff song, with notes that shiver and weep in the light breeze. All across the sweeping grounds, white-gloved hands of supervisors and officers alike – snap up in a final salute to the fallen comrade.

Closer scrutiny of this scene would reveal that, in addition to the bagpipes' plaintive wails and the trim dress uniforms were tears, openly shed by some, winked away by others intent on preserving that officer's decorum. The grief is real, a pain we all share, but there's more. It's that word again, creeping into our consciousness, whispering the message that we all know by heart: that this could be any of us being buried today. That, at any time, God's graces might shift, separate us from those assembled by a single fateful act. When the final pipers' notes have stilled and the crowd has long since dispersed, each of us must wrestle with the images fear conjures and recall those times in our own experience when it was ALMOST us. Almost our turn.

Like the time we respond to a "simple" domestic. Any officer with more than a week out of the academy knows there's no such thing as a simple domestic, or a simple anything that's police related. We learn early that danger lurks behind every door, that what appears to be a benign scenario can escalate in a heartbeat to untold violence. That word again – fear – murmuring low in our ear as we assess the distraught woman, the stumbling man who appears intoxicated…but just might have a weapon concealed in the waistband of his slacks. The weapon we might not see until it's aimed at our faces. Will it happen this time? Cops exit an assigned job in one of two ways – by walking out or being carried out. Which will it be this time?

Or what about those countless street stops that are a vital part of aggressive policing? Even as you curb the suspicious vehicle, fear has your gut clenching, cranks up those adrenaline levels another notch until you've got the occupants safely out of the car and in custody. And you're down to one big question that accompanies every street stop – that this time there are no surprises.

Like the gunman who lurks in the backseat, crouched out of view with an assault weapon, ready to pump a dozen rounds of teflon-pirecing ammo right through your safety vest. It could happen – a grim reality of our job that's illustrated by the walls of "fallen hero" badges in police departments nationwide.

And then there's the fear that strikes on a more personal level, permeates the game face and professional exterior of even the most seasoned veteran. The one that assumes a prominent place in every cop's mental chamber of horrors, relived as a nightmare for years to come. Like the babies we discover, butchered and discarded like so much trash in an alley dumpster. Or children so violated and abused their child's eyes are ancient with pain. In those tragic faces, we see our own children, dread the possibility of these unspeakable horrors befalling them. And wonder how we can protect them, if we can protect them… while the fear speaks louder, a shrill echo in our pounding hearts.

The worst fear is the one that brands itself in our consciousness like a searing kiss. Beyond our personal safety, beyond even the well being of our families, this is the most insidious fear, the one that cripples us more effectively than any bullet. And like a bullet, it can leave us paralyzed, another of the "living dead" unable to function as police officers.

This most obscene fear is the one that makes us doubt ourselves, question what we as police are required to do. We survey the crime scene – more death, more brutal carnage that we couldn't prevent. Or didn't. Fear seeps in like a cold dank fog, clouding our perception of our abilities.

A rape victim shudders away from our protective hand, too terrorized to recognize that we're the good guys come to rescue her. Or an old lady, brutally beaten for her two dollars bus fare, stares at us in mute reproach. Where were we? Why didn't we help her? There are a hundred different scenarios, all with the same bottom line: what are we doing out here? Are we making a difference – will we EVER make a difference? Do the scales of justice have a special street version that might some day tip things in our favor, give us a little edge in the battle of good and evil?

No one knows, will ever know, since most of what a cop does is damage control – a thumb-in-the-dike approach meant to stem the tides a day at a time. It's a war out here that can only be fought that way, day by day, minute by minute, all the while hoping we're able to make a difference, save lives, do all those noble things we dreamed of when we took our oath.

It's that hope and faith we need to hear more clearly. If, instead, we allow ourselves to listen to the fear that questions what we do, who we are, and lures us into the defeatist's arena of doubt, then we've lost the battle, and ourselves.

Some words are merely profane, but this fear is the ultimate obscenity. Let this be the one word we continue to ignore, refuse to acknowledge, and never taste on our lips.

Fear: the last dirty word. ★

COMMENTARY

BUT FOR THE GRACE
By Marlene Loos

Jen pulled the police cruiser into the marked stall at the precinct. She had been called in on a "10-12," which usually meant there was a female prisoner to be searched and transported. Jen checked in with the desk crew to find out who wanted her services, then she found her way to the vice squad. Jen worked with this unit quite frequently, and received a warm reception.

"Whatcha got for me today?" Jen's question was barely out of her mouth before she heard a commotion coming from one of the interview rooms.

"We went 'ho trollin' and came up with one of the usual suspects. She's being a BITCH!" Mark, the arresting officer said to Jen, directing the last sentence at the prisoner across the room and assuredly getting a reaction.

"Fuck you!!" yelled the woman who was sitting on the floor with her hands handcuffed to the side of a desk. The two chairs designated for that room had been toppled over, the desk was pushed halfway into the center of the room. Tears had made the remnants of makeup and dirt streak down her unwashed face. Her nose ran and she made no attempt to stop it. As she yelled, snot and spit flew in the direction of the officers.

"Listen Jen, you want another officer? She's a live one!"

"Nah, I can handle her Mark. What's this stuff?" Jen asked as she pointed to a plastic bag containing paperwork and assorted pieces of broken make-up, a glass pipe, and small metal rods. Jen already knew the pipe and rods were used to smoke crack and it belonged to the prisoner.

"She doesn't travel light. I'll make it easy for you." Mark picked out the pipe and dumped the entire contents of the plastic bag into the wastebasket next to his desk. Many of the papers missed the intended target. Jen bent down to pick up papers that were strewn about.

One piece of paper caught her eye, it looked familiar. Her alma mater's letterhead was on the worn piece of paper. Jen's stomach fell as she recognized the handwriting on the paper as her own.

Jen went to Mark's desk looking for the prisoner activity log, no longer hearing the voices around her. She read the name on the top of the log "Erika Malesh" and her address "homeless" and her medications "AZT." Jen caught her breath. Jen secured her Glock 19 9mm in her gun locker and grabbed a pair of latex gloves as she walked toward the woman who was now kicking at the desk.

"Jen, you sure you don't want anyone to help you?" Mark seemed a little concerned, especially since it was his actions that riled her up so much.

"No, I'm fine!" Jen was focused on the room.

"Well, at least keep the door open."

Jen walked into the room, bringing in the two chairs that belonged there and closed the door behind her.

"Do you know me?" Jen asked the woman.

"NO!" Erika said as she continued kicking the desk.

"Look at me! Erika look at my face, do you remember me?!" There was a certain sense of urgency in Jen's voice.

"Nah, I ain't got arrested by no female cop!" Erika still kicked at the desk, making little effort to identify Jen.

"Fine. 'There but for the grace of God go I.'" Jen was still looking at Erika. The kicking stopped, their eyes met for a moment.

"Oh God!" Erika's dull eyes sparked at the recognition of a past she had long since forgotten. "Jen." Erika pulled her knees to her chest and put her head down and began to quietly sob, covering her face from a friend of long ago.

Jen reached down and uncuffed her hands. She put the desk back in its proper place and set the chairs up. She then helped Erika to the chair, and searched the desk for some tissues, handing them to Erika.

"You never found out how it all ended, Erika." Jen's voice was soft. "Do you want to know what happened? I looked for you, did you know that?"

"I didn't fit in. I... I... I never b-b-belonged there." Erika was still sobbing, barely able to speak.

"It was never your fault. Never. People are cruel, you never deserved that. I just wish I could have convinced you of that." Jen sat in silence, allowing Erika to cry and to regain her composure. As she waited, her mind went back to the Fall of 1984, over fourteen years ago, to her freshman year of college.

Jen was terrified of her new surroundings. She came from a town of five hundred people, where she lived on a dirt road. She found herself going to a university with over ten thousand students on Long Island. When she stepped onto the campus, Jen became painfully aware of how out of place she was. On the wealthy campus, every freshman had a new car, a gift from their parents for graduating high school. Her wardrobe consisted of Lee jeans, and flannel shirts with old Nike sneakers, hardly blending with the Jordache and Guess jeans her fellow students were wearing. Jen was there on a scholarship for athletics and academics. One thing that the other students couldn't make her doubt was her mind. She knew she was smarter than most. That was her saving grace. For her, the freshman year was painful and maybe that was why she befriended the girl in her Psychology 101 class that always wore black and heavy make-up. Her new friend was Erika.

They didn't hang out. Jen was intimidated by her, she looked so tough. She even smoked cigarettes! But they were friendly toward one another, when Erika would allow it. Erika would come to class and usually say "Hello,"sometimes she'd even go further with "How was your weekend?" Jen didn't think she ever wanted an answer, which was fine with Jen because she had discovered alcohol and barely remembered her weekends anymore. Other days, the bad ones, Erika would come in late and just sit there, staring straight ahead. Jen wasn't so scared of her on these days, because Erika's eyes would water and Jen almost thought if she disturbed her, Erika might cry. Jen knew if she did disturb her, Erika would definitely beat her up, but she might even cry and Jen wouldn't let that happen to her friend.

The conversation on October 10, 1984 that took place in room 203 during Dr. Gould's Psychology 101 class changed two lives forever. They were beginning an overview on sexuality. The professor had more confidence in the maturity of his students than he should have.

"Today we are going to talk a bit about sexuality and abnormal behavior," the professor began.

"I'd first like to see if we have any victims of rape in this room. I'm sure there are cases, then we'll discuss it, if the victim is willing, with the rest of the class. So, with a show of hands, how many students have been victims?"

Jen was too nervous to look around. How could this stuff happen? she naively thought. She looked over to her right, Erika's hand was up! Jen quickly looked away. She heard laughter from the two guys behind them.

"Jesus! Look at her, I wouldn't do her if you paid me!" one of the guys said loudly to his friend. The class had fallen still. Erika's hand still remained the only one up in the air.

"Look at how she dresses, that screams 'do me! do me!'" They kept laughing.

Jen looked over to see tears in the corner of Erika's eyes as she struggled to maintain her stony defense. Jen tore out a piece of paper from her notebook, 'There but for the grace of God go I,' she wrote on the paper and placed it on Erika's book on top of the desk. Erika grabbed the paper and without looking at it, put it in the pocket of her leather jacket. Erika snapped, finally taking her hand down, she grabbed her books and spun around. She spit in the faces of the two male students screaming "Fuck you!" as she ran out of the room.

The male students were stunned. They wanted to run after her and beat her into the ground, but still she was a girl and it was ingrained into their being that you can't hit a girl. So they'd sprung up, acting as if they would run after her, and each of them acted as if he was holding the other back, trying to calm each other down.

"Bitch! At least she got what she deserved!" one of them said.

Jen was shocked. There were other students laughing and agreeing with the boys. The professor had walked into the hall in a vain attempt to look for Erika, but she was long gone.

Jen spent that afternoon looking for Erika, but Erika was elusive. In fact, Jen had never seen her other than when she was in her Psych class. Jen didn't know her friends and really had no idea where to search for her. It was the last day Jen would ever see Erika until today. Life was cruel.

"Do you want to know how the semester ended?" Jen asked Erika again.

"Yeah." Erika was calmer and nodded as she looked at Jen.

"One of our class assignments was to dedicate a day to someone who had made a difference in our lives and to tell the class how you would live that day in honor of the person you selected. It was an oral presentation. Remember how quiet I was? Thanks to you, I broke out of my shell!"

"What did I do?" Erika was confused.

"I got up and said 'This day is dedicated in memory of Erika Malesh,' and everyone looked around and said 'Who's that?' I pointed to your empty seat. Then everyone wanted to know if you died, and I said 'Yes, we killed her spirit that day on October 10th. Perhaps we all could remember that day? Or was it that insignificant?'"

Jen went on. "The room had fallen silent. I looked at the two guys who sat behind us. 'Have you always belonged to the in group? Do you find yourself laughing at anything that the two jocks say because you want them to like you? Even if it is cruel and hurtful to another?'"

"I wanted to belong, or so I thought. But then I saw how vicious people can be. No one noticed you had slipped between our fingers. We were there to learn, and everyone missed the most important lesson of the class, even the professor.

"I continued, 'This day is dedicated to the memory of Erika Malesh and to the human spirit. Erika was the girl who sat in the second row, first seat of our psychology class. She was a woman who was searching for her way through life. Tragically, we all let her down. Erika came from a hard life, but she believed in herself. I never asked her, but I'm sure that she did. After all, she was here trying to become a better person. Her spirit was fragile, it needed nourishment. That spirit was crushed by two men who felt they could get more popularity at the expense of another human being. That spirit was destroyed by the fact that no one had the guts to stand up to these two and show Erika that she mattered.

"I let her down too because I was scared of their wrath being redirected toward me. I had slipped Erika a note before she left. It said 'There but for the grace of God go I'. I'll never know if she read it, but after class I tried to find her. I realized that I wasn't following what I prescribed. Regardless of your religious beliefs, believe me, this isn't a lesson about religion, it's a lesson on life. She never asked for such hardships, she never wanted anything but acceptance. Isn't that what we all want? Then why couldn't we give her a fair chance?

"Was breaking her spirit as much fun as you thought it would be? People are fragile. In this class, we all strive to be psychologists or psychiatrists. What happened to empathy? Are you going to laugh at your patients when they bare their souls to you? I want to thank Erika for showing me my weaknesses. I feel if I were stronger, I would have stood up and tried to change the tide of events at that time. Perhaps this is too little, too late. But if this day were 'Erika Malesh Day,' I would have everyone live the day realizing that there are a lot of twists and turns in this lifetime, some expected, others not. But if it were for luck, fate, or whatever you want to call it, we are all one step away from being the homeless man on the street or the president of the United States.

"Don't ever forget that. You are no better than me, nor am I better than you. That would be the lesson of my day. We all have to live with the fact that we lost Erika, that we all are responsible for that. That is a heavy burden to bear."

"You did that for me?" Erika asked.

"Yeah, but as I said, too little, too late."

There was a knock on the door. "You okay?" Mark asked.

"Yeah, just a minute," Jen said toward the direction of the door. "Okay, Erika, remove all your clothing, your jewelry and your hair band. Do you have any needles or sharp objects in your clothing that I should know about?"

"No."

Jen invoiced the property, including the bag of papers that Mark had previously thrown out. It was back to business as usual. Erika went to the small sink and washed her face. She finger-combed her hair and redressed, taking the time to make sure her shirt was tucked in and her shoelaces tied.

"You ready?" Jen asked Erika.

"Are they going to be mean to me?"

"Erika, look at how you acted. You get back what you put in, right?"

Jen handcuffed Erika with her hands behind her back, then opened the door.

Erika's eyes caught Mark's. "Excuse me," she said.

"What do you want now?" Mark was ready for another verbal altercation.

"I'm sorry about my behavior before, I just wanted to apologize." Erika was nervous, and looked at the floor.

"Ah, forget about it." Mark was surprised. "Jen, you gonna transport?"

"Yeah, no problem."

Jen drove Erika to the holding cells before her arraignment.

"You know my life is almost over." Erika looked at Jen from the passenger seat of the police cruiser.

"I know, I saw your medication list."

"I don't want to die in the street."

"You don't have to, you know. There are services available to you, but, Erika, they only work when you want them to work."

"You never lost faith in me? I mean, I wouldn't have recognized you today. You didn't have to talk to me."

"Erika, you control your destiny. I just believe in the human spirit. I think it's similar to the phoenix, it can be reborn from the ashes to soar again. I know, I've seen it happen. You can die with dignity, you can do whatever you want. The choice isn't mine, the choice doesn't belong to two guys in a psych class over fourteen years ago, it belongs to you alone. So, make the right choice."

Jen escorted Erika to the matron in charge of the female prisoners at the holding cells.

"How is she?" The matron asked Jen about Erika's behavior.

"She fine. She's a lady."

Erika's slumped shoulders straightened and she looked at Jen.

"Thank you."

"Good luck, Erika."

Jen headed back to the office to drop off the paperwork.

"Hey, you really bonded with her, huh Jen?" Mark asked.

"I went to school with her."

"Really? I didn't know what to say when she apologized to me."

"Well, you could have apologized to her."

"Nah, that wouldn't happen! Why should I?"

Jen took out a blank page out of her memobook and wrote, "There but for the grace of God go I" and handed it to Mark.

"This is why." ★

COMMENTARY

WHERE'S THE CRIME?
By Ernie Dorling

He wasn't sure why he did it. He didn't think it was that wrong. Certainly he knew it was "unacceptable." Inherently wrong perhaps but certainly not a crime.

And, if he had to do it over, he wouldn't because he's been treated like a criminal ever since.

Mike Briggs had been stuck in the same job for almost nine years. He was feeling complacent. A sense of emotional exhaustion built up over those nine years. The job, supervising a large office of federal investigators, had all the classic features that contribute to burnout, especially the routine work requiring vast amounts of paperwork and a promotional system that offered limited career paths. Senior management in the agency, like so many organizations, turned a blind eye to burnout. Sometimes when they had to, they would deal with the problem. But almost always, they avoided addressing the symptoms. But that's another story.

Maybe it was just plain curiosity. Certainly, he couldn't rule that out. Or maybe he was just visited by the fuck-up fairy. Who knows? But he keeps asking himself, what did he do that was so wrong as to warrant this type of treatment? Mike was one of the most respected and successful agency supervisors in the organization. A former Manager of the Year he was less than two years from retirement.

It was just fucking dumb. Stupid. A juvenile act. A lapse of sound judgement. Yes, all these things. But the administrative sentence for this so called "offense" was harsh. And handed down with little to no due process. Why? What did he do that was so wrong as to warrant this?

Mike hadn't stolen anything, lied in court or to Congress or to anyone for that matter. He hadn't been caught misusing the government car, an offense that carries a mandatory thirty-day suspension and sometimes results in an actual firing. He hadn't screwed up an investigation, been caught sleeping with an informant, lost his gun or credentials or leaked sensitive information to the press. Instead, he ran one of the most successful and consistently productive offices in the agency. All of which appears to have been disregarded because of an 8-minute lapse of good judgement. But he still doesn't see that what he did was so damned wrong.

The office was quiet late that afternoon. In fact, it was empty. Most of the other agents had left for the day or had gone off pretending to meet an informant or follow up on some lead in close proximity of their homes. As so often happened, Mike found himself alone toward the end of the day. Actually, he was just plain bored.

Mike logged onto the Internet to run some basic searches and see if he could find some jokes related to Monica Lewinsky. The jokes were being told at a pace faster than anyone could keep up with them. Mike wanted to have a few in his repertoire. Mike didn't remember how many matches Yahoo produced after he typed "Lewinsky" in the search box, but there were dozens, maybe a hundred or more. He scanned a few jokes. Some were hysterical.

Then he saw a match that offered the daily photo of Monica with the notation, "adult oriented" highlighted. A quick click of the mouse and there she was; a topless photo, certainly done with some type of trick photography.

"It was humorous if you have a warped sense of humor like mine," Mike later said.

Several flashing advertisements appeared above the photo offering instant access to adult web sites.

Mike thought, why not?

He wanted to see what was out there these days. He was surprised by the magnitude of material. It was definitely porn, Mike thought. Or maybe it was just some peoples' way of celebrating the First Amendment.

A couple of more clicks and more wild stuff appeared. Mike told himself he'd better get out of those sites before he caused himself a problem. But the photos kept downloading. Photos he had just seen began reappearing on the screen.

"Who's doing this?" Mike asked himself. It was, in computer language doing a loop. This made exiting the sites difficult.

He could have simply turned the computer off, but he didn't. He had been trained not to do that out of fear of losing other data. So he kept clicking the X at the top of the screen until he was able to exit the program. He shut down the computer feeling a sense of relief as he went home for the day. Two days later, Mike's boss called.

"Mike, this is John."

"Hi, John, How're you doing?"

"Not well," said John. "Your computer has been detected by Headquarters as having accessed some adult web sites."

"That can't be," Mike said. "Not my computer. But wait a minute, let me check my history files."

There it was. He had completely forgotten about his short incursion into these sites. He wasn't trying to lie or hide anything, he was just suffering from CRS, that affliction that comes over so many people late in life and close to retirement in this business – "can't remember shit."

"I'm afraid it's true, John," Mike told his boss. "I did it."

Cops are the worst when it comes to confessing. Prisons are full of guys who will go to their graves swearing they are innocent. Cops. They confess right away.

Mike explained how he had come to enter the sites and that he had not intended to. John was calm but serious. He saw some humor in the stupidity of his act, even indicating that it reminded him of a time when he was young and stupid.

"What's going to happen now?" Mike asked.

"There's going to be some type of inquiry," John said. "I'll get back to you."

As soon as Mike hung up the phone, he deleted the history file, a common practice by most everyone, so those with suspicious minds can't find where others have been while on the Internet. Then, to ensure that no one on his network would discover where he had been, he deleted the cache. This is also a routine task for some especially since clearing the cache actually improves the operation of the computer. Little did Mike realize that deleting the cache would result in an agency charge tantamount to obstruction of justice.

An hour or so later, John called back.

"Mike, Headquarters wants you to secure your computer. Shut it down and lock it in the evidence room."

"You're shitting me," Mike said. "This is fucking ridiculous."

"I know, Mike. But they want to have one of our computer trained agents do a mirror image of your computer and I can't get one until next week."

"This is bullshit," yelled Mike. "They've made the detection. They have what they need."

"I know. They want to make sure there isn't a history of that type of activity. No child porn stuff, that sort of thing," John said.

"Well there isn't. I can assure you of that," Mike told him. John could sense the frustration and anger in Mike's voice. "It happened just the way I told you it did. I can't believe they're making such a big deal about this."

Mike was pissed. Not only at himself but also at the way the agency was handling this. "Now we have the damn Internet police," he thought. I guess Big Brother is actually watching. What I wouldn't give right now for an old Royal 440 typewriter, the kind I started with in this business years ago, he thought.

Mike disconnected the computer and locked it away that afternoon. This would go away, he told himself.

He was wrong.

The letter arrived about ten days later. It informed him that an internal inquiry was being initiated for having misused a government computer while accessing voyeur web sites on the Internet.

Mike felt sick to his stomach. He couldn't believe they were actually going to assign this to an internal affairs investigator and expend time and money on this. Moreover, he couldn't believe he had put himself in this position.

To Mike, they were turning this into a personal war. He wondered what ulterior motives they had for pushing this so far. Stuff like this would easily roll off some peoples' backs while others would feel a sense of outrage. He'd caught his own agents doing similar things and simply told them to knock it off. A simple warning or ass chewing was about all this warranted. Besides, the agency policy on such activity was vague at best. But not so according to Headquarters.

Mike's first call was to an attorney retained by the Federal Law Enforcement

Officers Association (FLEOA). Like thousands of other federal agents, Mike joined FLEOA to have legal representation in situations just like this. He explained in detail to Dennis, the FLEOA attorney, what he'd done and what the agency was doing to him. The lawyer explained to Mike that this wasn't going to be a big problem.

Two weeks later Mike went to meet with the inspector, Spencer Gaines. Gaines had been assigned to the case and flew out from Washington to conduct the interview.

Mike was advised of his administrative rights. These are called Kalkines warnings. These warnings are unlike the typical Miranda warnings. Under Kalkines, you are told that you will be asked specific questions concerning the performance of your official duties. You are told that you have a duty to reply to those questions, that agency disciplinary proceedings resulting in your discharge may be initiated as a result of your answers; that neither your answers nor any information or evidence that is gained by reason of such statements can be used against you in any criminal proceeding and, that you are subject to dismissal if you refuse to answer or fail to respond truthfully and fully to any questions posed to you during the interview.

When someone is charged with a crime, that person has the right to remain silent. As a federal employee, however, Mike could be fired if he failed to respond to a question that might ultimately result in being suspended, which in this case would be like receiving a large fine or actually being terminated from the job. Mike told Gaines that he understood his administrative rights. Then he was told to raise his right hand and swear an oath to tell the truth.

Gaines showed Mike several photos that had been printed out from the web sites he had accessed. He recognized a number of the pictures while claiming to have never seen about half of them.

"How did you wind up entering or accessing those pornographic sites?" Gaines asked.

"I was on the computer doing some work, and I went into Yahoo! and typed in the word Lewinsky," Mike said.

"Okay," Gaines said. "When we retrieved your hard drive the history of those sites had been erased. Can you elaborate on that?"

Mike explained that he wanted to avoid any further office embarrassment and deleting the history and cache files. He even apologized for his stupid stunt. The whole taped portion of the interview took eight minutes, the same amount of time he was logged onto the "adult" web site.

It would be more than two months before the disciplinary board would meet to decide his fate.

The board consisted of three senior managers who would review the internal investigative report and make a recommendation for punishment. Mike couldn't have drawn a more unforgiving group than the three who were selected to review his case. One was deeply religious. A Southern Baptist by birth and upbringing, he would never approve of such conduct. The second had moved more than anyone in the agency, taking the next new job and promotion no matter where it was for the sole purpose of putting himself in position to be the agency director. No one was safe if they got in his way. He would be quick to make an example out of someone just to demonstrate his authority. The third member of the board was the most technically competent, but he was also someone who saw the world in that dualistic sense of black and white. There was no middle ground with him. You were either right or wrong. And, he was more of a follower than a leader. He'd go along with the other two.

"I know I'm fucked going in," said Mike, after hearing who the board members were.

"Mike, I really think you're rushing to judgment," John told him. "My guess is, if you're telling the truth, this will result in a letter of reprimand."

"No way," Mike said. "These guys are going to make an example out of me. This is uncharted territory and they want to send a message. I'm going to get fucked on this deal."

Mike suspected John of being naïve about many things, having spent most of his career with the agency as a manager in one office. He was too trusting of his counterparts. Mike was sure John couldn't believe personal considerations would impact the board's recommendations. Mike was also convinced more than ever that any connection between his reality and John's was purely coincidental.

It was almost a month before John called to tell Mike that the review board had recommended that he propose a 14-day suspension. John could have deviated downward or disregarded the board's recommendation. But he didn't.

"Mike, I can't go against the board on this," said John. "I spoke to the people in personnel and I don't feel I can minimize this because of your having deleted the cache. The board had no real heartburn with your accessing the web pages and your admission. But they, and I, really have a problem with your deleting the cache."

"I can't believe what I'm hearing," said Mike. "You're the same guy who told me that this would probably result in a letter of reprimand, the same guy who said he'd stand by me and kept telling me to hang in there."

By recommending 14 days, the board was ensuring that Mike's appeal route was limited. Had the board recommended 15 days or more, Mike could have appealed the decision to the Office of Personnel Management's Merit Systems Protection Board (MSPB).

"Why didn't they give me 15 days?" Mike asked. "That way, at least I could bring an attorney with me and put on a defense in front of an administrative law judge. These gutless bastards in the agency's star chamber don't want to risk this being overturned by the MSPB. Nor do they want to pay to adjudicate it," Mike screamed. "This is just plain bullshit."

"Mike, you've got to understand where the board is coming from. You deleted the cache. I can't understand why you did that and neither can they. You took action after being told there would be an inquiry," John said.

"That's right, John, an inquiry. Not a major fucking investigation. Besides, I told you why I deleted the cache file. I didn't want anyone in the office to know where I had been. This was embarrassing enough without having others in the office learn about this. And I had no idea you guys were going to seize the damn computer," Mike told him.

"Listen, John, I never considered this a problem and neither did Gaines when he came up here. In fact, he seemed satisfied with the answer. Had I thought it was going to be such a big deal, I would have explained it during my interview with Gaines," Mike screamed.

"I agree Mike, that it could have been investigated better," said John. "It wasn't addressed in detail. In fact, I'm surprised they didn't interview me."

"You're right," Mike shouted. "They didn't investigate that thoroughly, and now I'm being sentenced for something that wasn't part of the initial inquiry. And what about the official notification I received that said I'd be notified in writing if the administrative inquiry would be expanded to include additional issues? I was never notified of that. What about that?" Mike demanded to know.

"Listen, Mike," John said. "I'm going to stand behind you on this. I told you, if you're right, I'll stand behind you a hundred percent."

"Fuck you, John," Mike yelled, risking the filing of even more charges. "When I'm right, I'll stand on my own. It's when I'm wrong I need you to stand with me. It was wrong to screw around for those eight minutes on the Web but that's where this ends. And you haven't stuck by me on this as far as I'm concerned. As for deleting the cache, I'll stand on my own on that."

When Mike hung up the phone, he knew that John would not take his outburst personally. He'd be pissed for a day or so and that would be it. They'd move on. But John knew Mike was more than disappointed in him. He was on his own.

Mike sat at his desk staring out of the window overlooking the city and thinking about his predicament. This was just fucking great, he thought. John's admitting that this could have been investigated better. And, he wants me to see it the board's way.

Mike knew that the building of the pyramids is considered one of the great mysteries of the world. Hell, that's no mystery, he told himself. About a million slaves were ordered to move large stones long distances and place them on top of each other. What is a bigger mystery is what happens to people when they get promoted so high in government or are transferred from the field to headquarters. How is it they lose touch with reality? Now, that, he thought, is a mystery.

An hour later he called John back.

"So, what is my recourse," Mike asked him, his voice now calmer and more controlled.

"You've got to write up your rebuttal and explain all of this in writing. Then present it to Tina. She's the deciding official. I believe you," he said. "I'll support you on this. But you have to explain it to her."

Tina Clark was the Deputy Director. Mike had met Tina just once, briefly at a conference just after the agency hired her from another agency in order to demonstrate its diversity in the workplace. Never mind that they had passed over several highly qualified white males who had come up through the ranks within the organization and helped make it what it was. The agency was hell bent on putting a woman in the deputy's spot to check the right box. And they were conditioning her for the director's job. Only the most naive thought otherwise.

Tina was certainly nice enough. Mike had no first hand knowledge of her investigative skills or track history in this profession. But at that level, it's not really important. Mike didn't know her and she didn't know him, other than by his reputation, which was still excellent by most standards. Nonetheless, she was gaining a reputation for being more concerned about where the agency was going and not where it had been. Something the good old boy network had not put much emphasis on. Regardless, Mike felt sure that he was going to remain screwed.

Several weeks later Mike flew to Washington to present his case. He had spent the time preparing a written summary of the facts as he had recalled them and knew them to be. Tina would have already read his brief and no doubt, made up her mind as to what her decision was going to be. This was all nothing more than formality. A way to embarrass Mike even more. But, he had no choice but to play along with the game. Refusing to do so, would only give the agency the ammunition it needed to stick with the 14-day suspension. By not playing the game, they could say that "Mike never disputed the charge or the sentence." Mike wasn't going to make it easy for them.

As he entered Headquarters operational section, he was welcomed by many of his former colleagues, all of whom had no idea why he was in town. Mike explained that he was just in on a day trip to meet with some attorneys from the Justice Department to review a major case. It was a simple but effective lie. No one questioned him further. The pleasantries dispensed, Mike was ushered in to see "her highness" where he would be expected to beg for forgiveness.

Tina had been given a nice corner office overlooking much of Washington. It was hot in her office. Mike tried to keep from sweating. She could have turned the air conditioning on a bit more he thought.

"Mike, please have a seat," Tina ordered. She was smiling, and her voice was pleasant. The meeting was starting off cordially enough.

"Thank you," Mike said.

"How was your flight?" she asked.

"Fine," Mike said, keeping his answers short. He didn't want to make small talk with her. He wanted this ordeal over with. Tell me you're going to stand firm by the recommendation of your senior managers, those judicial geniuses that are behind my execution, Mike thought to himself.

Tina sensed he was uncomfortable and wanted to get right to the issue.

"So, I've read your brief," she said. "Very well put together."

"Thank you," Mike said. "I tried to address the facts as I know them and to demonstrate that there was never any intent to cover up the accessing of the adult Web sites. Punish me for that if you want, something that is fair that is, even though, there is no specific agency policy against it. But, I can't accept this accusation of trying to cover this up."

As he spoke, Mike sensed something very familiar about her. He had only met her once, but it was as if he had seen her somewhere other than that brief meeting. The hair was different, both in color and style, but he had seen her somewhere before. He just couldn't place her.

Tina listened as Mike explained the entire incident again, including the sequence of events that led to access to those "adult" web pages and why he deleted the history and cache. She listened as if she actually wanted to hear it. Mike became more focused on where he had seen her than on his oral presentation of his defense. Where had he seen her before he asked himself? He couldn't ask, that would be too personal. It wasn't the time or place for that question. Then he realized it. He had seen a photo of her on the Net. It was a provocative photo of her and another woman. The hair was different but it was her. He didn't know if it was a recent photo or not. Nor could he recall which web site it had been that he had seen her on. But it was her. No wonder she was listening so attentively. It was clear now why she was so cordial, wanting to know every detail about Mike's intrusion into this world.

Mike ended his presentation by apologizing for his indiscretion. He told her it would never happen again and was sorry for any problems this had caused. It was, after all, the words he was expected to say as part of the game. But, he actually meant them. Not that anyone cared. These eight minutes had already cost the government several thousands of dollars in work hours and travel expenses. Mike had played out his role well.

Tina thanked Mike and told him she would make her decision soon. Mike didn't know if she knew or suspected anything. She didn't ask and he didn't tell. After all, that is one of the themes of the Clinton administration and Mike thought for once, he would actually benefit from one of the President's policies.

"Let me walk you to the elevator," Tina said.

As they walked together down the hall, Mike asked. "Tina, just answer one question for me."

"Sure, Mike, if I can. What is it?"

"Where's the crime here? I mean why all this for these eight minutes? Exactly what crime did I commit?" Mike asked.

Mike hadn't really intended to ask that question in such a frank manner. But now, he was intrigued by what her answer would be. He felt that he had some information that he might be able to bargain with later if he had to appeal Tina's decision. He'd cut similar deals in his career both for himself and to help some of his agents who had gotten themselves in some minor trouble for violating some agency policy. But these deals had all been cut with men who had allowed some secret they would have preferred to have kept hidden, become known. These situations had normally resulted in some mutual benefit to all parties. But in this case, there was a woman involved. He wasn't used to cutting such deals with a woman, especially one with whom he had no history. Mike hoped to never have to use the information. He wasn't sure he would no matter what the outcome.

But before Tina could answer, the elevator opened. And there she was, getting off the elevator. One of the women Mike had seen from the Internet. It was her, the hair, everything almost exactly like in the photo.

Tina never answered Mike's question. Or at least he never heard the answer.

What he heard instead was, "Mike, let me introduce you to Karen, my twin sister." ★

CRIME SOUTH OF THE BORDER

THE FEAST OF SAINT CECILIA
By Liz Martínez DeFranco

Consuelo sat on the hard pew and listened to the mariachi music drifting toward the back of the church. The musicians wore light green costumes, the color of the sea that rhythmically stroked Puerto Vallarta's malecón three blocks away. As she allowed the sliver of sunlight that made its way through the narrow window to caress her face, Consuelo closed her eyes and listened to the singer. He crooned in perfect harmony with the sweet chords of the guitarrón and the other instruments in the band.

The mariachis finished a set and a few people – all of them Americans – applauded. Consuelo felt no less enthusiastic, but she did not clap. Putting her hands together in a noisy fashion might be appropriate in a nightclub, but never in church. She knew that the gringos clapped only out of ignorance, but she had to wonder about their upbringing. Were they not Catholic? It seemed inconceivable that one could be anything else. And were their churches so different that applause was encouraged? It did not occur to Consuelo that some of the tourists sitting near her might not attend church at home, or that they might be ignorant of Mexican social graces.

As the band members genuflected and exited to the left, the next group of mariachis paraded down the aisle on the right-hand side of the church and spread out in front of the altar. Before them was a statue of Saint Cecilia. The altar was decorated beautifully, with garlands and colored lights. A spotlight bathed the statue in a beatific glow. Saint Cecilia, in turn, wore a gentle and inviting expression on her plaster face. The new group of musicians was clothed in salmon-tinted uniforms. As they moved about, assuming their places in front of the altar, the metal buckles that decorated the length of the outer seams of their pants legs rattled slightly. It did not take long for them to prepare.

The lead singer began serenading the statue. Consuelo closed her eyes and pictured horses and the medieval knights who rode them through her schoolbooks years, a lifetime ago. This is the way a smitten knight would sound beneath her window, she imagined. She saw herself clothed in a long, full dress of the middle ages, brushing her dark, luxurious hair at the upstairs window as the knight sang beautiful songs of eternal love from the garden below.

Lucky Saint Cecilia! she thought now. To have an entire day every year when the mariachis came to serenade her with their beautiful music. They sang and played for her in the hopes that she would bless them in the coming year and leave them without want.

Consuelo had heard that this custom was not universal. Some said that it was only in her seaside village that the musicians came to pay homage to their patron saint on her day. Right now she didn't care. She was enjoying the free concert. She lifted her head and glanced out the window. A woman was perched on the ground-floor window ledge of the building next to the church. Her head was lolling about. Consuelo thought she looked drunk. She was disgusted, but at the same time, too good a Catholic not to offer a quick prayer for the woman's salvation. She crossed herself. Gracias a Diós, she herself did not suffer from that problem.

Not that her life was worry-free. On the contrary. But Consuelo knew she was lucky to have work as a maid in a big house. Six days a week, she helped the señora cook and clean, wash the clothes and pick up from the ground the fruit that fell from the trees in the courtyard. All this she did in a quiet manner, so as not to disturb the señor, who worked from an office in another part of the house. He worked with words on a complicated looking machine.

Consuelo was always careful to avoid touching the machine when she cleaned. She wished to avoid displeasing both the señor and the señora. She was afraid that either the machine would mysteriously hurt her in some way if she came too close – perhaps by electrocuting her, or, no less frighteningly, by sucking the words right out of her brain. (Where else would all those words come from that she saw dancing across the screen when she peeked over the señor's shoulder as she cleaned the room? She was convinced that they came from the señor's mind. And if the machine could pull them out of his head, she reasoned, why not from her own?) Alternatively, she was frightened of doing damage to the electronic wonder in some way. (Although she secretly thought the señora might like that: more than once, Consuelo had heard her refer to the computadora as the señor's "mistress.")

The couple with the big house was good to her, no doubt. She was able to eat there each day that she worked, and once, when she was very ill, the señora had taken her to the doctor and paid for the medicine that she needed. No, her problems did not stem from her job, which she was lucky to have in any case. Her difficulties in life were brought about by Raúl.

Wasn't it always the same? she thought. Even in the days when the virgin Saint Cecilia was alive, men probably caused women the same problems they were causing them today. Consuelo didn't know anything about Cecilia's life, but she was sure that the virgin probably had been spared heartache from suitors. But perhaps not. After all, one did not become a saint without suffering. And men caused a lot of suffering.

Consuelo should know. She was subjected each day to the evidence of Raúl's cruelty. Oh, he would never hit her – not like her friend Dinorah, whose husband Juan came home more often than not late at night, stinking of booze. His heavy fists had left poor Dinorah looking quite frightful. That was Dinorah's lot in life, not Consuelo's, gracias a Diós. No, Raúl would not lay a finger on her.

In fact, that was the root of the problem. Raúl had been laying his fingers – and other things as well, Consuelo knew – on other women. Yolanda, who lived in the neighboring colonia, had paraded her swollen belly around for months. Consuelo knew very well who had caused that swelling. And now, each day as she made her way to the bus to go to work, she saw the niñito running around in his fine little shorts and tiny American sneakers, playing with the other children of his neighborhood.

She seethed each time she thought of the food that was taken from her mouth and given to that puta and her illegitimate son. And now she heard rumors in the streets that Yolanda was preparing to move to a nicer colonia, where the streets were cleaner and the buildings better kept. Consuelo thought about Yolanda in a new neighborhood while she was scrubbing the tile floors of the big house where she worked. As she cooked other people's meals, she imagined the little boy in his tiny finery growing up in – well, if not in luxury, then at least better conditions than those in which she herself lived. There were no shopping trips to the city for Consuelo. No, she thought bitterly, if she had new clothes, it was only because of the generosity of the señora who lived in the big house.

In the past two years, Raúl hadn't laid out a centavo more than was absolutely necessary for Consuelo to keep their home. He certainly hadn't bought her any new clothes – and why should he? He never took her out any more, so there was no need for Consuelo to look pretty.

Consuelo knew she should not have ugly thoughts, especially in God's home. She silently crossed herself again to ward off the evil brewing in her mind, but it was not helping. Concentrate on the music, she told herself sternly.

The full chords of the love ballads resonated throughout the church. The mariachis strummed and sang most sincerely as they courted favor with St. Cecilia. A tourist stood to take their picture. Consuelo pressed her lips together and shook her head. All that money, but they didn't know how to act.

Consuelo herself was a lady. You would never catch her taking a photograph inside the church or being loose with the men. She saw these norteamericanas draping themselves all over Mexican men so that the men became spoiled and expressed interest only in fair, light-eyed women. Where did that leave her? Consuelo wondered. She was dark-skinned, with a long black braid and eyes the color of night. So many men here were spoiled by the gringas who came down for vacation, bedded the local men, then returned home to their real lives.

Sometimes Consuelo was torn between wanting to laugh at the foolishness of the men and wanting to weep for them as their dreams of a green card were dashed time and again. What do you think she sees in you, pachuco? she was tempted to ask these men with their broken hearts. Consuelo might be a humble house servant, but she was not an idiot.

No, she was nobody's fool. She could see the writing on the wall for herself, not only when it came to others. And the picture that formed right now was of Raúl mounting his horse and waving good-bye to her. Claro, he didn't have a horse, Consuelo knew, but she allowed herself a moment of whimsy. In reality, he would climb into his broken-down Jeep that was kept together mostly by prayer, and chug off down the cobblestone streets with Yolanda and their son. In fact, Consuelo would wager that Raúl would put in an appearance at the church today just to pray that his Jeep survive another year. She permitted herself a tiny smile as she imagined the three of them – Raúl, his whore and his bastard – stranded up in the mountains somewhere, the vehicle having given up the ghost.

She sighed. That would never happen, she knew. Things like that did not befall people like Raúl, who lived a charmed life. Except that Consuelo would not bend to his final demand: a divorce. Oh, he hadn't come right out and asked her for one, but Consuelo knew he would sooner or later. But she would never yield. Never! She was a good Catholic, and while she could overlook certain things, she could never become divorced. No, the church dictated "until death do you part," and Consuelo was not going to part one moment ahead of schedule.

Consuelo suddenly heard something. She stiffened and turned her eyes slowly to the right. She knew it. She had known he would show up here. Raúl was with his buddies, all of them dressed in the finery of the mariachi. The buckles of their costumes rattled as they unpacked their instruments. They whispered quietly as they prepared for their turn before the altar.

How dare he show his face in church, she thought. The biggest sinner in town here to request a good year from his patron saint. Hah! thought Consuelo. That's what you think. Do you really believe that the virgin will listen to you? she mentally railed at Raúl. You fat tub of lard, she thought. I hope you rot in hell. How could you do this to me? Tears began rolling slowly down her face.

Consuelo wiped here eyes with the hem of her dress and scrunched down lower in the pew. She did not want her husband or his friends to see her, especially not like this. She did not want anyone to know of the pain that knifed through her heart. There was an envelope beside her, and she patted it in time to the music, as though for comfort.

The mariachi band that was playing completed their final note and left quickly. Now Raúl's group moved to the front of the church. She recognized most of them, but a couple were new members. Someone she didn't know hummed loudly for pitch, then the song began. "Cielito Lindo" indeed, thought Consuelo. Only her fury kept her tears in check.

It was too hard for her to sit there and listen to Raúl crooning to the virgin. Those were the songs of love that he used to sing to Consuelo in better days. She moved up the aisle and out the front door of the church, into the sunshine. That was the one constant in her life: the sun. Always there to warm her, to bake the earth and everything else it touched. Mariachis who had finished serenading Saint Cecilia called and waved to others who had yet to go inside. The steps of the church were awash in the colors of the mariachi costumes and the sounds of musicians in good humor. Blues mingled with blacks, whites and shades she thought of as Easter colors: salmon, sea green, lavender.

Consuelo turned her head and caught a glimpse of Yolanda and her son seated on the steps. Her stomach turned to stone. Yolanda was feeding the boy. He ate slowly, pausing to look around after each bite. His mother was busily encouraging him to keep chewing, wiping his chin, now smoothing his hair. She loved him, Consuelo could tell. Objectively, she could see that the boy was sweet. Inquisitive, looking at the world through those eyes that were miniature versions of Raúl's. Her chest knotted again and she tightened her grip on the envelope she had brought outside with her.

How could this be happening to her? Consuelo beseeched her Maker for the millionth time. What had she done to deserve this? she thought. She had done nothing wrong. She had cheerfully cooked and cleaned, tended to Raúl's every desire. And this was what she got in return? Mockery as her husband flaunted his affair and its fruits – "the fruit of thy womb, Jesus," she thought, and laughed a bit hysterically inside her head – Holy Mary, mother of God, why is this happening? Consuelo wanted to scream.

She backed against the wall of the church to steady herself. The brick was warm, and the heat soothed her. I'm all right, she told herself. It's going to be okay. She gripped the jamb of the huge doors that led in to the church and held on. Nothing can happen now that is worse than anything that has already occurred, Consuelo reassured herself. She saw Yolanda help the boy stand and brush crumbs off his lap. He took her hand as they started off. Probably to find a bathroom, Consuelo thought just as she heard the music draw to a close inside.

Her body tensed. Raúl would be coming out of the door any moment now. Consuelo's grip tightened around the envelope she had lifted from the señor's office in the big house where she worked. Her palms were sweaty, but she held it fast. She knew that what she had to do was God's work. Her heart beat faster as she heard Raúl's gravelly voice become louder as he proceeded up the aisle.

As he cleared the doorway, Raúl was blinded momentarily by the sunlight. Consuelo stepped forward at that moment – ah, you have forgotten what a good dancer I am, Raúl, what perfect timing I have; you have not held me close in such a long time – and thrust the envelope toward him. The sharp kitchen knife she had secreted inside slipped right through his ribs and into his heart – not for nothing had she spent years trimming fat and boning meat. Raúl's eyes widened and he gasped. As he fell backwards, he reached out as though to pull Consuelo to him, but she had already disappeared, her flat-soled shoes echoing lightly off the stone steps of the church as she fled.

No one had seen the event. The mariachis gathered around Raúl as he lay on the ground, sure he had suffered a heart attack. Well, with all his extra weight, that was no surprise. Yolanda and the boy reappeared just as the blood began seeping out of the wound. By some fluke, the envelope remained in place, obscuring the knife, adding to the confusion as everyone thought it was something Raúl was holding on to.

"My cousin," Raúl croaked. "Take care of my cousin – and her son." His eyes closed.

"His cousin?" asked Pedro, who played the guitarrón. "What is he talking about?"

Through the fog, Raúl could hear someone shouting for a doctor. ¡Emergéncia! Get the ambulance. Somebody call the Red Cross!

Who's sick? he thought.

"He means Yolanda," Raúl could hear Chava, the singer, reply. "He brought her here from his home village in the mountains. He has been taking care of her."

Oh, yes, Yolanda. Raúl had scraped together every extra centavo to help the poor girl, he recalled fuzzily. She had become pregnant out of wedlock and his aunt had thrown her out of the house. She had no one else to turn to. He had not dared to tell Consuelo – she would have disapproved also, she was such a staunch Catholic. The fog became a swirling red mist. Raúl thought he heard Yolanda crying, but it couldn't be because here was his grandmother, holding out her hand to him. "Come," said his abuelita. "Join the rest of the family. You're home now, where you belong."

Raúl tried to look back over his shoulder. All he saw were the white uniforms and black gunbelts of the "tourist police" who had been hastily summoned from their duties between beach umbrellas and in the Plaza, but they were very far away, and shrinking each moment. He craned for one last peek at Consuelo, his love, but he couldn't spot her. Suddenly it didn't matter any more, anyway.

Consuelo kept to the back roads until she reached the highway. A dark man in a truck offered her a ride. He was clad in a black cowboy hat and well-worn boots. "Where are you going, señorita?" he asked, and a while later, "Are you married?"

"I am a widow," Consuelo said, and burst into tears. ★

CRIME IN THE CITY

BABES IN GANGLAND
By Gina Gallo

The names are exotic, enticing. They sound like the titles of boys' adventure stories: The Spanish Cobras, The Counts, Insane Unknown, Latin Dragons, La Raza, The Vice-Lords, Two-Sixers. These are some of the street gangs in Chicago, more than one hundred forty all told, but the numbers grow daily. Asians, Hispanics, Blacks, Whites, all ethnic groups can now boast representation in the city's gang society. Like an ungainly pie, the city is divided into turfs fought for and presided over by resident gangs. In the most simplistic terms, Chicago gangs pledge their allegiance to one of two main groups. There are many sub-groups, minor factions and spin-offs of larger groups, but all of them are part of either the "People" or the "Folks." In Los Angeles, it's the "Crips" and the "Bloods." Whatever the city, the outcome is the same: invade the turf of a rival gang and you're teasing the Grim Reaper. It's not just a question of survival, it's about respect. And, increasingly, it's about big business. The name of the game is drugs, a never-fail supply-and - demand empire that can launch a gang's economy into the stratosphere. Drugs need dealers, suppliers and runners. A gang provides all of that.

Initially, most kids join gangs for support. They feel they're not getting it at home in their single-parent or absent-parent families. Or they're getting hassled on the street. In communities where strength lies in numbers, a gang offers them everything that's missing: loyalty, support, protection. Fuck with me, fuck with my brothers.

Some kids start young. At the age of eight or nine, when they're just "shorties," they're being recruited by older gang members. Young kids make good "mules" – the ones who transport money and drugs. They're too young to be locked up if they get caught, too young to do any real time in the Audy Home, Chicago's Juvenile Detention Center. So they run the money, sometimes four, five thousand at a time, between the dealers and the dope houses, learning the hustle. By age ten or eleven, they're junior gang members, as adept at gun usage as the older guys.

By now they've have a taste of the wares – the drugs, the girls, more highs than they ever imagined. They're part of the gang now. They run with the pack. For many, the story ends in death. A few lucky ones manage to get out, reclaim their lives.

For Rigo DeLeon, it was the fast life, a golden glamorous ride, that shot him light years beyond the boredom of home. His father Guillermo was a mechanic who worked hard every day, came home each night to his wife Alicia. His home where, amid the chaos of five lively children, he was happy to forget the long workday with some family chatter and a couple of cold cervesas. Devout Catholics with a strong sense of family, Guillermo and Alicia tried to instill the same values in their kids. Not the usual family profile for what Rigo would become.

He was the oldest child, a smart boy, quick in school, quicker on the street. He saw how much money the dope dealers and gangbangers were raking in, saw how hard his own father slaved to put food on the table. What was the point of killing yourself? Why be poor when you could be rolling? For Rigo, it was a no-brainer. He wanted to be his own man and enjoy the finer things of life- a flashy car, a flashier woman and a big wad of cash in his pocket.

So when some gang members approached him, just after his eighth birthday, and asked if he wanted to be a mule, he said sure.

Smart kids learn fast. At nine, he's running guns. At ten, he's a junior gang member. And is careful to hide from his father the gang's official pitchfork tattoo that's his pride and joy – proof that he runs with REAL men.

These real men wean him on marijuana, and then hash, and reward him with lines of coke when he's very good. Like, good enough to knock off a mom-and-pop grocery store, or pistol whip an old lady for the seven dollars she had buried in her purse. By the time he's twelve, Rigo is ready to move on. Show us you got some huevos, his fellow members tell him. Time to ride 'the horse,' man. Get some hair on your balls! Be a man!

Rigo is pretty sure he's a man already. Just the week before, they'd fed him some Dexamyls – an amphetamine that made him feel like he was flying, like he could do anything. So he did. They put a revolver in his hand and told him to kill somebody – anybody- just to prove himself. He shot an old man walking his dog in the alley, and then, because it felt so good, he shot the dog too.

But now he has to prove himself all over again. It's time to ride the horse, court the Lady Heroin. And so the seduction begins. At first, he just snorts up. Somehow, that isn't as scary as needles, and anyway, the high's the same, isn't it? Skin-popping comes next, and finally, the needle that slides into his vein bringing white heat and blind lust. At twelve years old, Rigo falls in love.

He becomes a lover possessed. More needles, more hits, more orgasmic blasts of ecstasy. So besotted is he, so eager to prove himself as a lover, he vows to devote himself to his new mistress. Every waking moment is spent thinking about her, every dream of sliding into her sultry embrace. But it costs. The money he makes with his gang doesn't cover it, nor do the proceeds from the purse-snatchings and petty thefts.

His lover is a demanding one. If he wants to be with her, he has to find a way. He decides that way is his father's car. He can steal it, sell it for a lot more money than he'd find in any old lady's purse.

A few nights later, the police are called about a 'domestic disturbance with the family.' When we pull up in front of Rigo's house, a crowd of neighbors are already congregating, murmuring in Spanish and English. Once inside, we shoulder past the screaming Alicia, the wailing children, to the bathroom where Guillermo is.

He'd been taking a bath, relaxing in the warm water while listening to his favorite music on the Spanish station, WOJO. And Rigo had gone in, on the pretense of relieving himself, but really to take the car keys from his father's pants pocket. When Guillermo shouted at him, Rigo grabbed the radio – still plugged into the outlet – and threw it into the tub.

When we put the cuffs on him, Rigo defiantly rotates his hand so we can see the pitchfork, his beloved emblem of manhood. And when we lead him outside, he swaggers, sneering at the gathered crowd. And waits until he's inside the squad car, behind the thick steel cage before he asks, "So now what? Where you takin' me, huh?"

The twelve-year-old murderer's voice quivers.

"You can't do nothin' to me. I'm just a kid." ★

CRIME IN THE CITY

VERTICAL PATROL
By Gina Gallo

On paper, it must have sounded like a great idea. Low income housing for as many as one hundred thirty families per building, families that could share a sense of community without bearing the obvious stigma of poverty. Design the buildings to mimic the Gold Coast high-rises along opulent Lake Shore Drive – with a few modifications, of course. Cinderblock walls instead of textured silk wall coverings, concrete floors in lieu of pastel terrazzo.

So what if the project dwellers didn't have much money? At least their buildings could look like those lofty penthouses with the breathtaking Lake Michigan view. Sort of.

The building architects must have broken their arms patting each other on the back after the City Council approved their designs. High-rise structures with a plot of land around each for parking lots – even a designated playground for the kiddies. The theory was that, even though these buildings were erected in the most crime-ridden areas of Chicago, the kids could enjoy a safe place to play while their parents kept a watchful eye out from the apartments above.

The problem was that each building had fifteen floors, which didn't allow for much parental supervision, not unless you peered through some high-powered binoculars. And if you did happen to notice something questionable involving your child – say, a fast transaction with a drug dealer, or a chance encounter with the neighborhood pedophile, there wouldn't be much you could do in the way of intervention. It's hard to get down fifteen flights in a hurry, especially when there are only two small elevators, each just a bit larger than a phone booth, and neither of them in working order very often.

Once the high rise projects were inhabited, the architects realized they'd made some major booboos. The space designated for the playgrounds was much too small and no parents felt safe leaving their kids there when gang bangers were humbugging on every corner. To let the children play there alone would be an outright sacrifice to the gangbanger gods.

And the physical placement of the buildings was nothing short of brilliant, if you were trained in sniping and high-powered weaponry. From the higher levels of the Robert Taylor Homes or Rockwell Gardens or the notorious Cabrini-Green, a sniper could pick off a rival gang-member, an innocent by-stander, the windshield of a police squad – anything he chose without being detected.

There were other glitches in the projects that never showed up on the drawing board. In some buildings, the apartments are entered, motel-style, from an outdoor balcony that spans the width of the building. A nice touch for the Gold Coast well-to-do's, a bad idea for the inner city. Too many bodies got tossed over the railings during domestic disputes, gang fights, or the random Saturday night 'get outta my face, muthafucka' attitude that went a tragic step too far.

In no time at all, the Chicago Housing Authority added steel mesh to the balconies from floor to roof, making the buildings appear to be what their residents had felt all along: cages of crime and violence where staying alive is a job AND an adventure!

In their infinite wisdom, the Housing Authority developed a tacit policy for apartment assignment, determined by each resident's frequency of police encounters. The peaceful families with little or no history of disturbances are assigned the lower floors, a convenience which meant they wouldn't have to heft groceries or laundry up a dozen or more flights.

The frequent offenders were given the higher-floor apartments, which does nothing to curb the cycle of violence. Climbing ten or more flights several times a day is enough to give anyone an attitude. Toss in some liquor, drugs and a mouthy mate who won't do right, and it's time to call 911.

For cops assigned to a project beat, it's vertical patrol every night – stairs and domestics, stairs and burglaries, stairs and guns, stairs and stairs. The first two commandments of patrolling the projects are that you never take the elevators, always wear your safety vest. And for those who don't share an appreciation of wildlife, it's a good idea to spray some insecticide on your shoes before going up those stairs so you don't leave with more than you came with.

There are no words to describe the onslaught of feelings a cop experiences when entering the projects for the first time. It's the darkness you notice first, a perpetual gloom that comes from insufficient light sources, windowless halls and lobbies that look more like grim tunnels than residential buildings. Rank smells, mixed with the stench of industrial-strength insecticide are strong enough to gag you. You learn to breathe through your mouth, creep carefully up stairwells littered with garbage, human waste – and the random body. All you want to do is take care of business and get out quickly. This is a dangerous place for cops who come as peacemakers, but arrive as targets.

You fight back the nausea, the flutter of fear each time you step into those dark halls. Fifteen dark and secret floors of eyes watching, untold crimes waiting to happen.

For residents here, there's a pervasive despair that comes from living in daily fear. Crime is as much a part of the project experience as the strong gang presence, poorly maintained facilities, nearly intolerable living conditions. With gunshots popping throughout the night, even during the day, just stepping out on the balcony is a risk. Living here means there are no simple household chores. Trips to the laundromat are an invitation to burglarize your apartment. And, if you are burglarized, the subsequent repairs to your door, locks, or shattered windows won't be made immediately. Maybe not at all. With 'property damage' incidents occurring on a daily basis, it's all the building maintenance people can do to keep up. Most times, they slap a sheet of plywood against a shattered window, advise the tenant to fix his own broken locks, or else just stay at home to protect what's his.

Nothing is easy here, not even the business of being a child. Play lots meant for carefree fun are instead the domain of gang members and dope dealers. Tiny people with ancient eyes staring out of children's faces linger on the fringes, witnessing the atrocities of a life few can comprehend. Injury, drugs, shootings are commonplace here, part of the bloody terrain these kids call home. Some families struggle to break the cycle of despair, work desperately to find a better life. Others become victims of that same despair, and victimize others.

Eleven year old Latrell Daniels was one of those who planned to find a better way. He never noticed the despair or squalor. He was a dreamer, his mother said, always with his head in the clouds. Latrell was a dreamer, but he hadn't made it to the clouds. Not yet. Not until he got a pair of Air Jordans, the creme de la creme of athletic shoes, so he could be just like Mike. He'd be airborne for sure then, soaring toward his dream of being an NBA all-star, the next world-famous Chicago Bull.

Dream on, his mother told him. With four kids to feed, she was lucky she could buy him shoes at all. Air Jordans? Why not a Cadillac? The likelihood of her being able to afford either was the same.

But Latrell was an enterprising kid. Nothing was going to interfere with his dream. He started working around the neighborhood, carrying laundry, washing cars, hauling stock for Mr. Patel at the corner grocery. It took a while to save up, longer than he expected, but he kept on striving toward his goal.

His dream came true on a Wednesday. The gray skies and persistent drizzle didn't dampen his excitement as he proudly strutted home, laced into immaculate red and black high-tops. He couldn't wait for the rain to stop so he could get out on the court and shoot some hoops. Go in for a lay-up, dazzling everyone with his vertical leap. Hang-time like no one else but Mike. In these shoes he could do anything. Drive the lane, go airborne for a sweet fade-away jumper...

Lost in the rarified air of hoop dreams, Latrell never saw the boys who loitered near his building's entryway. Didn't see them move toward him, barely heard their muttered, "Yo, Blood..."

The last thing he remembered was a flash, and finally, the sensation of flying.

It was a first floor resident who called the police. She'd heard a shot, she said. A scuffle near the stairwell. She was too scared to peek out. What could she have done anyway, an old woman like her? Them hoodlums, why, they'd kill her just as soon as look at her.

We found Latrell crumpled in the stairwell. He was conscious, barely bleeding from the .25 slug lodged near his spine. The new shoes were gone, stolen from feet that will never fly again. Latrell didn't know that yet. Even as he was carried to the ambulance, he was talking, about basketball and glory... and being like Mike. ★

CRIME IN THE CITY

WATER TOWER HILL
By Jim DeFilippi

Driving home on a hot Monday night, with the sun still out and burning orange because of the season, Detective Sally Boy Grippo was thinking hard about the Creep, Eddie Esternazi. Grippo needed a lever to use on the guy, something to jack the Creep up with.

Sally slowed down, checked the pull-off, and saw that the purple van was parked on the hill again.

Water Tower Hill. All the hills on the Island were made either out of sand dunes or out of garbage that the rest of the world had refused delivery on. Water Tower Hill had no water tower.

The pull-off was nothing more than a matted down little tan spot of dirt and sand, marked off by scrub brush and weeds. The entrance way had been blocked off by two creosote-soaked, ten-foot cut lengths of Lilco telephone poles. The poles were sawed off smooth, lashed together with rusty cable, and laid neatly across the paths worn by tire tracks. Very deliberate. To get in, you'd have to pull your vehicle up onto the scrub for ten yards, then back down, risking a scraped side wall or a ripped exhaust.

The purple van must have done that a lot, because when Grippo checked out the spot on his drive-bys, he would see the van parked there maybe three out of every ten times, mostly at night, but sometimes even in the morning, on his way in to work. Sometimes there was another car parked window to window to the van. The other car was a different one every time.

Grippo pulled his red Dodge Dakota off the road, up around the railroad ties, and he stopped halfway, before his vehicle did what it wanted to do because of gravity, which was to roll back down off the bank, back onto the flat part. He stepped hard on the parking brake and got out, checking his truck. There was no way out of the pull-off, no way to get around the telephone poles and his Dakota.

The van had all its windows dark-frosted. Grippo walked over to it. Closer up, he could see that the windshield tint was a nice job, had probably cost more than the van was worth. The sheet metal on its driver's side was all battered in, its chrome twisted and hanging off in a couple places.

Grippo stopped about five feet behind the rear driver-side corner of the van, reminded himself again that the first rule of police work is the only rule of police work – "Don't come home dead." All the other rules, they didn't matter.

Not if you did not come home with your life.

He could have gone straight procedure with this, but it was too late. He walked up to the driver's door, tried to look inside, pounded twice hard with his fist on the door panel. He held his gold shield up to the driver's window. Waited. Didn't want to wait too long.

Slowly, the window rolled partway down. Behind the wheel was a kid with a shaved head that had a twisted-up, yellow bandanna wrapped around it. There was another kid sitting in shot-gun. Grippo moved his chin up at them and the driver put his hands on the dash. Then the other kid did too.

Grippo told them to get out, as he backed off a few yards to watch. He relaxed only when he had both the kids leaning up against the driver's side panel of the van, their legs spread three feet apart, their hands also spread three feet apart against the hot, purple paint of the van.

Grippo didn't say anything. Both kids wore ear-rings in both ears, both their heads were shaved. Religious zealots, punks, maybe basketball players.

The driver had on a black and gray Raiders jacket. On a day about eighty-five outside. Grippo asked him, "You ignorant magrasto, why the hell you rooting for the fucking Raiders for? What they ever do for you? We got no home teams around here?"

The driver gave no answer. Along with the jacket, he had on faded, torn jeans with a black and yellow Michigan ball-cap twisted up and hanging out of the ass pocket, and black leather boots with chrome rings hanging all over them.

The other kid had black high-tops, short black silk socks just barely showing, shiny and baggy shorts that were fluorescent yellow and fluorescent blue – the two colors cut diagonally across – and a red muscle shirt that said Aztec, with pyramids on the side and on the back.

Grippo could see they were getting arm-weary from leaning against the van. He asked them how was business.

They both asked, "What? What business?"

"Oh, God damn it, boys," Grippo whined to them, "Why doesn't anybody ever say anything worth listening to anymore? Something that maybe will surprise me a little bit? Do I have to be so old that everything I hear from everybody I talk to has to be something I've already heard from somebody else, at least ten dozen-thousand times before? Huh? Does it?"

The boys didn't answer him, so he stepped between them, grabbed an ear-ring of each, twisted, and repeated his question, as closely as he could reconstruct it. Grippo had gone to Catholic school. He'd had the nuns for eight long years.

The boys still didn't say anything, they just twisted up to follow the pressure their ears were getting while they still were trying to keep their finger-tips on the side of the van.

Grippo let go and asked them if he could please look around inside the van. He asked the question like it had already been answered. The Raider asked, "What we do?"

Grippo just looked at him like he was a jerk.

The kid said, "Sure, go ahead, look, if you want to then." Grippo thanked him.

"You boys stay right there," he told them as he went around to the passenger side, opened the sliding door, pulled himself into the back of the van.

It was not worth a mini-grid search. Why segment the interior of the vehicle when you're dealing with morons? Just slop around on the floor in back, then in the glove compartment.

Thirty seconds later Grippo was sitting in the driver's seat. He rolled the window down all the way down, stuck his head out, and said to the boys standing there, "Boys, this is disgusting. This vehicle is nothing more than an opium den. Extremely disgusting. Is this what you two've been doing for your summer? You couldn't have a better job than this? Something more honest? Legal? Look. Look. Here, look at this, what I found. What it this shit?"

He put his right arm out the window and dangled three plastic-wrapped little packs of white goo. He jiggled the packs to try to get the boys' attention, but they just looked down into the dirt of Water Tower Hill.

Grippo told them again how disgusting this whole thing was to him, and how disappointed he was in them. He got out of the van, went through the moves of placing them under arrest, making up a bunch of different steps to the procedure – asking them their blood type as he studied their driver's licenses, and having them stand on one foot, close their eyes, and bring the tips of their thumbs together over their heads.

The kid in the Raider jacket said, "Listen, we're running for student council. We already run. We won. I'm a representative, and he's the alternate. We never done anything wrong before. You can ask anybody. Please don't tell."

"Please don't tell?" Grippo faked some interest, asked the kid, "What was your plurality?"

Kid looked at him.

"How much you win by?"

Kid said, "I don't remember. You mean the election? You remember, Clark?"

Clark shook his head. Then Clark said, so you could hardly hear him, "By a lot, I think it was."

Grippo told the Raider to draw a line in the sand with his boot heel. He told the other kid, Clark, to do that too. Then told them both to walk their lines, toe to heel. Then do it again, racing each other. He considered having them do it a third time, while imitating Johnny Cash singing his classic tune, "I Walk the Line."

Grippo was almost running out of stupid things for them to do when finally the kid in the Raider jacket started crying. Clark looked up and over at his friend, then looked back down. Grippo let the kid cry for a couple minutes, let the other kid just stand there, then Grippo told them both to follow him over to the telephone poles. Back around the Dakota. He told them to sit on the poles, and he groaned as he sat down beside them. Both kids hung their heads, looking down at the ground, the one still half-crying.

Grippo looked down too, asked them, "How long you been dealing?"

The Raider said, "First time."

Grippo said, "C'mon, Slicker, don't say shit like that to me. Please, sir. I been driving by here all summer long. You're always here, every time I drive by, you are, so don't tell me."

The Raider said, "All summer. We done a prom, a charity thing, for the junior class. We sold jewelry. It was the biggest fund raiser in the school. Ever. But somebody stole the money. Not us, stole it. So we had to make it back. So Clark's brother knows a guy."

Grippo held up the three packages of goo, swung them in the air. He told the boys, "One time, when I was a kid, I was working in a school as a janitor. Maybe the same school you are. Where you go to – the high school? Four Towns?"

The Raider said, "Yeah."

Grippo told him, "No, it wasn't that one. It was another one. You guys know anybody from Saint Anselm's?"

"Where the teacher was killed? Yeah, a couple kids."

"What'd you hear?"

"What?"

"What'd you hear about the teacher getting killed?"

"Not much. They said they used to rank on him an awful lot. In school. Right to his face sometimes. You know, give him a hard time."

"Oh, yeah? Anybody give him a real hard time, you know of? Like, want to hurt him or anything?"

The Raider gave a quick, "No, no way."

Clark said, "He was a real dip-shit I heard, though. With some kids. Really could try to act cool, make them feel like shit. When he thought he could get away with it."

Grippo said, "Oh, yeah well, teachers do that. That's their job, boys."

The Raider said, "Yeah. You do that to the wrong people, you're gonna pay. Sometimes."

Grippo asked him, "What wrong people? You know?"

Both boys shook their heads. Then Clark said, "We heard he was a homo."

Grippo nodded.

Then the kid said, "Yeah, we heard that devil worshippers did it."

Grippo said, "Go on, get out of here. Devil worshippers?"

The Raider said, "Yeah, well, I heard, though, that he did have this devil's thing he wore. Wore it on his arm. Everybody heard about it. It was, like on a chain."

Grippo said, "Yeah."

The Raider's friend Clark said, "Yeah. Somebody told me, he told a class of his once, like, there was more heaven and hell in that thing than, I don't know, than, than, they would know. Something like that."

Grippo said, "Oh, yeah, who cares? Anyway, boys, getting back to your little situation here. I'll tell you a story of my youth. As a summer-kid custodian. My friend and me, we were cleaning the language lab, you still got them?"

The Raider said, "Yeah, for Spanish and stuff? We got them."

Grippo said, "Yeah, so, me and my friend, found these tapes, that they used in there, the old reel to reel kind. Girl's voice, very sweet and proper – 'Que sera, sera. Now you, repete, por favor, que sera, sera.'"

Grippo said the phrase from the tape again, trying to imitate a young Spanish woman. "Que sera, sera."

Then he had the boys repeat the phrase. He let them use their own natural voices. They weren't so different from Grippo's phoney-girl voice.

Then he told them, "So, what do we care, you're young, silly, bored. Cleaning the language lab. What we did, we took a couple tapes, we recorded us singing, the dirty version of 'Louie, Louie' on them. You know that song." Grippo started singing it, "Louie, Louie, oh, no, we gotta screw." He looked at the boys. "You never hear it? It's old."

The Raider said, "Sure."

Clark said, "Not like that."

Grippo said, "Anyway, what happened is, they found the tape before we got our last pay checks. In September. The superintendent, I think he was, he called us in, played the tape for us. Very embarrassing. Like you boys are now. But, I tell you, the nice thing was, this guy who didn't even know us, he recognized us as good kids, just kids that'd made a dumb mistake. So, after scaring us a little bit, he laughed, we laughed. He gave us our pay checks."

The Raider looked up, wiped his cheek, looked at Grippo. The kid asked, "So does that mean you're gonna let us go?"

Grippo yelled at him, "Of course not, I'm gonna arrest you, lock up both your sweet asses and then call your family. I was just telling you a little story first, that's all."

The Raider started crying again, and he asked Grippo if there was please something they could do to avoid all this and to avoid what was coming.

Grippo said to them, "What is coming is worse than this."

The kid looked at him like a little dog that wanted to go outside, and the kid blew snot and asked Grippo, "Anything at all, please, sir?"

And Grippo pretended to think. He told them, "Nope. Jeez, I don't know, I can't think of a fucking thing. I'm fresh out of ideas. Do you kids have any suggestions at all?"

***

Wednesday, Eddie Esternazi was driving his Tuscany silver Diamante LS east on Northern State when he checked the mirror and spotted a cop-cruiser four car lengths behind and closing.

Eddie popped the cruise control down a couple of clicks, then used his thumbs on the buttons mounted at the base of the steering wheel to pop down the music – the Back Sliders, "Throwin' Rocks at the Moon."

The cop car slowed and held steady. Something funny about it jarred Eddie's thinking, but he couldn't quite nab what it was.

It wasn't passing, just sitting a couple lengths back now. Cops usually blew right by everybody – trying to keep a look on their face like they were heading off to a crime scene, in actuality heading off to an early lunch. Eddie looked in the mirror again. He flipped off the music, switched to the police band squawk for awhile. Nothing. The guy was a loser, so screw him.

Eddie checked his speedometer again, checked the time on his dashboard clock – a real clock, rotary, none of that digital crap. He was taking Northern State out to Huntington Station for a meet with an old Harvard Law buddy. They were organizing a celebrity golf tourney for a high school running back from Manhasset High, supposed to be the next Jim Brown, who had gotten himself paralyzed in a car wreck. After that, Eddie was scheduled to come back in for lunch with Audrey. Keeping the woman on track could be a full-time job.

The damn cop was right behind the Diamante now, tail-assing. Eddie tried to see what look was on the cop's face. Nothing. Eddie got bored with the jerk, punched the cruise control up a couple clicks. Cops were fools. Like this one Audrey was spending her time with.

Eddie's eye caught a quick blue flash in the mirror. The patrol cop was blinking his top-light and head-lights, coming around. Eddie looked up ahead to see who the cop was taking off after. The road was clear. The cop must have received a call. Eddie still hadn't heard anything on the police band. He pulled toward the shoulder and slowed, letting the jerk come around. As the cop's front was along side Eddie's driver's seat, the cruiser gave a short, loud siren-wail that sounded insulting.

Eddie looked up ahead again, still wondering. It took him a moment to realize, even as the cop lifted his right hand off the steering wheel and pointed at him, that he was actually pulling over Eddie.

Eddie cut the wheel and banged the undercarriage over the curb-way, partway up onto the grass. Whatever was going on was senseless and stupid.

The cruiser parked right in front, as if Eddie were preparing to make a run for it. An old patrol cop with black, oily hair sticking out from his cap climbed out of the cruiser, walked up to the Diamante. Eddie powered the window down.

He didn't know this cop – some big corporal with a Polack name on his chest. The cop asked him, "Are you all right, sir?"

Eddie said, "Yeah, I am. Why?"

The cop pointed at the bruises on Eddie's neck and arms. Eddie told him, "They're old."

The cop waited awhile, then pulled back to look at the car and said, "I remember when Japanese automatically meant cheap." Eddie didn't respond and the cop said, "Course, that was a long time ago."

Eddie told the cop he didn't remember that, and the cop said, "Okay," and asked for Eddie's paperwork. The cop took out some big, old-fashioned glasses and put them on. Then he went over to his cruiser. He stood by his driver window, looked back at Eddie, leaned into his cruiser and took the mike off the dashboard, started talking into it, still looking at Eddie.

The cop stood and waited, didn't stop looking. He nodded once. Eddie stayed still, hands on the wheel. After a while the cop said something quick into the mike, hung it back up, then came back up to the Diamante.

Eddie didn't say anything.

The cop said, "Sir, everything's fine here, except that your tail-light's broken out. That's the brake light's too included. Both out on the left side."

"Not working or actually broken out? What'd you mean?"

"Glass actually broken, sir. I'm gonna have to citation you."

"Citation me? I just had it into the dealership." Eddie had just had the Diamante in for servicing and a wash – everything on it was perfect.

"It could be," the cop told him.

"Let me see this please. I'd like to see for myself. I'm getting out of the car, is that all right? I'm coming around?" Eddie took his hands off the steering wheel, held them up.

"Please, c'mon around," the cop said and he stepped back.

The cop and Eddie stood equidistant between the two tail-lights, with the traffic going by, everyone slowing down a little to look. Eddie looked at the broken glass. He said "Fuck" quietly to himself. He told the cop, "It must've been in a parking lot just now. I don't know."

"Yeah, that could be."

"People clip your freaking car and they don't even care. They throw garbage out on the road. This used to be a God-damn nice looking parkway, corporal, at one time. Take a look at it now."

"Yeah, I know it was. You're right." The cop was writing on the sensitized paper in his summons book. He finished and said, "Yeah. Yeah, maybe. Must be."

Eddie said, "God damn it." He told the cop that the light would be fixed – his dealership would do it.

The cop said, "Yeah, it will be, I'm sure. Within forty-eight hours, as the citation I'm filling out here says to. You'll have to come in and show proof."

"Yeah, I know how it works, Corporal. I'll have it done." He would switch cars and have Audrey take it in; he had no time for crap like this.

As the cop was flipping closed his citation book – after ripping off the yellow page, making a big show of it – Eddie's mind finally clutched onto what had been bothering him. Eddie turned around, looked at the cop cruiser. This was a Four Towns cruiser, the cream color with the blue and orange stripes along the side. Township P.D. So this cop, he was a town cop. On the parkway, it should be a trooper, driving one of those ugly dark blues with the dirty yellow stripe.

Eddie took the yellow paper from the cop and said, "I'm heading off now, okay, Corporal?"

The cop took his glasses off, moved his eyes around, seemed to focus in on the Diamante's trunk. He took a step over to the keyhole. He bent over so that his eyes were a foot away from it, maybe less. He put his glasses back on.

Then the cop said to Eddie, "Hey, Mr. Esternazi – did I say it right? – could I ask you about this?"

"About what?" Eddie went over, saw a little white smear around the little chrome keyhole on the trunk.

The cop ran a finger through the little smear, smelled his finger, put it up to his tongue. "Could I ask you to open up your trunk, Mr. Esternazi. I'll ask, but you have to do it."

"You'll see my golf clubs, officer," Eddie told him.

Eddie went around, leaned into his driver's window, feeling the cool air draining out. He braced one palm on the leather seat, reached down by the floor, and pulled the trunk release lever.

Then it took him maybe two seconds to get back there to the town cop and to the trunk lid.

But by then the cop was already leaning back out and looking at these three plastic-wrapped little balls of white goo. ★

CRIME IN THE CITY

GOING TO MANHATTAN
Robert B. Cohen

They sat in the car, not talking. The only sounds were the engine idling and the windshield wipers. Quiet nights were nice, Frank thought, especially Sunday nights, although when it was quiet he tended to smoke too much. It wasn't even ten o'clock yet, and he was lighting the last cigarette in his pack. He crumpled the empty pack, dropped it on the floor of the car and then rolled his window down. Eddie shook his head and smiled. He knew that Frank's right elbow was out the window and that in a few minutes the drizzle would soak the right side of his shirt. Frank explained once that since he was soaking wet underneath his vest anyway, what difference did it make? He might as well cool off a little bit by getting his arm and shoulder wet, too.

The portable radio lying on the seat between them sputtered weakly to life. Frank picked it up instead of making it louder, and held it near his head. Making it louder just made the static louder. "Unit covering Seventh Avenue on the 'F,' Seventh Avenue, come in to central." Silence. "Unit covering Seventh Avenue, come in to central." Another voice came over the radio: "Central, what's the condition at Seventh Avenue, kay?"

"Unit calling, what's your shield?" Silence again. Eddie laughed and said, "I guess he's got radio trouble."

"They're playing tag," Frank answered. If there was something serious, like a robbery in progress, central would broadcast the job straight out and cops would be tripping over each other to respond. When they called for a cop covering a specific post it usually turned out to be something like a drunk or a dispute, so instead of just blindly answering the cops would try to find out what the job was. On the other hand, the dispatcher would try to get the cop to identify himself on the air before giving out a distasteful job, just in case an anonymous cop should have a change of heart. It would seem to make for a pretty good game, except that if central couldn't get a foot cop to answer up for a job, they'd refer it to the patrol sergeant. The boss would check his rollcall to see which cop had the post, and if he couldn't get that cop, he'd assign somebody else. Then he would spend the rest of his night hunting down the missing cop and generally trying to make his life miserable. The game then, was basically futile. They still played it.

"I think Murphy's got Seventh Avenue," Eddie said. Frank checked his rollcall. "Nope, we do. Murphy's out to meal until ten-thirty. We've got the whole 'F' line down to where district thirty-four picks it up. Looks like we're covering half the borough. What's it now, a quarter after?" Before Eddie could answer, the car's radio came on. "Thirty Robert, thirty Queen on the air, thirty Robert or thirty Queen?" The dispatcher was calling either of the two police cars assigned to the section of Brooklyn's subways known as district thirty. The car's radio was a different frequency than the portable radio. It was loud and clear; you really couldn't play tag. Frank reached forward and keyed the mike without removing it from the dashboard. "Thirty Robert, go, central."

"Yeah, Robert, Seventh Avenue, female outstretch, blue ski jacket, southbound side. Call's from the railroad clerk, kay." He answered, "Robert, ten-four."

The first time he had heard the term 'outstretch' used, he thought it was pretty bizarre. It meant, quite simply, a person laid out. An outstretch could involve a wide range of underlying circumstance, but by September of 1988, it was usually nothing more than a homeless person sleeping in some objectionable place. Without realizing it, he had become numb to the term, and was now just trying to do some mental arithmetic. "Ed, how far out are we from Seventh?" Eddie said, "Maybe ten minutes. Why don't we let Murphy take it? He'll be coming off meal in a few minutes. It's his post, anyway." Frank didn't answer. It was bothering him that it was a female outstretch. It wasn't normal. Most police contacts with homeless people in the subway were with men, not women. "Nah, Eddie, we gotta take it. It might be a victim of a crime or something. I mean, if it ain't, I'll have Murphy pick it up, but we gotta go." Eddie put the car in gear. "Yeah, I guess," he said as he pulled away from the curb. He put on the defrosters, but the yellowish haze on the windshield was from weeks of cigarette smoke. They drove off slowly, partly because of the rain.

Frank had been looking at his rollcall when Eddie said, "We're here, Sarge." He eased the big black and white Suburban into a bus-stop, placed the shift lever in park and turned off the ignition. The engine started dieseling and the car shook as if it were having a seizure. "Shit," he said as he turned the ignition back on, instantly restarting the engine. When he turned it off a second time, the car lurched once, sighed and fell silent. "How embarrassing," he said, "I hope nobody seen this." As they opened their doors and stepped down out of the car, Eddie pulled out his nightstick from where it had been jammed between the seat cushions. With a familiar cadence they locked and closed their doors, and disappeared down the stairwell beneath the green globes.

It was like entering a different world. The stairway led to a long, narrow corridor with a concrete floor, ceramic tile walls and very bright fluorescent lights. There was a stench of urine as they entered the corridor. As they walked along, the smell eased a bit. Frank wondered if his nose was simply adjusting. The corridor, like most of the subway, was an echo chamber. Some cops liked to make cop noise; they'd have all kinds of jinglingthings hanging from their gunbelts and they'd keep their radios turned up. Maybe they were hoping for a scarecrow effect, that the cop noise would precede them and shoo the mopes and the mutts away. Frank and Eddie were both from the quiet school. Neither of them jingled and they both kept their radios low. Eddie was even wearing black sneakers. As stealthy as they tried to be, there was still no mistaking the sound of the two uniformed cops in the Seventh Avenue station.

The corridor finally ended by opening up onto the subway station's mezzanine, an area about the size and shape of a football field, not as brightly-lit as the corridor. There were floor-to-ceiling fences and gates of dismally painted wrought iron everywhere, like jailhouse bars. Combined with dozens of steel pillars, the effect was visually disturbing. Maybe it was the low ceilings that did it, maybe the lighting. Frank knew that his eyes would adjust to this surreal view, as his nose had already adjusted to the smell.

There was a deep and increasingly louder rumble as a train pulled into the station down below on another level. Then abruptly, silence for a few moments. Then more rumbling as the train pulled out. They could feel the power of it through their feet as they walked. At the other end of the mezzanine, Frank saw several shadowy forms come up the stairs from the platforms below and disappear into the stairwells that led to the street. He heard a noise behind them, conversation and giggling. He turned and saw a group of teenaged girls exiting through the corridor that the two of them had just come from, all wearing skin-tight stretch pants and bulky, oversized sweaters with the sleeves pulled out over their hands. As they disappeared into the corridor, he noticed that they even had identical hairstyles.

At the center of the mezzanine, they came to the token booth. The clerk didn't acknowledge the cops as they approached. Frank walked up to the front of the booth. The clerk was sitting and appeared to be reading something. He didn't look up. Frank waited a few seconds, then he tapped on the glass. There was a microphone in the middle of the bulletproof glass, but he leaned down and spoke into the change slot, "How ya doing?" The clerk, a cheesy-looking guy with coke bottle glasses, looked up for a second, said something he couldn't make out, and returned to whatever he was doing. Annoyed, Frank dropped his smile and said, "Hey, did you call us, or what?" The clerk looked up again and smacked the microphone with the back of his hand, "I said, she's down on the plat. Southbound side."

"Who's down on the plat?"

"Hey, what do I know? I'm up here. Go look." Rather than say something nasty, Frank turned and walked away while the clerk was still talking. Yeah, fuck you too, he thought.

They walked to the closest stairwell leading to the southbound platform and went down. At the foot of the stairs, they stopped and looked up and down the platforms. The station was nearly empty. There were less than a dozen or so scattered people that they could see. From where they were standing, they could see just about everything, except for what was behind the other stairways which came down to the platforms about every hundred feet – exactly where an outstretch could be. Frank said, "I'll go this way." Walking together, it would take them twice as long to check the station.

Frank was nearly at the end of the platform. He had one more stairway to go and his end was clear. He was hoping Eddie's end would be clear, too. He noticed a small pile of rags near the last stairway. He was just thinking that he could use a cigarette and remembering he was out when he saw the rags move. He stopped right in his tracks and watched. He couldn't make anything out, in the rags or anywhere around them. He turned and saw Eddie coming back from the other end. He knew Eddie would come to him if he didn't go back, so he started moving slowly toward the last stairway.

When he rounded the stairs, he saw that it wasn't a pile of rags at all. On the concrete floor was a girl. She was trying to sit up but it looked like the best she could do was to prop herself up on her elbows. As he approached she weakly pulled her legs toward her body, knees together. What he had thought were rags appeared to be a bag of her possessions. She seemed obviously aware of his approach, but she didn't look at him as he walked to within a few feet of her and stopped. "How you doing?" he said softly. She glanced in his direction briefly, then turned away, looking across the tracks to the other side. "Okay," she said, her voice not much louder than a whisper. Frank studied her. She was a white girl, maybe Hispanic, with dull, matted black hair down to her shoulders. She was terribly thin, with big, blank-looking brown eyes. She was breathing through her mouth. Her face was so thin it made her look bucktoothed. She was wearing a cheap, down-filled navy blue ski jacket that was filthy and stained brown in places, and a very odd-looking pair of baggy black plastic pants. She had no socks and only one sneaker, although the layers of dirt made the missing sneaker less obvious. Her ankles, and the foot he could see, were covered with festering, ulcerated sores.

She seemed afraid. He didn't perceive her as much of a threat, considering her physical condition, so he squatted down next to her, resting his rear end on his right heel. He took off his hat, leaving his sweat-soaked hair plastered to his head in the strange shape formed by the headband of the hat. "What are you doing here?" he asked. "I'm going to Manhattan," she said. Frank looked around to see if there was a sign they could see, but there was none. "You're on the wrong side. This train goes out to Coney Island. The train to Manhattan is on the other side." Expressionless, she said, "I know. Can you help me get to the other side?"

Eddie quietly walked up and said, "Spike." Frank turned and saw he was standing over a hypodermic needle about five feet from her on the side opposite where he was squatting.

He had missed it. "Is that yours?" She shook her head without even looking toward Eddie. Frank nodded to him, and Eddie stepped on the needle, crushing it. He casually kicked the pieces onto the tracks. "What's your name?" She didn't respond. He stood up slowly, his right knee making a popping sound. "Listen," he said, "you don't look so good. You want to go to the hospital?" For the first time, she made eye contact with him: "What are they gonna do for me?" Then she looked away, back to the blank stare across the tracks. "Well, I can't do anything for you, don't you understand? All I can do for you is take you to the hospital." Still staring, she said in a weak monotone, "I don't want to go to the hospital. I'm going to Manhattan."

"What's in Manhattan?"

"I got people there." If you've got people, how the hell did they let you get here, he thought. "Can you walk?" She nodded. "Go ahead, get up and cross over to the other side. Then you can go to Manhattan." She made a few weak, jerky motions with her legs, then she simply stared. He slowly removed his portable radio from his belt. "Thirty sergeant to central, kay." Static. Then, "Thirty sergeant, go."

"Ah, central, have EMS respond to Seventh Avenue on that outstretch job, kay."

"Ten-four, Sarge. What's the pedigree and condition on that aided, kay?" The city's understaffed emergency medical service was backlogged, and the hospitals were worse. Frank knew that all ambulance requests were prioritized based on the information that the dispatcher was asking for. If you exaggerated the seriousness of the condition, then somebody else might die waiting for the ambulance you got. If you minimized it, you might not get your ambulance as quickly as you needed it. Or at all. "Central, that's a female, uh, twenty-five years, kay."

"Ten-four, Sarge. Condition?" He had been looking at the girl the whole time. Suddenly he realized something about her strange pair of pants. They were supposed to be skintight stretch pants. The girl was so emaciated they were baggy on her. "Thirty sergeant, kay?" He thought, how do you say, 'dying, no rush?' "Thirty sergeant, come in to central, thirty sergeant?"

"Thirty sergeant, go."

"Sarge, what's the condition on that aided, kay?" He felt very tired. "Exposure, central." There was a long pause. It was September. "Uh, ten four, sarge. Ten-four."

There was a jingling noise coming from the other end. "Well, Murph finally made it." Frank turned and saw another uniformed cop walking down the platform toward them. He recognized Tommy Murphy by his gray moustache and his big belly. Tommy's voice boomed out, "Hey, Big Ed! What do you got?"

"Hey, we got your aided here, you fat bastard. You done stuffing your face, or what?" They both laughed. Frank wasn't laughing. Tommy walked up, saluted Frank, and said, "Hey, boss, I'll pick up this job, no problem. Wanna scratch?" He handed Frank his memobook. There was a steady beeping echoing down from the mezzanine, the signal that a train was coming. While Frank was signing his book, Tommy was putting on a pair of work gloves.

"How you doing?" he asked the girl, "You want to go to the hospital, dear?" Without looking at him, she said, "No... I'm going to Manhattan." He turned to Frank and said, "Hey boss, she's gonna refuse. The skell squad's probably at the end of the line down in Coney Island, they'll take her off to a shelter. Let thirty-four worry about it." A southbound train was coming into the station. They couldn't see it yet, but the rumbling had started. Frank shook his head, and said, "Bullshit, what if they're not down there?" Tommy frowned: "Then the train pulls outta Stillwell, heads north, and she goes to Manhattan. Everybody's set."

The rumbling was getting louder; they could see the reflection of the train's headlights moving down the ceramic tile walls of the station. Frank had to raise his voice now: "No, no good. No good! You can't do that!" Tommy, also raising his voice over the incoming train, said, "What the hell we gonna do with it then?" As the train was barreling into the station, Frank yelled over the noise, "I'm gonna EDP her!" The letters stood for emotionally-disturbed person. Only a sane person had the right to refuse medical attention. Visibly stunned, Tommy stood there for a second with his mouth hanging open, then suddenly he grabbed the girl, trying to pull her to her feet. Frank yelled something at him, but it was drowned out by the screech of the train braking to a halt. Frank grabbed his arm, his face inches from Tommy's ear. Tommy relaxed his grip on the girl as the screeching reached a crescendo, and an instant later as she slumped to the floor, there was silence as the doors on the 'F' train opened. They all just stood there. The girl was moaning. The few people leaving the train just stepped around them. Three cops standing over a girl lying on the floor and nobody paid any attention. The conductor's bored voice crackled over the train's speakers: "Stand clear the closing doors…" The doors closed and the train rumbled out of the station.

Before the noise died down completely, Frank started yelling again. "What the hell was that all about? What's wrong with you! Jesus Christ!" Tommy quietly said, "Sarge, can I talk to you a minute?" Taking the hint, Eddie said awkwardly as he started up the stairs, "I gotta go, uh, get something from the car, I'll be right back…"

"Tommy, I say she's an EDP, she's an EDP! You don't turn around and do something else!" Tommy said calmly, "Frank, it's a bad call. She's not an EDP."

"Bad call? Who the fuck you talking to?"

"She's not an EDP. She's a skell. She's just a skell. She probably got AIDS or some fucking thing." Frank could feel his face getting hot, but he said nothing. Anyone overhearing this conversation would think that Tommy was a callous scumbag, he thought. They had known each other a long time, and he knew this wasn't so. Only two months ago, at Jay Street, a drunk had fallen to the tracks and was run over by a train. Officer Murphy, with seventeen years on the job, crawled under the still-electrified train to get to him. The terrified man spoke no English, so Tommy just held his hand as he bled to death. People said that that took balls, but Frank knew that wasn't what it took. He looked at Tommy's face, in his eyes, and saw there was no malice.

He looked down to the girl. She had apparently tried to drag herself away while they were arguing. There were tracks of some type of bodily fluid on the concrete, and she was nearer to the stairs. He felt the frustration rising within him. He hated these jobs, when nothing he could do seemed right. He was looking at the girl, wishing she had gone some other place, any other place, when he noticed that the dirty shirt beneath her dirty jacket was a very feminine floral print, probably very pretty once. Once. He had a sudden urge to leave.

"Yeah, okay. Fine," he handed Tommy back his book. Tommy saw the look on his face. "Hey, Frank, I'm sorry. I'll take care of this, alright, whatever you want to do." After a long, uncomfortable pause, Frank said quietly, "When I put this job on the air, it went out as a straight aided. I didn't put it out as an EDP, you understand? Just an aided." Tommy understood. The two men stood there in silence. What Frank had told him was that if the girl got up and walked away, that he should cancel the request for an ambulance. If she got up and walked away – or if she left on a train. "Okay, boss, I'll take care of it. Go on, I'll see you later." Frank turned and walked away quickly.

Eddie was waiting for him up by the token booth. Frank didn't stop, and he had to jog a few steps to catch up. They walked out through the long corridor, up the stairs, down the street back to the Suburban. The rain had stopped. They climbed back into the car, and as Eddie started the engine he asked, "Where to?" Frank threw his hat on the back seat and said, "Cigarettes."

They drove to an all-night diner a few blocks away and made polite small-talk with the aging waitress as they had their coffee. When they got back into the car, Frank lit another cigarette, even though he had just smoked two in the diner. On the portable radio, central was calling for the unit covering Bay Parkway, a few stops further down the 'F' line. They paid no attention. "You know, I can't believe him sometimes. That little scene back there looked really terrible."

"Frank, there wasn't anybody there to see it. Besides, nobody gives a shit." Throwing his just-lit cigarette out the window, he turned in his seat, facing his partner. "Maybe I give a shit. The law says if an emotionally-disturbed person is a danger, then I can take her to the hospital against her will, right, and if she wants to lay there and die on a subway platform, then I can say she's nuts and she's gotta go, okay?" Eddie didn't answer. The dispatcher was still trying in vain to raise the cop covering Bay Parkway. "Alright. Okay. I know she ain't crazy, I know she'd end up sitting in the goddam psych ward at Woodhull for eighteen hours until some doctor says, sorry, you're just screwed, next!' So what are we supposed to do? At least I could say I tried to do something..." The game of radio tag continued. "Hey, Frank, I'm not arguing with you. As far as I'm concerned, you didn't do anything wrong back there." Then the car radio came alive:

"Thirty-four William on the air, thirty-four William? Bay Parkway on the 'F,' female outstretch, blue ski jacket, southbound side, kay." Frank looked away and they sat in the car, not talking. ★

CRIME IN THE CITY

THE SPECTACLE CASE
By Liz Martínez DeFranco

I was on foot patrol on East 85th Street when the call came over the radio. My partner and I were to go back to the house to meet Sgt. McGonigal. We looked at each other, shrugged, and hopped on a city bus going downtown. We would find out why the sergeant wanted us soon enough.

It turned out that cops were in short supply that night and they needed to secure a crime scene, so they were rounding up all the auxiliary police officers who were working their volunteer shifts in the precinct that night. We were to stand around looking official to make sure that nosy neighbors and reporters who listened to the police scanner didn't gain unauthorized entrance.

What they didn't tell us was how we were supposed to keep anyone out. Okay, we wear uniforms that are almost identical to the ones that the regular N.Y.P.D. officers sport, but we don't carry guns. We have nightsticks, but they're hardly the weapon of choice against any armed and dangerous person who really wants to get past us. To tell you the truth, the self-defense instruction the department gave us wasn't even that good. Believe me when I say that I am basically trained to call 911 in an emergency.

You might ask why I wander around the streets of New York without a firearm, dressed like cop and looking like a target for anyone not observant enough to see the word "Auxiliary" above the police sleeve patches. And it would be a good question. Sometimes I wonder how I got into this myself. In real life – during the day, that is – I am an optometrist. I spend my days in a (mostly) dark, narrow room flipping lenses in front of patients' eyes, saying, "Is it better like this, or like this?" and writing out contact lens prescriptions for people too vain to perch a pair of specs on their nose.

The answer is that deep down, I truly want to make a difference. Anybody can write a check and mail it off to some group that claims to use it to feed starving children in Africa, but not everybody wants to actually do something to improve society. So if I put in my four hours a week patrolling the streets of Manhattan, I can feel as though I am at least "providing a police presence and serving as the eyes and ears of the N.Y.P.D." Or so the recruiting literature assured me when I signed up three years ago.

The rest of the truth is that I am basically a lazy person. I became an optometrist because being a doctor seemed like a good way to ensure a decent income, and I don't have to deal with blood and guts. Yuck. Even though I am

101

a slug at heart, it started to sink in that I should do something active and interesting with my life when my boyfriend announced that he was leaving me for someone younger and cuter, oh and by the way, more fun. I picked the auxiliary police because they don't have physical fitness standards. Not that I am tremendously out of shape. I'm just a little short for my weight. I'm 5'4" and I weigh 140, but I have big bones and I carry it well. Or so I tell myself as I'm downing chocolate-fudge Slim-Fast. But I have long red curly hair and blue eyes with long lashes, and I think that the dark blue N.Y.P.D. uniform is flattering to my 32-year-old figure.

Plus, auxiliaries get to meet lots of cops. Most of them are either way overweight and married (isn't life so unfair? If they were women, their husbands would leave them in a New York minute), or act like they're about 12 years old. I don't date married men and I don't date anyone who hasn't entered puberty, either. So that left very few prospects in the precinct. But I'm still hoping.

Sgt. McGonigal, who took us over to the crime scene, was good looking and unmarried, but I knew his boyfriend so I didn't think it would work out between us. The assignment turned out to be pretty easy. They didn't actually leave us in charge of anything – we were just supposed to stand there and help to fill up the hallway with blue uniforms. The real cops took care of the interesting parts of the job, like telling neighbors and onlookers, "There's nothing to see here, move on."

Apparently, someone had expired in one of the apartments and it had been a while before the neighbors checked into the source of the odor. Don't want to get involved, you know. I could sort of see the point. If someone's dead, why bother rushing to the phone? Nothing you can do for them. But one of the tenants had finally broken down and called in an anonymous report. I knew this because I overheard the sergeant discussing who had phoned in. The poor slob obviously didn't know that the 911 center captures every caller's phone number and address. So the do-gooder would wind up answering questions anyway. What can you do? That's life in the city.

They brought the deceased out in a black body bag, just like you see on television. That was a first: something that actually worked as advertised. I figured it was an old lady whose time had come. Probably had a bunch of cats who were her only friends. I was constructing an entire fantasy around the dead person to keep from going insane with boredom. I was lost in my reverie, imagining that the poor soul had children who didn't call her because they were too selfish to be bothered with their poor mother who had sacrificed to put them through school when I heard the radio squawk with a name I knew.

"Carlyn Valentine," someone said over the air, and my head jerked up. Carlyn was a friend of mine. She was a veterinarian who belonged to the same professional women's group as I did. We would see each other at the monthly luncheons, and sometimes in between. But why would they be talking about her here? I asked the cop next to me.

"Huh?" he said.

"What are they talking about on the radio?" I repeated. "They just mentioned Carlyn Valentine. I know her." I pointed to his radio.

"You know the D.O.A.?" he said.

"The D.O.A.?" I repeated, surprised at this lug's brain-dead qualities. "No. I was just wondering why they were talking about my friend, Carlyn Valentine. On the radio." I pointed again, trying to use hand signals to communicate with the moron.

"Yeah, Valentine. That's the stiff's name," he said tactfully. He narrowed his eyes. "What do you know about this?"

My stomach sank, and the room started spinning. "Carlyn?" I croaked. "Carlyn's the one who's dead?"

He put his arm out toward me – not to offer me comfort, but to prevent me from leaving the scene. I couldn't have gone anywhere anyway. I couldn't believe that my friend was the one in the body bag. I had just seen her last week.

I thought about the last time we met. We got together at Paolucci's Restaurant in Little Italy, famous for its six-dollar pasta specials. We had lunch and chatted. It seemed impossible that we would never laugh over linguine again.

The sergeant suddenly appeared. "Betsy, do you want to come with me?" he said.

I just looked at him, numb. My mind was going a mile a minute, but I was having difficulty following the conversation. He took me by the arm, gently but firmly, and led me to the patrol car. He hadn't really been asking.

At the precinct, I got to find out what it felt like to be questioned. They took out a tape recorder and everything. McGonigal and some detectives took turns asking me about Carlyn. Even though I liked her and we had fun together, we hadn't been all that close. More acquaintances than good friends, but I felt we had been on the road to a deeper friendship. She had spoken briefly about her ex-boyfriend, a man who, reading between the lines, I gathered had been abusive. She even mentioned to me that she had moved recently to "put some distance" between them. At the time, I guessed that she got tired of being beaten up on a regular basis. Although I silently applauded her decision, I didn't say much about it to her because she skirted the issue. I figured that when she was ready, she would say more.

Now she would never talk about it again. My eyes filled with tears.

"Would you like some water?" Sgt. McGonigal asked, concerned.

I shook my head. "No, thanks. I'm okay," I managed.

"Betsy, if you can think of anything else to help us, anything at all…" he said.

I shook my head again. "I'm sorry. I really don't know much more about her," I said. And I was sorry. "But maybe if you check into her old boyfriend…"

"You told us already," one of the detectives cut in.

McGonigal shot him a look. "You sure you don't remember his name?" he asked me gently. "Anything that would be helpful to us?"

"I didn't know him," I repeated.

"Do you know what kind of work he did? Whether he was older or younger?"

"No," I answered. I thought about our last conversation. "Wait! I do know something. I think he's a vet." I started to get excited.

"You mean he collects benefits?" the other detective asked.

I gave her a disgusted look. "A veterinarian. Like Carlyn." I turned to McGonigal. "I think she mentioned that he worked with her or something. But I got the feeling that it wasn't a regular thing. I'm not sure exactly."

The cops exchanged exasperated looks. Did they think I was holding out information deliberately? Maybe they did. Maybe I was a suspect. I started getting paranoid.

"You're not a suspect, Betsy," McGonigal told me. "I could see that panicky look on your face," he said, reading my mind again. He looked at the detectives. "Are you finished here? Because I think Betsy would like to go home now. I'll have a car take you back to your place," he told me.

It wasn't easy to sleep after seeing my friend's body being bounced out the door of her apartment building. I lay awake and thought about death. I was only 32 – how could my friends be dying already? Some of us hadn't even begun to live yet.

The morning's Post showed a photo of Carlyn under the headline "Who Put Dog Doc to Sleep?" My eyes filled with tears, and I reached for the Daily News instead.

I had a hard time concentrating. I couldn't forget Carlyn's sunny smile, or the way she was prone to breaking into spontaneous hearty laughter that filled an entire room. What would happen if I died suddenly? Would anyone care?

My boss came in around noon to send me home. Apparently, I wasn't discreet enough about crying in the exam room, and patients were noticing.

What to do on a sunny summer afternoon with no place to go? I took a cue from the pit of despair in my stomach and went into the first bar I saw. It was a dark cave of a place with a few shaky old men sitting around the bar. Perfect. My misery could keep everyone else's company.

A few drinks later, the bartender, Brian, who had become my new best friend, was suggesting that it was time for me to go. He put his arm around me and steered me toward the door. "There's a girl," he said. "Come back any time, when you're feeling better."

"But my friend…" I started. I was blubbering again.

"…died. Yes, I know, sweetheart," he said. He gently wiped the tears from my eyes with a bar napkin. "But you're still here," he told me. "You'll have to do the living for the both of you, now, won't you?"

I hiccuped. "That's right," I said. I suddenly felt on top of the world. I was going to live two lives, by God. I tripped going out the door and righted myself just before meeting the ground. I had never felt so good.

"Darlin,'" Brian said to me, "when you're through being sick, why don't you call me up. Here's my number. I'd love to talk to you when you're feelin' better." He pressed a folded matchbook into my palm.

I would! I would call him and we would go dancing…. I thought about these things right up until I started worshiping at the porcelain altar. I dropped into bed, and my lights were out before the sun went down.

The noise made my head pound. I reached over and tried to turn off the offending clock, but it wasn't working. A few more swats at the alarm, and I realized that it was the phone. The receiver felt like it weighed forty pounds.

"Hello," I managed.

"Dr. Arnold? Betsy, is that you?" came the frantic voice.

"Who'z this?" I croaked.

"Betsy, it's me. Melanie. Are you okay?"

"Melanie," I sighed. Melanie was one of the assistants in the office and a good friend. "I don't feel too good. I'm not coming in today." My mouth tasted like cotton candy. Chicken-liver flavor.

"Betsy, are you all right? You're not scheduled to come in today. It's your day off." Melanie was whispering.

"Oh," I said. Then, "Speak up. If I'm not supposed to come in, why are you calling at this ungodly hour?"

"It's 11:30 in the morning. I didn't think you'd still be in bed." She sounded slightly offended.

"Oh. Why are you whispering?"

"A policeman was in here just now, asking about you. I wanted to let you know," she said.

"What policeman? Who are you talking about? What was he asking?" Now she had my attention.

"Some cop. I'm not sure what his name is. He was asking about your schedule and stuff. Wanted to know how close you and your friend were before – well, how close you were. That kind of thing."

McGonigal had lied to me. I was a suspect. Now everyone knew it, too. "Which cop was it, Melanie? Who came around to talk to you?"

"No problem, Mrs. Smith," she said loudly.

"What? Are you talking to me?" I was confused.

"We'll call you as soon as your contact lenses come in. Good-bye." She hung up on me. One of the doctors must have come into the room while she was on the phone.

Damn. I got up and took a shower. I fixed myself up as best I could and headed down to the precinct. McGonigal wasn't in yet, but the female detective from yesterday took me into the interrogation room.

"Why did you go to my office and ask questions about me?" I was really pissed. "Sgt. McGonigal told me I wasn't a suspect."

I thought I saw a flicker of surprise in her face, but she masked it immediately. "Routine," she said. "By the way, we'll need you to turn in your auxiliary shield and ID card. Temporarily," she assured me.

"I'm suspended?" I couldn't believe this. Suspended from a volunteer job for knowing someone who died. I was getting really angry. The mayor would hear from me, by God! "I'm a doctor. I have a practice. Patients. You go into my office and start asking the staff questions about me, then you suspend me? You want to arrest me too?" I was shouting now.

"Calm down," she said, not unkindly. "It's just routine. You can come back to work after we find out what happened to your friend. It's just a little close for comfort when the APO guarding the deceased's premises is a friend of the DOA. Appearances make a difference," she explained.

"Then you don't think I did it?" I asked her, more confused than ever.

She fixed her eyes on mine. "Did you?"

"No! I told you what I know about this. Christ, I'm not big enough to kill anybody. Carlyn has to be – had to be – 5'10"."

The detective shuffled some papers. "We have to get your shield and ID from you," she repeated. "Will you bring them in, or do we have to come and get them from you?"

I was angry and confused, but I put on my best manners and promised to return the six-pointed star and identification card before the end of the day.

The wheels kept turning in my head. Was she killed by her ex or not? I braved the tabloid journalism of the Post to find out, but their reporter hadn't printed that information. Either the police asked the press to keep quiet about the cause of death, or no one knew how Carlyn died. Given the reporter's deadline, the information might not have been available before press time last night. I decided to go right to the horse's mouth.

I found out that journalists like to receive information, but they're not too generous about giving it out. I tried explaining to Brenda Starr on the other end of the telephone that I had been on the scene last night, and all of sudden, she was interested in what I had to say. I agreed to meet her in a diner nearby.

I felt bad about calling her Brenda Starr, even if I only did it in my mind and not out loud. Ann Howard seemed like a nice woman who just wanted to get a story because that was her job. She didn't look like a vulture or sprout wings or fur or anything during the conversation.

The NYPD has a rule about not speaking to the press unless it's cleared through DCPI: the Deputy Commissioner of Public Information. But since they had suspended me, I didn't feel obligated to keep a lid on anything I knew – which still wasn't much, because I couldn't pry any information out of the reporter.

After we danced around for a while, I finally said, "Look, Ann. You have a job to do – you want to get information from me so you can do it. My interest is in finding out about my friend's death. Now, how can we work together?"

She thought about it for a moment, then said, "I have an idea. Let's exchange information. I do an interview with you, the grieving friend, and you get to find out what I know about Carlyn's death. How does that sound?"

It sounded good, but I wanted to be sure there weren't any loopholes. "Everything? You'll tell me everything you know?" I raised one eyebrow.

"Yes, everything I know," she emphasized.

"Uh, uh." I shook my head. "Not good enough. I want to hear everything. Stuff you heard, stuff you're not supposed to talk about. This was my friend who died."

She smiled a little at that. "Okay, you're on. But not until after I get the interview." She pulled out her pad and pen.

We talked for about half an hour and I told her what I could.

But when it came time for Ann to uphold her end of the bargain, it seemed that she had received the better end of the deal. The information on cause of death wasn't being released. But her eyes lit up as she spoke to me about a plan she had for getting the scoop.

"Oh, no," I told her. "I could lose my license. I won't be a party to something like that." Famous last words.

I didn't exactly lie – after all, I am a doctor – but the medical examiner's office still didn't have much to tell me. All they knew was that it looked as though Carlyn had died of natural causes.

"That's impossible! She was 28 years old," I told Ann.

"Hmm. That's unusual. They don't usually say something like that unless they really think that's the way she died," she said. "But I have another idea."

Custer's last stand all over again. Don't ask me how she did it, I don't even want to think about what she had to do to get us in there, but Miss Howard's cleverness was enough to get us inside Carlyn's apartment. Before I knew it, we were past the seal on the door.

I had never been inside Carlyn's new place – or her old one, for that matter. I discovered that she had been a neat, orderly person. The modern furniture was clean, and everything seemed arranged in a logical sequence.

"Don't touch anything," Ann reminded me.

Sure, just what I needed – to get my fingerprints inside Carlyn's apartment. I tucked my hands into my pockets while I wandered around. Her bedroom contained a floral print comforter over a double bed, and I noticed towels in a matching design in the bathroom. The apartment wasn't large by New York standards, which meant that it would make a generous broom closet in the rest of the civilized world. But the bathroom was more than adequate, with a full-size tub. There were a few tchochkes out, oddly shaped perfume bottles and whatnot, but everything was neat. A few pairs of Victoria's Secret panties were hanging over the shower curtain rod, and her contact lens case was empty and open so that it would air-dry. I spied a pair of glasses on top of the toilet tank. I recognized the frame as one that was popular with patients who wore thick lenses. Mentally I congratulated my friend for having good vision-care habits: she rinsed out her contact lens case and carefully set her specs down so that the lenses wouldn't get scratched. Occupational hazard: I tended to notice things like that.

I also noticed that Carlyn apparently had been in the middle of making breakfast when she died. The small kitchen had a couple of used cups half-full of cold coffee in the sink, and a fossilized piece of toast was displayed on a plate beside the toaster. The only sign of disorder in the place was a broken piece of china with a design that matched the plate. The shards of the bowl were mixed in with Cheerios on the floor.

Ann and I must have had the same thought at the same time. "Do you think – " she started.

"Does it look like – " I began.

She motioned to me. "Go ahead."

"I was going to ask you, doesn't it look like she was interrupted while she was fixing breakfast?" I said.

"My thoughts exactly. The ME's office didn't pinpoint the exact time of death, but…" Ann riffled through her notes. "Here it is. The estimated time of death is between 3 and 11 a.m. That fits."

It fit, but what did it mean? Carlyn's apartment was neat and clean, and except for the cereal bowl, there were no signs of any struggle. The windows were shut tight, and they were all fastened securely with key locks. There were no scratches around the door locks, meaning that no one had attempted to break in that way. I knew from the police radio transmissions the night they found Carlyn's body that the super gave the cops keys to the apartment, but they had to break the safety chain on the door in order to get in. So for all anyone knew, Carlyn Valentine was home alone, safely locked in her apartment, when she expired of natural causes.

No. I refused to accept that explanation. She was too young to die, just like that. And I didn't think that the cops accepted it either, or they wouldn't have gone nosing around, checking into my story. Her ex-boyfriend didn't seem to be in the picture – she wasn't killed violently. And her apartment was neat, not trashed the way it would have been if a burglar had been caught in the act. Besides, how would the burglar have gotten in? Not through the windows – there was no way to lock them behind himself when he left. He could have gone out the front door, but how could he have fastened the chain from the other side of the door? It was impossible.

I had another thought. "If Carlyn let someone into the apartment..." I began slowly. "No, that couldn't have been what happened. Look," I said, pointing to the spot where the Cheerios decorated the floor, "she dropped the cereal bowl and died right here. Whatever happened to her must have taken place here."

I thought some more. "If someone knocked on the door and Carlyn went to let the person in, she would have put down the bowl first. If she dropped the bowl while the visitor was here, she wouldn't have gone to the front door to let the person out, then locked the door, then come right back to this spot to die."

Ann shook her head. "No, you're right. She would have cleaned up the mess. It doesn't make any sense that someone entered the apartment, killed her, then locked up behind himself." She gnawed on her lower lip. "I just can't figure it."

She checked her watch. "Cripes! Do you know how long we've been here? Let's get going." She pulled out her camera and took several shots of the interior of the apartment. I cringed to think about the captions that would accompany those photos in the newspaper.

Sleep eluded me for a while that night. I kept chewing over the facts of Carlyn's death, but they didn't add up. Finally, the Sandman came and rescued me from my thoughts. My mind didn't stop while I was asleep, though. I had vivid dreams that I couldn't quite recall in the morning.

While I was dressing for work, the interior of my closet spurred the same thought I entertained fleetingly every day: I needed to clean up. Optometry school textbooks crowded shelves next to Monopoly and Clue games left over from childhood. I chuckled at the Coca-Cola puzzle that I had never managed to put together, and a flash of memory came back to me from my dream.

Ann Howard called me just before the end of the day. "Can you meet me at the diner in an hour?" she asked.

"Did you find something out?" I got excited.

"I'm on deadline, so I can't talk right now. But I think you were on the right track with the boyfriend."

I took up a table for forty-five minutes before I called Ann at her desk. I got her voicemail. I decided to give her another fifteen minutes before I packed it in. Maybe she got caught up in a story at the last minute. I kept tossing around what she said about the boyfriend. I tried to think how he tied in. I knew that statistically, women who got out of abusive relationships were at the greatest risk for being killed when they left, not when they stayed with the man. So that would fit, if Carlyn had been killed. But the medical examiner thought she died of natural causes. I went around and around with it again.

Yeah, solve the puzzle. Like I needed that kind of direction from my subconscious mind. A crystal ball was what I needed to tell me what had happened. I remembered reading a story in which a detective explained his methods: "I figure out who has the answer, then I ask that person the question," he said. Great advice. If I could figure out who had the answer, then I wouldn't need to ask the question. Too bad detective novels didn't offer better tactics.

But if Carlyn's boyfriend was also her killer, then he would be the person to ask about her death. Sure. I don't even have my trusty Auxiliary Police shield to impress anyone with. Not that it worked anyway. A couple of times I had shown it to friends, only to hear, "What's that?" as though I had saved it from a box of Cracker Jacks. But I didn't need a badge to ask questions.

I played tug-of-war with myself all the way to the animal hospital near the 59th Street Bridge, where Carlyn had worked. Maybe I could find her ex-boyfriend. If he wasn't there, I figured one of the employees would know something about him. If veterinary techs were anything like optometric staff, they thrived on gossip. I could probably pry something out of a loose-lipped assistant.

The guy who spoke to me in the waiting room should have been named Igor, but his nametag said "Brad." He was a creepy kid who looked like he might have taken the job just for the sheer fun of all the animals he got to snuff. In fact, he explained that that was part of his job. He was a morbid geek who spoke in a monotone until I mentioned Carlyn. Then his face lit up, highlighting his acne and overbite.

"She was so nice," Brad told me. "She was always very gentle with the animals, especially when she had to put them to sleep. She didn't want them suffering any more than they had to. She was nice to everyone. Even me," he whispered.

I could see how that would elevate anyone in Brad's eyes. He probably didn't get much positive attention. Maybe if I was nice to him, he would give me more information. I decided to try that ploy.

"You must be very good at your job if Carlyn had you helping her out," I said, stroking him.

He stood up straight. "I'm a certified technician," he told me huffily. "I have extra training in putting animals to sleep."

Oh, shit, this isn't working. I tried to smooth it over. "I mean, if you assisted Carlyn personally, then she must have thought quite a bit of you. Personally," I stressed.

"Well," Brad said, a trifle mollified, "I did help her out a lot."

I didn't think it was possible, but his zits seemed to get worse by the moment. This guy was really revolting. I couldn't imagine how Carlyn put up with him.

"Yes, that's what I mean," I said in my best oily manner. The kid seemed to eat it up. "Did you know of any…trouble…she was having?" I asked delicately.

"She had a lot of fights with Dr. Redmond," he confided. "I could hear them in the back sometimes."

"Who's Dr. Redmond?"

"He's a part-time vet. He works here sometimes, but he has another practice too. He wasn't nice to Carlyn, I mean, to Dr. Valentine."

"What do you mean, not nice to her?" I asked, my heart quickening.

"Well, like, I think he hurt her," Brad confided. His features twisted with pain. "She never shoulda had to put up with that. She was way too nice. She always thought about other people, you know, like remembered their birthdays and stuff."

His face brightened. "Once, she went on vacation and she brought me back a T-shirt. It was a really nice one, with an animal design on it. I still have it," he told me proudly.

I was more interested in hearing about Dr. Redmond than Brad's crush. "How did Dr. Redmond hurt Carlyn?" I asked. "Do you mean he physically harmed her?"

"I don't know," the kid said sullenly. "I just know that if she was my girlfriend, I never woulda treated her like that. Even animals don't deserve that. That's why if they're too sick or hurt too bad, we put them to sleep. Not even animals deserve to suffer."

This kid was really creeping me out. I tried to cut the conversation short. I pumped him for more details about Dr. Redmond so I could get out of there as fast as possible. He reluctantly fished out a card from his Rolodex. It was grimy and disgusting. I tried not to think about what left-over animal parts were deposited on it. I copied the information into my book and made my getaway before the kid could describe the joys of animal surgery or something.

I called Dick Redmond's home phone number and got an answering machine. I would try him again tomorrow. In the meantime, I would try to get a good night's rest. Just before I closed my eyes, I spied a matchbook cover on my nightstand. It had a phone number inked in – Brian, the bartender, had given it to me. I decided to pursue that avenue tomorrow. I fell asleep thinking of his big strong arms holding me as we waltzed around the dance floor. We would go to a club and dance and share frosty tropical drinks….

I awoke with a start, sweat making my pajamas stick to my skin. The alarm clock read only 11:14, but I felt as though I had been asleep for weeks. I turned on the light and frantically dialed Ann Howard's number. Naturally, I got her voicemail. I punched numbers until I got a live person. Well, a person, anyway. I begged and pleaded, then tried threatening when that didn't work. Finally, the sadist on the other end got tired of toying with me and promised to call Ann at home and have her call me back. I paced around, wide awake now.

The phone rang. "This better be good," Ann growled at me. "I have company."

"I know who killed Carlyn," I said.

"Can't this wait until tomorrow?" she pleaded.

"Hey," I said. "You stood me up today. The least you can do is listen to me now."

There was a brief pause. "Oh, yeah, I did, didn't I? Sorry about that." Then, "You sure it can't wait?"

"Come on!" I said. "Do you want to break this story or not?"

"Yeah, yeah," she grumbled. I could hear the rasp of a lighter and a deep inhalation on the other end. "Okay, give it to me."

"Uh, uh," I said. "Meet me at the precinct."

She protested until I convinced her that this would be her best shot at getting an exclusive on the story. Her journalistic ambition won out over her biological instincts, and we descended on the station house together.

Sgt. McGonigal was finishing up some paperwork from his tour, so he was still there. The two detectives who had interviewed me the night Carlyn's body was found were processing an arrest. The sergeant corralled them and they set us up in an interview room. The detectives started the tape recorder.

I had visions of pacing the room the way detectives in old movies did it, calmly ticking off the facts and bringing everything to a neat conclusion. All I lacked was a pipe. The reality was a bit different. The cops made me recite my vital stats (name, address, etc.) until I thought I would die of boredom, then they led me through my theory step by step. I was fond of that part, I must admit. I got to feel important, being the first one to figure out how my friend had died and who had killed her. I tried to stretch the suspense as long as possible, relishing my moment in the sun. Sgt. McGonigal rolled his eyes, but I ignored him as I announced my dramatic conclusions.

"I know who killed Carlyn Valentine," I began.

The female detective started to interrupt with a question, but her partner elbowed her in the ribs. "Let her tell it or we'll never get out of here," he muttered.

I glared in their direction and continued. "And I know how she was killed." I stabbed the air with my index finger. "All the clues were evident in her apartment, but you had to know what to look for."

I paused for effect. The detectives were sighing heavily, exchanging weary glances. Sgt. McGonigal looked annoyed. Ann Howard was the only one who seemed interested in what I had to say, so I directed my efforts toward her.

"Allow me to point something out in the crime scene photos," I said. "If you look closely, you will see that in Carlyn's bathroom, both her eyeglasses and her empty contact lens case are out. Clearly, she had removed her glasses in order to put in her contacts. Now, she inserted her contact lenses into her eyes, then rinsed out the case and left it open to dry." I indicated the items in the pictures. Everyone looked, but no one seemed impressed. Yet.

"Now, when you put contact lenses into your eyes, there is always an excess of the solution that is used to hydrate the lenses," I continued. "That excess liquid leaks out the corners of the eyes. However, a certain amount of it also drips down the tear ducts." I looked around smugly. All I got in return were blank stares.

"What that means," I said, scrambling to capture their fascination, "is that the killer slipped a poison into Carlyn's contact lens solution. It was not a

111

poison that killed her immediately." I paused for effect. "It made her gradually become drowsy. She went about getting dressed and making breakfast until she came under the influence of the drug and could no longer stand up. That's when she dropped her cereal bowl."

No one said anything for a moment, then the female detective looked up at me. "Is that it?" she asked.

"Well, yes," I said. I couldn't understand why no one seemed interested.

Her partner cleared it up. "She was still locked in the apartment, you know. How do you account for that?" he asked.

I knew I had forgotten something. "I'm glad you asked," I told him. "Carlyn let her killer into her apartment, but probably not that morning. I postulate– " I had always wanted to use that word – "that the killer slipped the drug into Carlyn's contact lens solution the night before. Then he left her apartment. He didn't have to be present in order for her it to kill her."

The detective started to say something, but I anticipated his question. "You want to know who killed her, right? I can tell you that. The killer is…" – I paused for effect – "Brad, the veterinary technician."

Everyone looked puzzled. I ticked off the points on my fingers. "He is trained in putting animals to sleep, so he has access to the drugs that are used to kill. He told me that Carlyn was suffering, and that 'even animals don't deserve that. That's why if they're too sick or hurt too bad, we put them to sleep.'" I looked around triumphantly.

Sgt. McGonigal put his head in his hands. The female detective snapped off the tape recorder. The male detective put on his coat. "Stay here for a while, okay, Betsy?" the sergeant said to me.

"Okay," I said, unsure about what was happening. "Are you going to arrest Brad now?"

The cops all exchanged glances. "We have to do some more investigation before we can arrest anyone," McGonigal told me.

"You don't believe me?" I asked, incredulous. "You don't think this is the way it happened?"

"Like I said, we have to do more investigation," he said, edging toward the door. "Just sit tight. We'll be back." They left Ann and me looking at each other in the small room.

"What do you think they're doing?" she asked me.

"I have no idea. Don't you think my theory was right?" I was almost pleading with her.

"It's hard to say," she told me kindly. "But we'll find out soon enough."

Soon enough turned out to be hours later. Ann and I staked out either end of the conference table in the interrogation room and put our heads down. I shook myself awake when I heard the door open. McGonigal and the two detectives entered, all of them looking worse for the wear.

"You're free to go now, Betsy," the sergeant told me.

"Did you arrest him?" I asked excitedly.

"Ah – no," he said. "Your theory wasn't quite right."

I was crushed. I had been so sure I had figured everything out.

Ann jumped in. "Well, what happened? You people owe me an exclusive, and I want to get it," she demanded, her pencil and notepad at the ready.

McGonigal wearily ran his hands through his hair. He sat down at the table. "You were on the right track," he told me.

Then he described what the cops had been doing for the last several hours. The crime scene technicians had gone back to Carlyn's apartment to examine her contact lens case and bottle of solution. Neither had shown any sign of tampering or any trace of poison.

"However, the medical examiner did more tests on Carlyn," Sgt. McGonigal told me. He gave me a strange look. "She died from – " he pulled out his memo book and consulted it – "an overdose of sodium pentobarbital."

"Truth serum?" Ann asked.

"No. Sodium pentobarbital is the euthanasia solution that's given to put animals to sleep." He turned to me. "Even if it had been slipped into Carlyn's contact lens solution, the ME said that the amount she would have absorbed that way wouldn't have been enough to kill her. Besides, she would have detected it before she put her contacts in," he said. "For safety reasons, the pharmaceutical companies that manufacture the drug always color it purple, red or blue," he finished.

"So how – ?" I started.

McGonigal put up his hand. "We tested everything in the apartment that could have been contaminated. The killer slipped the euthanasia drug into her coffee cup. The color of the drug was masked by the dark coffee. We found traces of sodium pentobarbital in one of the cups in the sink."

I was disappointed that I hadn't been quite so smart, but I had one ace in the hole. "I was right about the killer, wasn't I? Brad did it, didn't he?" I had to be right about something.

"You were right, but not in the way you thought," the female detective told me.

"What do you mean?" I asked.

"Her boyfriend was the one who killed her," she said. "He talked his way into her apartment, slipped the sodium pentobarbital into her coffee, then left. Carlyn automatically put the chain on the door after he was gone, then she went back to fixing breakfast. She died the way you said," she admitted. "She got sleepier and sleepier until she collapsed – after Dr. Redmond was gone."

I looked at Sgt. McGonigal for confirmation. He nodded. "He confessed," the sergeant affirmed. "We have it on tape. He's going to go away for a long time."

Even though I hadn't been right about Carlyn's death, I was glad they caught the killer. Dr. Redmond did go away, but not for as long as he should have. He'll be out in a few years, but the closest he'll get to puppies and kittens is sweeping out their cages once the veterinary licensing board finds out about his record.

Ann got her exclusive and was thrilled. She even forgave me for interrupting her date. Sometimes we meet for coffee, but I'm afraid to get too close to a new friend right now.

I got my auxiliary shield and ID card back. It's not so thrilling patrolling the streets any more. I'm always afraid of what might happen next. Sgt. McGonigal spoke to me about it, and told me that this is what police work is like. "Welcome to the brotherhood," he said wryly. Great. Now I'm a member of a club I never wanted to join in the first place. But he told me it gets easier with time.

Poor, pathetic Brad remained just a creepy little guy who had a crush on Carlyn. He moved on to another veterinary practice, where no doubt he's pining away after someone else.

I went to visit Carlyn the other day. I brought a bottle of Italian red and shared it with her by pouring it on the grave. She would have enjoyed it, I think.

Brian the bartender came with me and held my hand. He's not too young, he's not overweight, married or gay, so he definitely has potential in the long-term department. Besides, you almost have to marry a guy who comes with you to the cemetery.

His only flaw is that sometimes he teases me about being an optometrist. We were in bed the other night, and he said to me, "Is it better like this, or like this?"

That kind of teasing I can live with. ★

LEARNING THE JOB

TRAINING RIDE
By Charles Padias

1958: SUMMER
SOUTHERN CALIFORNIA

The young man closely studied himself in the full length mirror. He picked a piece of lint from his black, breakaway necktie, straightened the brass tie bar, then stepped back to look at himself full view. Pretty good, Clay McTavish thought. The cleaners had done a good job. The military creases in his tan shirt and forest green trousers were razorsharp. He looked down at his spitshined, black shoes. They sparkled like mirrors, a technique he learned in the Marine Corps. He had polished his sixpoint sheriff's badge so that it glistened brightly. He was careful, though, not to rub too hard on the bear. Taking "the hair off the bear" was a not a smart thing for a cadet to do. The instructors at the academy didn't like that.

Clay took in a deep breath and straightened himself to his full height of five-ten. He felt good. The physical training at the academy had paid off. He was in great shape, a lean, mean, one-eighty-five. He could run for miles now, no problem. He couldn't help but smile at himself just a little. Then he glanced around, sheepishly, hoping no one had seen him.

He was in the locker room at Alondra Station. It was his fourth Saturday night ridealong since he had begun his training at the Sheriff's academy. Rollcall and briefing were over and the ongoing evening shift crews were about to go out into the field. Clay turned away from the mirror, glanced at the mimeographed "Vehicle Inspection Sheet" he had picked up in the briefing room and looked around for Deputy Frank Schmidt who would be his partner for the next eight hours. Not seeing him anywhere, he went out to the hallway then through the rear door to the parking lot outside. Dep. Schmidt was standing at the rear of a radio car holding the shotgun and laughing as he chatted with two other deputies. When Schmidt saw Clay, he stopped laughing, took a drag from a cigarette then flicked it to the pavement.

"I'll take care of that," Schmidt said in an irritated tone as he reached for the vehicle inspection sheet. "The last time I let a recruit fill out the inspection sheet the dipshit missed something and I got accused of damaging the radio car. See if you can check out the shotgun without having an accidental discharge."

Clay handed the inspection sheet to Schmidt without comment and obediently took the shotgun. He had learned there were two types of 12 gauge shotguns now being carried in radio cars – the Winchester M97 and the Remington M870. This one was a Winchester, which he preferred to the Remington because it carried one more round.

The Winchester had a five round magazine capacity where the Remington's magazine held only four rounds. You could add a round to each gun by carrying one in the chamber, but, that was against Department regulations. The Remington didn't have an exterior hammer, and the Winchester did, therefore, some deputies preferred the Remington.

He held the shotgun with his left hand, resting the butt against his side, and removed five live rounds from the magazine. Clay pressed the slide release button and jacked open the chamber. A live round flew out, landed on the pavement of the parking lot, and rolled underneath the radiocar.

"Look, when you open the fuckin' chamber, do it gently so the round will come out slow and easy," Schmidt said. "Then put your hand up to the chamber opening and catch it. Do you think you can handle that?"

"Sure," Clay said, "but I thought the chamber would be empty. I didn't think we were supposed to carry a round in the chamber."

"That's just academy bullshit they feed you guys. Believe me, if you get into a shootout, you'll be damn glad you have that extra round. The instructors at the academy don't have to worry about getting into shootouts. Street cops do. Now, get down there and get that round you let roll under the radiocar."

"Why not just move the car?"

"Look, clown, who in hell's running this crew, anyway, you?"

"No, sir."

"Then get down on your hands and knees, reach underneath the car and get the fuckin' shotgun round, okay? Let's see if you can do what you're told. You know, you're not getting off to a very good start with me. I'm going to remember this bullshit when I fill out your evaluation form at the end of the shift."

"Okay, okay," Clay said as he leaned the shotgun up against the side of the car and bent down to get on all fours.

"No, no! Jeesus! Put the fuckin' shotgun in the shotgun rack first! All I need is for it to slide off the car and go off."

"Yes, sir, sorry," Clay said as he opened the car door and placed the shotgun inside the car in the vertical rack next to the dashboard. He returned to the side of the car, got down on this hands and knees and reached for the shotgun round. He stretched but it was just out of his reach.

"I can't reach it. We're going to have to move the car."

"Bullshit. Just get the fuckin' thing, will you? And hurry up. We got two details from the desk. It would be kind of nice if we could get started sometime this evening."

Clay got back down, this time all the way on his stomach, and wriggled underneath the car far enough so he could reach the shotgun round.

"Hey, Schmidt, what's your recruit doing, changing the oil?" asked a passing deputy with a chuckle.

Schmidt laughed and said, "Naw, I think he's looking for something to eat."

Clay came out from under the car with dirt all over the front of his previously immaculate uniform and his tie askew.

"You look like shit, smart ass. I see I'm gonna have to mark you down for your personal appearance," Schmidt said with a smirk on his face as he lit a cigarette.

Clay made no comment as he brushed himself off. Glumly, he got in the black and white radiocar and sat in the passenger seat.

"Okay, do you know how to handle the spotlight when we're making a traffic stop?"

"Yes, sir."

"Alright, now, what I want you to do is just back me up and keep your mouth shut. You got that? I don't want to hear any of your chatter and I don't want you butting in or saying anything while I'm talking to somebody."

"What about the daily log? Do you want me to fill that out?"

"No. The last time I got stuck with one of you asshole recruits, the log was so fucked up the sergeant chewed my ass and I had to do it all over. I'd have been better off to do it myself right from the beginning. You just handle the spotlight, back me up, and keep quiet. That's all. Think you can remember that?"

"Yes sir. I've got it."

Clay could see this was not going to be a pleasant shift at all. His other weekend training rides had gone exceptionally well. They were exciting and he enjoyed them. He had ridden at Manchester, Belvedere, and Las Tunas stations. He actually had fun at all of them – didn't even seem like work. The rides were interesting, exciting, and got his blood pumping. He loved the experience. But this guy, Schmidt? Not a good beginning.

Schmidt looked to be about twenty-five or six, was of medium height, skinny and appeared to be a chain smoker. He looked scuzzy, needed a haircut and shoeshine. His oily brown hair gave him ring around the collar.

Clay wondered how in the hell the sergeant let him get away with it. But then, briefing had been held by the desk sergeant and he was sort of a grandfatherly type who probably didn't want to rock the boat. The other sergeant on duty, the field sergeant, had rolled out to a hot call just prior to briefing. They said he was pretty tough, so Schmidt had lucked out. Too bad.

Clay knew some of the deputies had their ways. Like the crew he rode with at Manchester. They ran people out of town, called everybody an asshole or a nigger, and were much too quick with their fists. Those deputies punched people, usually in the gut, at the slightest provocation whether they arrested them or not. They even went into a movie theater, grabbed bags of popcorn for themselves, and sat down and watched the picture for awhile. All without paying, of course. Clay didn't think too much about the movie thing but he didn't like the way they smacked people around. If somebody took a swing, then fine, they were bought and paid for. Better that they go the hospital than him, but, he sure as hell didn't like the idea of just beating on people for the hell of it. It disgusted him.

Outwardly, though, Clay had gotten along okay with the Manchester crew. At least he thought so. He certainly didn't say anything about how they conducted themselves to anybody, didn't fink to the sergeant. He was no fool.

Usually, the regular deputies kept their distance and had superior attitudes toward the cadets on their weekend rides, but, at least for the most part, they treated them pretty well. Sure, it was a stress academy and the instructors acted similar to drill instructors in the Marine Corps, and that was expected, but out in the field, among the public, it was different. The cadets were there to observe and to learn by practical application. They usually rode as third man in two man cars, but sometimes, they were the second man and had to be depended upon for back up. Most deputies didn't want their recruit partners to be so skittish they wouldn't react during an emergency or a physical confrontation with a suspect. Schmidt seemed different.

Clay had ridden as third man at Manchester and Belevedere stations. Last week he rode as second man at Las Tunas Station and thought he did quite well. At least his partner said so. They got along and he enjoyed the evening.

So here he was tonight, at Alondra Station, riding as second man again, but getting off to a rocky start with Deputy Frank Schmidt. Well, he would do his best. Keep his mouth shut, do what he was told, and try to get through the shift with as little friction as possible. This too would pass. He sure as hell didn't want to do anything to jeopardize his chances with the Department. The more he worked, the better he liked it. Not only did he desperately need the job to support his wife and newborn son, but he also found it exhilarating. He loved it. He swore to himself that he was going to be the best damned deputy the Sheriff's Department ever had.

During the course of the shift, Schmidt mellowed out a little toward Clay. Evidently, he had begun to see that Clay wasn't the nerd he originally pegged him to be. Schmidt was still a pompous, officious prick, however, who snarled at nearly everyone. The only people he was friendly with were attractive waitresses in the coffee shops where they stopped to eat or have a cup. He was a prime example of the kind of deputy that the academy was trying not to turn out. How in the hell did this guy slip through? Clay wanted to believe the Sheriff's Department was the best, just like the lieutenant at the academy had said. But, the more he saw, the more he realized that a lot of the lieutenant's talk was just hype. Hype and wishful thinking.

In fact, the lieutenant had a lot of asshole in him, too. He took delight in firing people. Every Wednesday, after a stress interview called the "Benny Board," he would take the badges and identification cards from the recruits he had just fired and line them up on a table at the rear of the classroom. The class was then ordered to file by and take a look. To add to their embarrassment, those recruits who had been fired had to clean out their lockers in full view of the class. Sad, but better them than him, Clay thought.

Now, Clay had to face his immediate problem of getting through the shift without pissing off Schmidt so much that he would write a lousy performance evaluation on him. He sure as hell didn't want to have to write a memo or, worse yet, appear before the Benny Board.

They were patrolling a residential neighborhood in the city of Woodlake. So far, the evening had been rather slow – only two reports, both residential burglaries. Neither deputy had said much. The silence was uncomfortable, but

Clay preferred it to Schmidt's arrogant prattle.

Suddenly, the silence was broken by the female voice of the radio dispatcher, "Forty-three, Alondra unit Forty-three... A 211 now at Frosty's Liquor... Carson and Cherry... Code two. Forty-three?"

Clay wrote down the time, location, and nature of the call in his notebook. "Forty-three... ten-four... forty-three," he replied into the car's microphone in an unemotional monotone.

Two-eleven, now. Wow, that's an armed robbery. Clay felt a rush of adrenaline. He reached down and flipped on the red lights of the "Christmas tree" on the roof of the radiocar. He took out his key to the shotgun rack and unlocked it. He was ready to go.

Schmidt's knuckles turned white as he tightly gripped the steering wheel and drove at a dangerously high rate of speed toward the location. He almost lost it going around a corner as the radiocar fishtailed and the rear end struck a parked car. The tires spun, burning rubber as Schmidt accelerated and kept going.

"Forty Sam... did you copy Forty-three's call?" the radio dispatcher asked amid static. "Forty-three, no units available for back up except Forty Sam. Forty Sam's ETA is five... Forty-three, you copy?"

"Ahh... Forty-three, that's ten-four... Forty-three," replied Clay.

"Fuckin' sergeant! A two-eleven now and the only back up I have is an academy recruit and the fuckin' field sergeant!" yelled Schmidt in and excited voice.

"We'll make it. We'll be okay," replied Clay, calmly as he hung on to the barrel of the shotgun for support as Schmidt slid around another corner narrowly missing an oncoming car.

Upon their arrival at Frosty's Liquor, Schmidt struck the curb and bounced up over it. He stopped the radiocar, diagonally facing the front door about fifteen feet away. The red and amber lights remained flashing as Schmidt positioned himself behind the open car door and pointed his revolver toward the illuminated front door of the store.

"Forty-three, ten ninety-seven at Frosty's Liquor... Forty-three," Clay said into the car's mike before replacing it in its carrier. He then, quickly, removed the shotgun from its rack, opened the car door and got out.

"Take the rear," Schmidt shrieked.

Clay ran around the gravel parking area to the rear of the store. A car was parked about ten feet from the back door. He made sure it was unoccupied, then found a good position where he could take cover behind the car and still have a good view of the rear door. He took the shotgun off safe and waited, his heart pounding.

After what seemed like an eternity, another radiocar arrived and drove around the store with its headlights out. It was a one-man unit, the field sergeant, Clay thought.

A short while later, Schmidt yelled at him to come on back around to the front of the store.

"The suspect is g.p.a.," Schmidt said, "I want you to listen in and take notes while I question the clerk so you can put out a broadcast. Think you can do that?"

"Yes sir. I can do that," Clay replied, calmly.

The suspect was "gone prior to arrival" so Clay needed to get a physical description – clothing worn, weapon used, amount of money stolen, and the direction taken when leaving. Also, he needed to know if there were more than one suspect, and if a vehicle was seen or heard.

All of this information was necessary so he could request a clearance on the radio and give it to the dispatcher, who would then broadcast it to all units.

He listened attentively and took copious notes as Schmidt questioned the nervous, overweight clerk. The field sergeant, a tall well built, serious man in his mid-thirties, stood by observing quietly until Schmidt was finished. The sergeant's name was Lon Elway.

After obtaining the necessary information, and while walking outside to the radiocar, Clay overheard Sgt. Elway tell Schmidt that he wanted to have a word with him in private. Clay got the feeling that the sergeant was a no-nonsense type.

Clay requested a radio clearance via a "Ten-thirty-four" and gave the broadcast information to the dispatcher. Sgt. Elway and Schmidt both stood by the open car door and listened for a moment or so, then moved a short distance away to have their "chat" out of earshot.

When he was finished with his broadcast, Clay saw that Schmidt was obviously getting his ass chewed by the sergeant. They ended their conversation in time to come over to the open door of the radiocar and hear the dispatcher put out the broadcast to the other units.

Clay got out of the radio car, and with his flashlight nestled in the crook of his left arm, continued to put some finishing touches on his notes. He wondered if Schmidt wanted him to write the report or if he would insist upon writing it himself as he had with the daily log. "Good job, McTavish," Sgt. Elway said. "You used good radio procedure and gave complete information to the Radio Room. You conduct yourself well. I like that. I want to see the report you write on this, too. When you turn it in, be sure to tell the desk sergeant that I want to read the report before you leave. Okay?"

"Yes sir. Thank you, sir," replied Clay, who couldn't help but feel a sense of pride at the compliment.

Sgt. Elway seemed like a real class guy. Clay had learned there were quite a few class people on the Sheriff's Department... and also that there were some with little or no class. Some of the academy instructors had class. The Manchester crew he worked with, and Frank Schmidt, did not.

"Don't let that 'atta boy' crap go to your head," Schmidt said as they pulled away from the liquor store to resume normal patrol. "Elway is a prick. What he said to you was mainly for my benefit. He just chewed my ass for my uniform appearance and told me to get a haircut. He never likes my reports, either. Nothing would please him more than for you to turn in a good report so he could say that even a bootassed recruit writes better reports than me. So, you better start writing, McTavish. Just don't expect any help from me. Elway wants you to write it, so you're on your own. I'm not gonna park for you to write it, either, and don't turn the dome light on. That's dangerous. Not only does it make it hard to see out, but it lights up the inside of the car and makes targets out of us. You just write the sonofabitch with your flashlight tucked under your arm."

Clay said nothing and resigned himself to do as he was told. He didn't want to start writing the report right away, though, because they were cruising the area looking for the robbery suspect. The clerk didn't see or hear a getaway car so, apparently, the suspect fled on foot. Of course, that didn't mean he couldn't have had a car parked nearby.

The suspect was described as a very large male, white, in his early twenties, wearing a black stocking cap, and a blue, long sleeved shirt. He had obtained a little over two hundred dollars by displaying a blue steel, possibly .38 caliber, revolver.

Clay doubted if the guy would still be wearing the stocking cap but who knows? He might. They checked the immediate area for about twenty minutes with Clay diligently using the radio car's spotlight, shining it down alleys and into parked cars.

Finally, Clay started writing the armed robbery report using his flashlight for illumination. He had just completed filling in the face sheet, when he remembered something.

"Hey, what about that parked car we struck on the way to the liquor store? Shouldn't we go back there and check it out? Make a report or something?"

"Fuck no! Nobody saw it happen. We didn't hit that car very hard, anyway. Just tapped it. Why should I hang myself out to dry with another traffic collision on my record. I just had a fender bender last month and got a written reprimand. I'll get some days on the bricks with another one. So, just forget it. Forget it and keep your fuckin' mouth shut! Got that?"

"Yeah, I heard you but I don't like it. You did more than just tap that car. I've got a job to think of too. A family to support. I keep my mouth shut, then I'm just as guilty as you are and could even get fired if it all comes out."

"Don't be such a pussy, McTavish. One thing you have to learn riding radio car is that you have to back up your partner. That's the most important thing you'll ever learn. If your partner can't trust you or depend on you, then you might as well pack it in. The word will get out you're a fink and nobody'll want to ride with you. In fact, nobody will even talk to you. You'll get the old silent treatment, my boy, and your life will be hell. So, if I were you, I'd be very careful before I even thought about getting diarrhea of the mouth. You want to keep your job? Then you better not screw me up. You do, I'll write some paper on your ass that'll put you before the Benny Board and get you fired. Ya hear what I am saying?"

"Yeah, I hear you, but you listen to me for a change, Deputy Schmidt." Clay said in an even tone. "I'm getting to where I really don't give a shit what you say. Right is right and wrong is wrong. Hitting that parked car is one thing, but not going back and doing what is right is another. It's not just trying to save my job, damn it, it's doing what is right. Some poor bastard had his car hit. We should own up to it. Besides, there's probably some damage and paint transfers on the radio car, anyway. The next driver assigned to this car is going to make out a vehicle inspection sheet and discover it. You're going to get caught, man, so why make matters worse by trying to hide it? You don't know if anybody saw us hit that parked car or not. The way we were screeching around corners with the red lights on, anybody around would certainly be watching and could have reported it to the station. Probably the Watch Commander. You call me a pussy, well, it takes a better man to face this kind of bullshit than to hide it. It's going to come out anyway. Hiding it is the same as lying and you can get fired for lying even if you aren't a recruit in the academy."

Schmidt slammed on the brakes and skidded to a stop. He got out and walked rapidly around to the rear passenger side of the car with his flashlight in his hand. At first, Clay thought maybe Schmidt was so mad that he was going to start a fight. Well, if that was what he wanted, it was okay with him.

Clay got out and met Schmidt at the rear of the car. Schmidt turned on his flashlight and bent close to the fender to check for damage. There was a dent the size of a baseball and some paint transfers from the other car.

"Okay, so there's some damage," Schmidt said. "You know, the guy who owns the parked car will still be able to collect from his insurance company even if we don't go back."

"Yeah, so what? That's not going to save your ass when you get caught trying to cover it up. And you will get caught, so don't be so stupid."

"Okay, okay. We'll do it your way. I still think you're a pansy ass, but we'll do it your way."

Clay got Sgt. Elway on the car-to-car radio frequency and asked him to meet them at the location where they struck the parked car. Sgt. Elway arrived shortly and examined the damage to both the parked car and the radiocar. Although he controlled it well, he was obviously disgusted with Schmidt and didn't bother taking him off to one side this time. He asked Schmidt why in the hell this wasn't brought to his attention earlier when they were at the liquor store? Did his recruit ridealong have to convince him to report it? Evidently, Sgt. Elway had admonished Schmidt earlier for jumping the curb at the liquor store, which probably knocked the front end out of alignment and could have caused even more serious damage. And now, this bullshit comes to light. His voice was calm but his irritation couldn't be hidden. Fire shot from his eyes like blasts from a cannon. Yes, Sgt. Elway was a master at the art of chewing ass with class.

The presence of the deputies drew several onlookers and one of them said that the car's owner saw the radio car strike his car and was quite angry about it. The owner of the car walked up a short while later and approached Sgt. Elway. He said he had just called Alondra Station and wanted to know what the Sheriff's Department was going to do about repairing his car. He said he didn't want to report it to his insurance company because he didn't want his rates to go up. Sgt. Elway used his radio to order a traffic car to come to the location and write a collision report.

The Sheriff's Department had a contract with the City of Woodlake to provide them with full law enforcement service, including traffic accident investigations. This was the first such contract in the entire country and there had been a lot of publicity in the law enforcement community about it. The City of Woodlake and the County were now jointly involved in the construction of a new Sheriff's station within the city limits of Woodlake. In the meantime, the Woodlake units worked out of Alondra Station.

The traffic deputy arrived, took some Polaroid pictures, and gathered information for his report. He looked sharp with his white gloves and the white cover on his seven point hat, but, Clay didn't think he would enjoy working traffic. He preferred a criminal car.

After about thirty minutes, Clay and Schmidt were free to resume regular patrol and answer their calls that had been stacking up. There were two petty theft reports and a malicious mischief report waiting. They responded to the given locations, handled those calls, and then handled a prowler call. They also made a couple of vehicle stops for traffic violations. Schmidt warned one driver for a tail light being out and cited another for failing to dim his headlights.

It was getting close to the end of their shift so they stopped at a telephone booth in a gas station lot so they could call the watch deputy and clear their calls. After doing that, they sat in the parked radio car as Schmidt worked on their daily log and Clay finished writing reports.

Although report writing was new to him, Clay worked extra hard to sharpen his ability and paid close attention during the report writing classes at the academy. He always arrived early at the stations he was assigned for his Saturday ridealongs. This allowed him time to read the various reports on the arch files in the briefing rooms. Other cadets did this too, but they read the reports mainly for the sensational content. Clay read the reports to help him learn the appropriate style, format, and word usage.

Clay had no problems with the petty theft and malicious mischief reports, but this was the first time he had ever written an armed robbery report. He was concerned about the modus operandi, or "MO" section. He was fairly sure it was okay, but thought Schmidt should read it. After all, his name would appear at the bottom of it, too. Schmidt refused, saying Clay was on his own. If the desk sergeant didn't like it, he could get his ass chewed all by himself.

Clay thought this attitude was crazy. Schmidt would get his butt chewed anyway because he was senior man in the car and Clay was just a mere academy recruit. Maybe the desk sergeant would approve the report without any problem and nobody would get chewed. That's what he hoped would happen.

The two men walking across the gas station's lot appeared startled when they saw the black and white Sheriff's car and seemed to change course in midstride. Clay and Schmidt saw them at the same time. One of the two men, the larger one, was wearing a blue, long sleeved shirt. Clay and Schmidt both got out of the radiocar and shined their flashlights on the men.

"Hey, hold on there a minute!" Schmidt said. "Come here. We need to have a word with you."

"What's the matter, officer?" asked the larger man as they stopped, turned, and slowly began to approach the deputies. "Is something wrong?"

"Just walk over to the front of the radio car and place your hands on the hood," said Schmidt who had withdrawn his revolver.

"Hey, no need for the gun," the shorter man said. "We're coming."

Although shorter than the man wearing the blue shirt, he was stockily built and walked with a cocky swagger.

Clay said nothing as he circled behind the approaching men and followed them to the front of the radio car where they both placed their hands on the hood as Schmidt had told them. Clay stood back, holding the flashlight in his left hand and resting his right hand on the butt of his revolver. Clay hadn't drawn his gun yet, but had unsnapped the strap on his swivelhip holster and was ready.

Schmidt had the two men move their feet back and spread them apart while keeping their hands on the hood of the car. Schmidt still held his revolver in his right hand as he started to frisk the larger man with his left. Clay thought maybe he should withdraw his weapon as the larger man certainly fit the description of the armed robbery suspect and, if he was the right guy, may still have the gun on him.

"What's this?" asked Schmidt as he felt the man's crotch. "It feels a little too hard and heavy to be your tallywhacker. Stand up and drop your pants, asshole."

Clay was withdrawing his gun from its holster when the man suddenly whirled off of the hood of the car and struck Schmidt directly on the jaw with a round house right. Schmidt dropped his gun and the shorter man sprang from his position on the car's hood and dove for it. Clay quickly reacted by moving forward and planting a lightning fast kick to the shorter man's face. Snot and blood flew but the man still had Schmidt's gun. As he was falling backward from Clay's kick, the man brought the gun up, pointed it toward Clay and fired. Clay felt his hat fly off as he fired two quick shots in return.

The short man flopped down on his back. Blood was beginning to ooze from a bullet hole in his throat and a hole in the center of his forehead.

Clay then whirled toward the larger man who was now on top of Schmidt, pummeling him in the face with both fists. Still holding his weapon and flashlight, Clay took a quick step forward, made a quarter turn to his right, brought up his left leg, and snapkicked the man on the side of his head. The man fell sideways off of Schmidt and rolled away. He appeared stunned and was starting to get to his knees when Clay caught him in the face with another kick, this time a powerful upward smash with his right foot.

The man fell in a heap, bleeding profusely from his mouth and nose. Clay then stepped back, with both arms extended, flashlight in one hand, and pointing his revolver at the man's head with the other.

"Don't move or I'll kill your fuckin' ass!" Clay said in a firm voice. Then, without turning his head, he said, "Schmidt! Go cuff him."

Deputy Frank Schmidt did as he was told. ★

LEARNING THE JOB

SPECIAL DELIVERY
By Roger Fulton

"I need an ambulance," the young man blurted out as he came through the door of the police station.

As the junior trooper assigned to the midnight shift, I was on duty at the front desk of the state police station just south of the Canadian border. While looking out the window, I had seen the young man's car turn into the parking lot and had heard the crunch of the newly fallen snow under his tires. That meant it was cold out there, even for mid-January. It was now 4:00 in the morning, and for this young man to have braved this brutally cold weather on this January night, it must be an emergency.

"Why do you need an ambulance?" I asked, meeting the young man's original tone, but with much less urgency.

"My wife! She's in the car and she's going to have a baby!"

I instinctively reached down for the telephone, but some inner force temporarily slowed me. His last response had triggered thoughts of the last time I had heard those words.

In that case I had stopped a motorist for speeding late one evening. As I got out of my patrol car and started to walk up to his car, the driver jumped out of his car and blurted out, "Officer, my wife is gonna have a baby. That's why I'm speeding."

Without hesitation, I said, "Okay. Stay calm and follow me." Running back to my car, I flipped on all of the emergency lights. Pulling out around the would-be father's car, I motioned for him to follow me.

I called the dispatcher and directed him to call the emergency room to alert them that there was an emergency case on the way – a woman about to have a baby. I put on my siren to lead the way as we approached other traffic, driving aggressively to clear the way for the soon-to-be parents.

Arriving safely at the emergency room entrance I jumped out of my patrol car and ran to the passenger's side of the other car to assist in getting the woman out of the car and into the emergency room. As I opened the door on her side, I looked into the woman's eyes and got a blank look from her. Before that could register with me, the husband popped up from driver's side door, and said, "Okay, you got me."

"What?" I asked in a voice clearly denoting my confusion.

"I was speeding, right? And my wife is going to have a baby, but not for another four months."

As my brain tried to make sense of all of these conflicting sensory assaults on it, I was temporarily stunned. In a couple of seconds it all started to become unbelievably clear.

Did I just hear this guy right? He pulled a trick like this, got everybody ready to handle an emergency delivery, and all for nothing. Just because he wanted to get out of a speeding ticket?

My thoughts collected well. A few minutes later, he drove out through the hospital gates, a lot slower than he had come in, and with a well-deserved speeding ticket in his pocket.

But now, it was several months later, and this young man standing in the lobby of the state police station wasn't trying to get out of a speeding ticket.

I now looked squarely into his eyes and asked, "When's she due?" not one to be burned twice.

"Actually, she's overdue," the young man responded. "I guess her water broke a while ago and she didn't want to wake me up, then the ambulance was out on another call... "

His eyes were honest and I realized that this was the real thing. The young man continued, but I wasn't listening as I punched the phone number of the ambulance dispatcher into the phone.

A female voice answered. "Fire department, is this an emergency?"

"Yes, it is. This is Trooper Green at the state police station on Route 22. We have a motorist here reporting that his wife is about to have a baby in our parking lot. Please dispatch an ambulance."

"They'll be on their way!" she replied.

"Thanks," I said, as I hung up the phone.

"The ambulance is on its way out from the city," I told the young man. He seemed a little relieved, but still appeared very concerned. I decided to go out and check on his wife, just to make sure she was okay and to reassure her and this anxious young man.

"Sarge, can you catch the phones for a few minutes?" I yelled toward the back of the station.

"Yea, but what's the problem?" a gruff voice yelled back.

The old sergeant had been doing reports in his office down the hall. A 30-year veteran of the state police, he was still an imposing figure of a man. Standing more than six feet tall, and about 250 pounds, he could intimidate the toughest of criminals, to say nothing of those young troopers who worked for him – like me.

"I've got a woman out here who's about to have a baby. The ambulance is on its way, but I'm going to check on her." I didn't wait for an answer. I knew better.

The crisp cold shocked me as I took my first breath outside. It was well below freezing. I walked over to the car and opened the passenger's side door. I saw a young woman in her early twenties, slouched down in the passenger's seat. She was staring straight ahead and clearly uncomfortable. She was initially oblivious to my presence.

"Hi," I said in as smooth and calming a voice as I could muster. "How are you doing?"

She gave me a side glance as if to be sure I had the right to ask that question. My uniform apparently reassured her and she responded with an unconvincing, "Okay."

Thinking back to my training, I asked, "How far apart are the pains?"

"I don't know!" she shot back at me sharply. Just about then, she moaned and said, "Oh, no!" and started to convulse in what could only be a contraction.

I had been trained in the police academy for this situation. I remembered watching a video of smiling people performing an "emergency" delivery under nearly ideal conditions. I remembered the class, but the details of that video were pretty fuzzy at this point.

I looked at my watch and noted the time. Somehow I remembered that three minutes was the magic number. If the pains were more than three minutes apart... this would not be my problem. The paramedics would be here soon and they would handle the situation. After all, they did this every day. They delivered babies. Troopers fought crime. No need to mess with the natural order of things tonight, I thought to myself.

Suddenly, the young woman moaned again. Her eyes shot wide open and she took a deep breath. It was another contraction. I looked at my watch. Only a little over a minute had passed! I remembered the three-minute threshold, but I would swear they never told me what to do about a one-minute threshold. At this point I was very concerned and a little scared. This was too close! It was well below freezing outside, with very little light, no help and in the front seat of an old Dodge, in a state police parking lot in the dead of Winter. I couldn't deliver a baby under these conditions. Both the mother and the baby would be in serious jeopardy. Yet, Old Man Winter and Mother Nature seemed to be calling the shots at this point.

"Lie down on the seat," I directed the young woman in as calm and yet as authoritative a voice as I could find under the circumstances. The discipline of my training was taking hold as I prepared both of us for a challenge with a questionable outcome.

My knees were shaking. Was it the cold or was I that scared? I wondered. It was definitely cold. My mind ignored the other option and returned to thinking about the young woman in front of me. She no sooner had laid down across the front seat than another contraction hit her and she let out another painful scream. "Relax," I said calmly, "Just let nature take its course." Although I wasn't entirely sure what that course would be.

For the first time, I was aware of her husband leaning in the driver's side of the car. He was holding both of her hands in his and looking at her with mixed emotions, wanting to do something to ease her pain, but not knowing what to do. He glanced up at me and gave me a look that said, "I know you will help us."

My knees stopped shaking as I resolved to rise to his expectations.

Another contraction and I learned what the term "crowning" means. I could hear the siren of the ambulance in the distance, but it was clear we were going to run out of time. This baby wasn't waiting for any ambulance. In the

ies the man just had to boil water. I thought about that, and realized there was nobody boiling water in that video I had seen. What was all that hot water for, anyhow? I briefly wondered.

Another contraction and another scream. The baby's head was now in my hands. This innocent child was coming into the world in freezing weather, with no medical attention, and was being delivered by a state trooper with minimal training in such matters. Moving in closer, I tried to shield the emerging child from the cold of the open car door. I thought about how such a quiet night had turned so suddenly into a life and death situation. Would this baby survive in this brutal cold? What about the mother? Both of their fates seemed to depend on how harshly the cold and Old Man Winter wanted to treat them.

I had been supporting the baby's head but nothing else was moving – one contraction, then another. The mucous around the baby was starting to freeze and I feared for its life. Realizing that something had to happen soon, I yelled, "Push!" just as another contraction was starting. She did, and the baby's shoulders finally passed through. In short order, I had a complete newborn in my hands, but I was still afraid the brutal cold would take its toll.

Without any prompting from me, the baby instinctively began breathing on its own. The thought passed through my mind how this child had been warm and comfortable in its mother's womb, and then suddenly was forced to take its first breaths in a truly cold and cruel world. Relieved that the child had been shocked into breathing, I again remembered my training, and placed the baby on the mother's stomach and covered both with a blanket of sorts from the back seat.

Completing that, I turned my head and caught a glimpse of a fireman's hat behind me. The ambulance had arrived. I remember the relief as I turned to the first fireman and said, "You have to know more about this than I do," and stepped aside.

Following his direction, we both went to work to get the equipment to clear the airway and keep the baby breathing. But it was still cold. It took us a while to get mother and baby out of the car, but we finally put mother and daughter into the ambulance and sent them on to the hospital.

As I returned to my desk duties, I replayed the delivery over and over in my mind. Did I do everything that I could have to help them survive? I asked myself that question a dozen times with no definitive answer.

About 15 minutes after I had returned, the old sarge came up to the front desk area, and pulled up a chair backwards in front of my desk, sat in it and looked at me over the chair back. "Well, did you deliver that baby?" he asked.

I nodded. "Yeah, Sarge, but it was awfully cold out there. I don't know how they are going to make out."

He stared at me for a few seconds without saying anything. When he spoke again, it was in a softer voice than I had ever heard him use. I was so surprised by his demeanor that I missed his first few words. I tuned back in as he confided to me that in his 30 years, he had never had to deliver a baby. "I always got them to the hospital on time," he said proudly. "It's an awful lot of responsibility, though, I would imagine," he continued. He hesitated for a moment, then looked me directly in the eye and stated, "But, all you can do is what you can do." With that said, he got up and walked back to his office.

His words conjured up an image of baseball's Yogi Berra who said "It ain't over 'til it's over." A smile came to my face as I thought how alike Sarge and Yogi Berra might be. They were two old curmudgeons, a little rough around the edges, but both having a thorough understanding of human nature. They were both wise men in their own rights.

Another half hour went by and Sarge came out of his office again.

"Well, how are they?" he asked, back to his usual gruff and demanding tone.

"I don't know."

"Well, call the hospital and find out!" he ordered.

Something grabbed my stomach. Did I really want to know? By this time, I was pretty well convinced that I had done the best I could. Under Sarge's powerful gaze, I punched in the emergency room number. When the nurse on duty answered, I identified myself and explained why I was calling.

She interrupted me in mid-sentence by saying, "Mother and daughter are doing just fine!"

"You're sure everything is OK?" I asked just to be sure.

"Just fine. Are you the trooper who helped in the delivery?"

Having been reassured by this time, I said, "Yes."

"Well, according to the parents, you did a great job. They think you're a hero."

"Thanks," I said, and hung up abruptly, not knowing what else to say.

Relieved beyond belief, I looked up and saw Sarge headed for his office. Just as he turned the corner, he looked back at me and winked.

The media hyped the whole incident, mother and daughter were pictured on the front page of the local paper with accolades to everyone. The other troopers called me "Doc" for weeks. But the most moving part was when the parents invited me for dinner at their home a few weeks later. I accepted and got to see the beautiful young lady that I had helped bring into the world. This time though, we were all warm and comfortable as we sat down to a nice home-cooked dinner.

Old Man Winter was still firmly in control of the North Country, but as mean as he can be, apparently even he can't resist the lure, charm and innocence of a newborn child. ★

129

LEARNING THE JOB

ON THE JOB
By Lou Savelli

NYPD had been a dream of the rookie cop, Larry Santoro, since he was a child. The son of Italian immigrants, he was twenty-three years old and his dream had come true. He used to watch the television series, NYPD, religiously. Someday, he knew, he would live the excitement just like he watched on his parents' black-and-white television screen. He couldn't wait till someone would ask him what he did for a living. He wanted so much to say what people in New York, especially cops, say to one another; "I'm on the job!"

Standing in his first roll call, the six-foot tall, thin young man with short dark brown hair eagerly awaited his first assignment. He stood with twenty other police officers in the seven-eight precinct in Brooklyn. This was Santoro's first taste of police reality.

The peeling, drab green paint on the interior walls of the building, built in 1928, seemed to reflect the attitudes of some of the seasoned officers. The others, just out of the academy a few days, were eager, proud and upright. These new members of The Finest wore their uniforms to precise regulations. The eight-pointed, navy blue hats were situated squarely on their heads. The bright silver cap device glistened at the crown while a black leather band accented the black patent leather visor across the front. A two-finger space from the bridge of the nose caused the hat to make their eyes barely visible to the public but just enough to see what a cop's eyes will see during his tour of duty. They were alert, anxious and waiting to volunteer for any assignment given by the sergeant at roll call.

The hair bags, the salty, less polished officers, would smirk in the back of the lines. They would never volunteer. Barely remembering the years past when their eagerness for the mostly thankless job was evident in their demeanor, the hair bags wore unkempt uniforms and sideburns left over from the seventies. The years on patrol in the streets of New York had taken its toll. Some, not all, had taken to alcohol as a therapy to cope with the job and the casualties of the streets.

"Attention roll call!" shouted Sergeant Tony Vecchi.

The tall, barrel-chested sergeant held a clipboard as he entered the dingy, hot, muster room. Santoro could hear the shuffling of feet and clanging of nightsticks as the 4:00 P.M. to midnight shift snapped to attention. The excitement sent a chill down his spine. He was the real thing, finally! This is what the six months at the police academy had prepared him for. He was ready to take on the world – or at least the Big Apple, New York, New York! The hair bags grumbled and joked with each other as they slowly shaped up at the back of the muster.

"Okay, quiet down!" yelled the sergeant. " Make two straight lines and dress it up! The Captain's coming to talk to you guys! Look sharp!"

The twenty, hat clad, uniformed police officers stood at attention in two straight horizontal lines holding their wooden night sticks at their sides as the Captain entered the large, dimly lit, room. Even the veterans and hair bags stood tall, glaring directly to the front in a military fashion that would make the United States Marines proud. Light royal blue shirts contrasted the navy blue hats and navy blue pants. Black gun belts, black shoes and shiny silver badges, called shields in NYPD, shone brightly across all the rookies' chests at the front of the muster.

"Ahem, mm!" The captain cleared his throat. "Good afternoon men!" he said in a heavy Irish accent. The room was silent. "It has come to my attention that some of you, not all, have neglected to wear your hats on jobs! Now you know I ain't a stickler for wearin' those eight pointed, poor excuse for a topper, shower caps, we have to wear!" Laughter came from the old-timers as the rookies stood stern faced. "But!" he continued. "The brass thinks that every copper should be wearin' them at all times because it presents a professional image. And if the brass wants us to wear 'em, well… we are gonna wear 'em! I don't have to tell you people that shoo-flies are out there lookin' to catch one of you with your hats off." The captain was referring to the group of high-ranking NYPD supervisors assigned to each borough who spent their time documenting uniform and minor procedural violations. "If they do, you're gonna get one and there is nothing I can do about it! So, when you get out of your radio cars, put your hats on your heads! That's all I gotta say!" The red-faced captain walked out of the room as the veteran officers began to relax and start grumbling.

"All right!" shouted the barrel-chested sergeant to the officers. "Those are the rules and we gotta follow them. Now. let's get down to business. Pay attention for your assignments! Murphy!"

"Here Sarge!" responded Dan Murphy in an eager clear rookie voice.

" Sindone!"

"Sarge!" shouted Dennis Sindone who was Murphy's partner and also a recent Police Academy graduate.

Brown!"

"Here Sarge!" quickly responded Tom Brown. He was just out of the Academy and the son of a well-respected sergeant with the department. He was barely twenty years old. He was just under six feet tall and had rosy red cheeks.

"Santoro!"

" Present, Sarge!" shouted Brown's rookie partner, Larry Santoro.

"You guys have Sector Boy-Eddie-Henry in RMP 1185 with a twenty hundred meal."

"Pisani!"

"Sarge!"

"Zietek!"

"Sarge!"

"Sector Charlie-Frank-Ida in RMP Fourteen-Fifty-Four with a twenty-one hundred meal!"

"Quiles!"

"Here Sarge!"

"You're driving me in R-M-P 2265. Get the property inventory in order and hand out the radios.

"The rest of you, since you got some time on the job, are flying to Manhattan for a detail. Take the van and get there immediately after roll call." The grumbling from the senior officers grew louder.

The sergeant continued "It seems that there's a major demonstration at the U.N. (United Nations) and it's starting to heat up. The Chief of Patrol's Office, downtown, called the borough and ordered us to leave the rookies in the precincts. The Chief felt, with the demonstration getting violent, the rookies might be too overzealous and escalate an already volatile situation. They are flying the desk officer to the detail and I am the only sergeant working in the division tonight. I gotta finish up my entries in the command log so you rookies are on your own for an hour or two. Don't cause any major problems out there! Got it!" shouted the sergeant.

Sergeant Vecchi hoped his last statement might keep the rookie officers from getting involved in some of those situations rookies tend to get involved in during their first few days on the streets. He was also worried. It was going to be busy for the rookie radio car teams on their first time on patrol. It was an unusually hot, humid night. The streets were already crowded. Several residents had already stopped into the precinct and picked up the last few sprinkler caps for the fire hydrants. There would be hundreds of kids cooling off in the heavy spray of hydrant water onto the hot asphalt streets. The sergeant only hoped his new officers would be busy on some minor radio calls for the first hour of the tour until his driver and he could get out on the streets and supervise their actions.

"Okay! Let's hit the streets!" the sergeant shouted as he walked toward the muster room door. The sergeant stopped and said, "Hey... be careful out there, you guys... and wear your vests. That's an order!"

Santoro and Brown looked at the front of the old station house for their assigned RMP. As they arrived, together, at the corner of Bergen Street and Sixth Avenue, just a few feet from the steps of the seven-eight station house, they noticed the numbers of the police car that would be their chariot for the next eight hours. It was a 1980 Plymouth Fury four door with blue and white paint. On the roof were red and white emergency turret lights. It had more dents than a car entered in the demolition derby, but to Santoro and Brown it was better than a brand new Cadillac.

"Why don't you drive, Tommy," asked Santoro of his first partner.

"You bet, Larry! I can't wait to drive this exquisite machine with the lights and sirens blasting at over a hundred miles an hour on our first call!" responded Brown catching the keys his partner tossed him.

Larry Santoro, with his hat situated perfectly atop his head, looked toward nearby Flatbush Avenue and watched the heavy traffic of yellow cabs, cars and trucks engaged in gridlock blocking Sixth Avenue. The car horns and shouts of drivers' comments filled the air. He knew, even as rookie, the odds of racing at high speeds through the streets of Brooklyn were unrealistic and unsafe because of the heavy traffic and countless pedestrians walking. It was also the summer of 1984 and things weren't that good in New York. Few jobs, the heat was unbearable and the drinking age was still eighteen, which made the rookie cop aware that they would probably be busy on their first night on the job.

They entered the tired patrol car and fought through traffic on Sixth Avenue across the gridlock of Flatbush Avenue. As the RMP drove slowly east on Sixth Avenue, just past Flatbush Avenue, the officers were alerted to the many people in the streets cooling off in the spray from the fire hydrants. Young boys were playing Johnny on the Pony, while young girls were performing expert moves of Double Dutch with their jump ropes. Everyone seemed to be having a fun time in the heat.

With no air conditioning in their RMP, Brown and Santoro quickly felt the heat. Their bulletproof vests made a hot situation even hotter. The only consolation was that they didn't have to wear their uniform hats in the car. Brown, with an obvious expression of frustration, pressed the horn portion of the steering wheel in a futile attempt to get the siren to work. His partner, who was four years older, laughed as he watched his persistency with the broken siren.

"I can't believe this damn siren doesn't work!" said Brown. "I need a siren, I waited a long time to have a siren. My father used to bring me to his precinct when I was a kid and let me play with the old radio cars. I loved to turn on the sirens. And now, in my own..." Brown was interrupted by a voice on the portable radios carried by him and his partner.

"Any unit available to respond to five-one-four Eighth Avenue, crossing Fifth to Sixth Streets, in the seven-eight, for a barricaded E-D-P (Emotionally Disturbed Person)?"

Without hesitation, as Brown punched the gas pedal of the struggling RMP, Santoro quickly pulled his portable radio from its holder to answer the dispatcher.

"Seven-eight Boy to Central!" shouted Santoro into his radio. "We'll respond to that E-D-P. Do you have additional information?"

The dispatcher responded immediately in an equally excited voice, alerting the rookie officers, "The E-D-P is a female, black, on the third floor and she is armed with some sort of cutting instrument and threatening to throw her two young boys from the third floor window!"

Looking at his partner, Santoro spoke into his radio. "Seven-eight Boy is a few blocks away, Central. We'll advise you of the situation when we arrive."

Brown maneuvered the RMP through traffic and pedestrians crossing the street. He knew he didn't need a siren because in this situation he wouldn't have used it. He needed to make a quick, but quiet, response, using the tactics he learned in the academy. As the RMP neared the area of the incident, the officers observed a crowd gathering at the rear of the three-story tenement that was situated on the corner of Sixth Street and Eighth Avenue. Brown pulled the car to the curb and the two partners rushed out of their RMP, forgetting to wear their uniform hats. When they ran to the rear of the building, which was adjacent to an extra parking lot used by Methodist Hospital, separated by a wrought iron picket fence, they couldn't believe what they were seeing. And they surely knew the academy had never prepared them for this.

Looking up to the third floor window, the officers saw a tall, large heavy set black woman standing on a window sill cradling two small boys. With one in each arm, she clutched a large shard of broken window glass in each hand and held it to the throats of each boy. The boys were no older than two years old and very thin. Frantically crying, the children were obviously terrified as they each yelled, "Mommy!"with each crying, gasping breath. The obese woman, who was wearing a pink, dress, had obviously broken the entire double window frame and pushed it out onto the ground below. Should she jump or throw the boys to the ground, either would be impaled by the old iron fence.

The crowd around the window stepped back for the rookie cops with the respect afforded a veteran officer.

"Holy shit!" shouted Santoro to Brown. "Do you see the size of those pieces of glass?"

"Yeah, Larry and look at the boy on the right. He's bleeding from the face where she's got the glass touching him. We gotta do something, right away!"

"Tommy, I'll stay here and try to talk to her while you go to the apartment door and see if you can get in if we have to. Don't make any noise because she may hurt the kids if she hears us trying to break down her door. Call Central and get the other two units, the Sarge, emergency service and an ambulance immediately. This is it partner, we're really on the job!"

Before Brown carefully slipped away from the woman's sight, he quietly said good luck to his partner. Brown immediately arrived at the front of the building and stopped to call on his radio.

"Seven-eight Boy to Central, I have an emergency message!"

"Go with your message Seven-eight Boy!" responded the dispatcher.

"Central, be advised, we have a confirmed barricaded EDP who is armed with large pieces of broken glass. The EDP is a female, black, approximately 30 years old. She is holding two children hostage and is now standing on the window sill of the third floor window holding the children and threatening to throw them to the ground. We need the sergeant to respond, emergency service unit and ambulance and back-up units to the corner of Sixth Street and Eighth Avenue!" Brown authoritatively informed the dispatcher.

"Affirmative!" answered the dispatcher

"Seven-eight Boy to Central!" again stated Brown on his radio.

"Go ahead Boy!"

"Central, advise the units no lights, no sirens upon nearing the proximity of this location!"

"Ten-four!"

Brown ran into the building to find the apartment door and assess his ability to gain entry in case it was necessary. Larry Santoro had taken an old mattress that was lying in the adjacent parking lot and draped it over the wrought-iron picket fence. He looked up at the woman who was now staring at him with a frightening, deranged expression. He wanted to shout but stopped himself and took a deep breath to calm down.

Someone in the crowd gave him information about her. Her name was Thelma Martin. She was a thirty-three-year-old housewife. She didn't work and was raising two-year-old twin sons. The boys' names were Samuel and Tyrone. She's was a manic-depressive who hadn't taken her medication in three days. Her husband abandoned her and the boys last year.

"Thelma!" Santoro said loudly but in a calm voice as he looked up toward the desperate woman.

She looked at the young, light-skinned-officer who glowed with a recent suntan. She seemed almost shocked that he knew her name or that he used it.

"My name is Larry!" he said clearly. He didn't want to use Officer Santoro, fearing it would put the woman on edge. "I want to help you and your sons!" He watched her face change from anger to sadness at the mention of her sons. He knew she cared for them but was still an extreme danger to the boys.

"You can't help us!" she said with tears in her eyes in a raspy voice.

"Yes I can," he replied.

"How can you help us?"

"If you tell me what's wrong, I can get you help," he answered. He didn't know what techniques and words to use because of his lack of experience, so he chose his words carefully.

"You want to kill me, don't you!" she shouted.

"No, no... I want to help. Please let me help you. Tell me what's wrong."

"Leave me alone or I'll kill the three of us, I'll... I... I... will jump!"

Giving her a chance to calm down, he stepped back a few feet and met with his back up. The four other rookie officers working the four to midnight tour were the only backup.

"Where's the Sarge, ESU and anyone else?" he asked of his backup officers, who were recent academy graduates like himself.

"We're it!" muttered Dan Murphy who was a big burly twenty-one-year-old. "ESU is stuck in the nine-oh with a shooting, the Sarge was called to Manhattan right after roll call and now he's stuck in the Brooklyn Battery Tunnel in traffic trying to get here. He probably won't be here for another half-hour. Oh and there is no hostage negotiator available. Central is trying to locate one. It's just you, Larry."

"No," answered Santoro. "It's us. We're it. We gotta be ESU, the Sarge, Hostage Negotiation, everything."

"But we're just a bunch or rookie cops!" exclaimed Al Pisani.

"No, we're just a bunch of cops," replied Santoro, with a determined look on his face. "And a bunch of cops is what those two kids need right now. And their mother. Let's get going. This is what we're gonna do: Danny, go into the building and join up with Tommy Brown. You two are the biggest and strongest of us all. Get ready to break the friggin' door down if we have to. Stan, you go to the apartment next door and try to jimmy the locks on her window that shares the same fire escape as her neighbor. If you can get in quietly, we can sneak someone into the apartment and pull her and the kids inside and, maybe try to get the kids away from her without them getting hurt. Go! Call me on the radio if you have any luck."

The three rookies ran to their assignments. Santoro told Pisani to back the crowd away so Thelma wouldn't get nervous looking at the crowd. Pisani calmly and carefully moved the crowd back. Santoro again started a conversation with the woman.

"Thelma!" he called to her.

She ignored his calls. Now she seemed to be oblivious to what was going on. She began pressing the glass into the cheeks of the two boys. Both were now bleeding from the face. Fearing that she was getting worse and closer to the point of harming the children, Santoro realized that something had to be done right away. He asked Pisani to continue talking to the woman calmly. Al had a way about him. Everyone liked him. He was a soothing person.

Al went right at it. He began talking to her and for a while she seemed to be listening and then she'd fade away. She was sweating profusely and her dress was soaked from the perspiration. It began to cling to her body and some onlookers began to laugh. She became more enraged.

"I can't take you people anymore!" she screamed at the crowd. "I can't have my boys live with you people in this world!"

Realizing it was too late to get through to her, Santoro ran to the third floor and joined Brown and Murphy. "How does it look?" he asked. "I think we have to break it down."

"It's a steel door with two dead bolts and we don't know what she barricaded the inside with," responded Tom Brown. "I got a sketch of the apartment's layout from the woman downstairs. Her apartment is the same. If we get the door open, all we have to do is run ten feet straight ahead. The living room, which is where she has the kids on the windowsill, is the first room on the left. The window is only ten more feet."

Santoro spoke into his radio and asked Zietek what he could see from the fire escape.

"I can see the apartment door," Zietek replied.

"What does she have barricading it?" Santoro asked.

"It looks like it's just a bookshelf of some sort. Nothing else! It doesn't look too heavy."

"Seven-eight Boy. Are you on the air, emergency!" Al Pisani's voice was clearly heard by his fellow officers.

"Go ahead Al," replied Santoro.

"She became enraged and started squeezing the boys and crying hysterically. She jumped back into the apartment. I don't know what she is doing."

"Ten-four!"

Listening at the door, Brown heard the woman talking to the boys. They began to scream. "You're hurting me, you're hurting me!"

"It'll be over soon!" she shouted.

Hearing that, Brown looked at his partner and said, "I think we gotta do it now. She's going to kill them."

Santoro, again took charge.

"Danny, Tommy," he whispered to the three fellow rookie cops who were standing outside the apartment door. "You guys try to force in the door. If you get it open, I mean, when you get it open, we'll rush to the living room. I'll grab her, throw her to the ground, while you guys pull each kid from her arm. Dennis, when I pull her to the ground, you try to cuff her right away!"

Each cop shook his head in acknowledgment and immediately took his position. As Brown and Murphy started ramming their bodies against the metal door, Santoro radioed to Pisani in the front to get ready in case she threw the children from the window. He also directed Zietek to continue watching her actions from the fire escape window.

Everyone was in agreement. They weren't scared any longer; they were determined. Santoro knew his hasty plan wasn't perfect, but neither was the situation. He knew it was now or just pick up the pieces later.

"She hears you hitting the door!" Pisani yelled into the radio. "She's climbing back onto the windowsill with the kids! Hurry! Hurry!"

Within seconds, Brown and Murphy slammed their bodies so fiercely into the door that the locks were shattered. The door swung open and pushed the bookshelf barricade over at the same time. The four rookies burst into the apartment and dashed for the living room. There was broken furniture everywhere. The floor of the living room was covered in broken glass, chips of paint, wood and blood. They hoped to get to the windowsill before the distraught woman was able to throw the kids, or herself and the children from the window. Brown, unaware that he had broken his shoulder, was the first to reach the woman. He grabbed onto the child in the woman's left arm while Murphy, now bleeding from the knee, grabbed the child on the right. As they struggled with the woman's grasp, Santoro wrapped his arms around the three-hundred-pound woman's legs and pulled as hard as he could. Surprising himself, he was able to force her backward toward the interior of the living room.

Feeling herself falling backward, the screaming and crying woman loosened her grip on the shards of glass now covered with blood. Her arms still held tightly onto her sons. The large shards of glass fell to the ground and shattered among the debris.

Slipping and sliding on the debris from the floor, the rookies pulled the woman into the apartment and onto the floor. She fell on top of Santoro. Brown pulled one child from his mother's arms. He was bleeding from the face and crying hysterically. Murphy struggled with the mother's grip on her other son. He stared into the innocent eyes of the boy and pulled harder and harder.

"Ahhgtt!" Murphy grunted, again and again until he bent her arm away from the boy.

By now, amidst the screaming, crying, grunting and shouts on the police radio, sirens were heard from responding backup officers racing to their assistance. The seven people, so tragically brought together, rolled on the hardwood floor in the sparsely furnished room. The crunching and scratching of glass and wood could be heard among the fighting. Blood from the children, their mother's hands and Murphy's knee smeared across the dark floor.

Finally, the team effort of the four rookie cops neared an end. Each boy was pried from his mother's grip and pulled away from her side. Santoro and

Sindone were able to push the woman over and onto her stomach. They wrestled her fighting arms behind her back. Sindone was barely able to place one handcuff onto the thick wristed woman. Santoro grabbed her other arm and squeezed a pair of handcuffs onto her wrist. The two pairs of handcuffs were pulled together by the struggling officers until they met in the middle and locked together.

"My sons! My sons!" shouted the woman lying in the dirt and glass on the floor held down by the two rookie cops.

"Tyrone and Samuel are okay, Thelma! Please calm down!" shouted Santoro.

The woman slowly relaxed and abandoned the fight.

Santoro and Sindone helped the woman to her feet, grabbed a nearby blanket and covered her to cloak the handcuffs from her children's view and the view of the awaiting onlookers.

"We are going to take you to the hospital, Thelma. Is that okay with you?" asked Santoro.

"Yes," she said, in a quiet voice.

The two young officers escorted the woman out of her apartment, down the narrow stairwell and into an awaiting ambulance now manned by backup officers ready to bring the woman to Kings County Hospital for psychiatric treatment. By now, cameras were everywhere.

Santoro and Sindone met with Brown and Murphy at the side of the building. They still had the two boys clinging to their necks. The boys didn't want to let go of their new police friends.

The four rookie officers, who half an hour before stood spit and polished at their first roll call, looked like they had just gone through a war.

Television crews were set up and reporters were asking questions of the neighbors. Video cameras filmed the officers as they walked down Sixth Street, with the twins to the entrance of Methodist Hospital. They all disappeared into the entrance as the media was turned away by hospital security. Doctors and nurses attended the injured bunch. None of them were seriously injured – at least not physically.

Later, as they sat in the large triage room, a familiar smiling face came in. The jolly sergeant, whom they left at roll call, smiled and shook his head. His hat was squarely on top of his head and his uniform was neat and clean.

"So! You rookies didn't wait too long to get yourselves involved in some shit, did ya?" said Sergeant Vecchi like a parent to his young children.

"We're the police, Sarge. That's what we do," responded Brown holding his broken shoulder.

"Well, rookies! You did it well! I am very proud of you and very glad I have all you maniacs in my squad. Cops like you guys make my job a little tougher sometimes, but a lot more rewarding! You guys will definitely be some of the finest!"

Sergeant Tony Vecchi turned and walked toward the way he came in. He stopped, turned around, and said, "Oh... by the way! The captain called me on the radio a few moments ago and ordered me to call the station house."

"Did he say to tell us we're gonna get a medal for this Sarge?" asked Murphy.

"He said the Borough Shoo-fly called and said he saw you all on TV. It turns out that you're all getting complaints for not wearing your hats," he frowned and walked out the door.

"Gee," Santoro said. "I guess, now, we're really on the job!" ★

LEARNING THE JOB

LUNCH ENCOUNTER
by Robert B. Shaw

Probationary Officer Peter Ignatio Newly rolled the black and white cruiser into the curb in front of Chico's Lunch Counter and killed the engine. He stepped out into the heat of the late morning. The .44 magnum revolver on his wide belt was a solid, confidence-building weight over his right hip. Surreptitiously Newly brushed his fingertips across the big gun. He loved the cool, sleek steel, the scent of gun oil, the exotically grained wood of the handle, checkered to ensure a good grip.

Instead of eating breakfast that morning, Newly spent the time putting a light coat of oil on the big revolver and wiping it down with a soft, lint-free cloth. Sliding the gun into the holster, Newly had been struck by the latent power of the firearm and the authority it represented. He told himself that he hoped he never had to use it, but great care of the weapon and hours of practice on the shooting range guaranteed that if he ever had to, he would be ready.

The young officer put these thoughts aside as he pushed through the double glass doors of the restaurant.

Across the street two men got out of a large sedan. One of them, the man in the battered leather jacket, followed Newly with his eyes. He drew on the butt of a cigarette and then tossed it to the pavement and stepped on it. The tall, roughly dressed man caught his own reflection in the window of the car. He paused to look at himself and what he had become. Thin to the point of being gaunt and pale. Unhealthy complexion, lifeless dark hair that was too long. He hadn't been close to a razor in a couple of days.

The man shook his head angrily. Life had not been treating him real well lately. Claire was talking about leaving him. The kids barely acknowledged his existence and worst of all, on the job they were checking up on his performance. The sour expression on his face matched the sour curdling in his soul. He tossed a glance across the hood of the car to the "front office man" who was dogging him this morning.

"C'mon, Lou," he growled. "Let's get it done."

The two men dodged across the busy street and followed the young officer into the dim interior of Chico's Lunch Counter.

Officer Newly didn't have the automatic self-confidence that some years on the force would have given him. So he was quick to take offense when the truck-driver-looking guy on the stool next to him made a loud remark about "baby cops." The words were said in the direction of the older guy sitting next to the truck driver, but he meant for Newly to hear. Newly could feel the back of his neck and his face getting red.

Newly lifted his cup and sipped at the steaming liquid, eyeing the second crispy brown doughnut with less pleasure. He glanced at the truck driver.

"Take it easy, Mister. Okay?"

"Take it easy? Why the hell should I take it easy? Because you say so? A baby cop like you?" The truck driver swung on the stool and looked at his companion in mock outrage. "Ain't this still a free country?" he demanded. "Can't a guy say what he wants?"

His companion nodded approvingly and truck driver swung back toward Newly.

"You in here practicing Doughnut 101 like they teach you up in that fancy academy up the state capitol and telling me to 'take it easy'?" He flicked a strong looking hand at the officer's meal. "Probably don't plan on payin' for that either. You coppers are always looking for a free ride. Livin' off my taxes and free handouts in the diners."

The lean, sour looking man glanced around at the diner's other patrons. Most of them were paying attention now, a touch of wariness in a few eyes but all interested to see how the cop would react. The truck driver was interested in that himself. *I wonder if I can get this kid to leave the diner. Better yet, maybe I can get him to take a swing at me.*

To Newly it seemed like the other customers were all grinning at him, some of them nudging each other, delighting in his discomfort. No help there. The young man struggled to remember his academy training. "When the situation gets hot, you get cool," his instructors had drilled into them. "Don't escalate the situation."

He fought down his rising anger and directed a level look at the truck driver, not sure what he was going to say. He took in the sallow complexion, the collar length hair. Suddenly he was struck by something familiar in the thin, be-whiskered face. *I've seen him before. Where?*

It could only be one place, the wall of wanted posters in the roll call room. That morning Newly had studied the dozens of grim, official portraits of society's dregs that cluttered the bulletin board. *That's where I recognize this asshole from,* he thought in triumph. *There must be a warrant out on him.* He couldn't remember exactly which poster bore this man's likeness, but it was definitely one of them. Of that he was sure.

The officer slid backwards off the green vinyl stool and faced the man.

The truck driver noted the instant of recognition in the young cop's eyes and the grin was gone from his mouth. *Looks like the kid is on to me. He's either going to be really pissed and start jerking me around or —*

"Sir, I'm going to have to ask you to step outside to my patrol vehicle. Just put your hands where I can see them, get up and walk outside."

Newly said a quick prayer that the guy would do what he was told, that he wouldn't have to force the issue or – please, God – call for backup on a simple arrest. His sergeant would never let him live that one down. Newly grasped the butt of his revolver.

141

Grinning once more, the truck driver placed his palms flat on his thighs and turned away from Newly toward his companion. "I tell you, Lou. They aren't making baby cops like they used to." He tossed a derisive glance over his shoulder at Newly. "An old timer would have had me on the ground and in cuffs by this time."

The dismissive words and contemptuous tone grated on Newly's ears. He glanced around at the wide-eyed and silent patrons. Even Chico's guy in the kitchen had come to the see through to check out the action. They all expected him to do something.

He reached out with his left hand and grasped truck driver's upper arm. "Outside, Mister," he said. "Now!"

The truck driver angrily swung back on the stool to face the police officer and easily batted the hand away. *Young punk. Who the hell does he think he is?*

Newly had the .44 magnum half way out of the holster now and he took a step backwards. He was about to speak when the truck driver's companion, the older guy called Lou, leaned forward and spoke into the man's ear.

"Okay, okay," Newly heard and the truck driver stood up and away from the stool to face him. The lean man slid a hand inside the leather jacket and down toward his belt.

He's reaching for a gun!

The young police officer yanked the big revolver out of the holster and clasping it in two hands aimed it at the top button of the leather jacket. "Hold it right there." His voice was loud, cracking with tension and what sounded like fright.

The truck driver checked in place. "Hey now, buddy-boy. Just take it easy, okay? This isn't what you think." *Dumb kid is gonna' screw around here and get himself hurt,* He grinned at the wobble in the gun barrel and the wide eyes staring at him over the iron gun sights.

"Tell you what, asshole," he sneered. "You start puking, turn your head, okay?"

The truck driver was mistaken. Probationary Officer Peter Ignatio Newly, "Pin" to his friends, wasn't the least bit afraid. He was completely pumped on the adrenaline crashing through his system. Every sense was feeding information to his brain at a million bits a second. As he saw truck driver's hand grasp an object under the leather jacket and begin to bring it into the light, he was totally aware of the older man, Lou, fumbling to extract something from inside his jacket. He always thought he would be scared in a situation like this, but he wasn't. He was exhilarated. *Jesus, these pricks are begging for it.*

"Put your hands in the air," he demanded. His eyes flickered to the other man. "You too!"

The lieutenant nudged the sergeant in the back, nervous, whispering urgently. Training Sergeant Danbury, on probation himself and pissed off at the world, shrugged off the older man.

"Yeah, yeah okay, Lou." *If I don't know how to break off a routine training evaluation exercise, what the fuck do I know? All these newbies act the same. Jumpy. Scared. Goin' for the gun. If it wasn't so damned boring it would be* funny. Time to badge the kid and get the hell out of here. Go somewhere and have a beer and a shot. Wasn't too early for a shot, was it?

He knew how to break off the exercise.

Danbury never took his eyes off the young man he thought of as a scared kid. His badge was shoved down inside his belt next to his gun. He flipped back the leather, hooked the badge carrier in his fingers and in a practiced motion jerked it out from under his jacket. The Lieutenant followed suit.

The kid will piss his pants when he sees a couple of gold badges lookin' at him.

Sergeant Danbury raised the gleaming metal toward the young cop.

Witnesses said later that the two booming explosions of the powerful revolver came so close together they sounded like one. A black hole appeared where the top button of the leather jacket had been. Immediately following that was the appearance of a neat, round crater under the older man's left eye.

Danbury was swept off his feet by the force of the bullet and flung into a booth alongside, upsetting the table. He landed in the ample lap of a screaming woman where he died from shock and gushing blood loss. The lieutenant was slammed back against the counter and off the stool onto the floor. There was a huge hole in the back of his head and his brains splattered all over Chico's cook.

Officer "Pin" Newly spent a year behind a desk, telling anyone who would listen about that morning in Chico's Lunch Counter. He described again and again what he saw, what he heard, what he believed was happening; justifying how he killed two fellow officers in a "good" shooting. They sounded in his own ears like whining, but the recitations went on. After a few months even his girlfriend stopped listening to him and turned away.

When Newly didn't come to work for three days in a row, his sergeant sent a patrol to ride by his apartment and check up on him. That's how they discovered that Probationary Officer Peter Ignatio Newly had used his big .44 magnum revolver this time to resign from the force. Permanently. ★

LEARNING THE JOB

YET ANOTHER CRIME FOILED
by Stormy Barton Apgar

It was Libby McBride's second week as the Field Training Officer for Nate Gibbons. While Libby took law enforcement very seriously, she was able to balance that with a good sense of humor. Nate was levelheaded and had good common sense. He and Libby got along well even though the field training period is always stressful for everyone concerned.

Dealing with the unpredictability of police calls is never easy. Even tougher on the new officer is knowing that everything you say and every move you make is being watched. How you converse with dispatch on the radio, how you drive to the call and then how you react to the problem presented when you get there is judged and rated by your training officer. To relieve as much tension as possible from Nate, Libby tried her best to keep things light and interject humor during the shift. A call to respond to a woman who had been raped, however, didn't leave much to joke about, so things were pretty quiet in the patrolcar as they rolled up to the hotel entrance.

The Middlebrook Hotel was one of those run down places you didn't often notice when driving through downtown. If you had to walk by the entrance on your way to a downtown restaurant or store, you usually found yourself picking up the pace a bit as you passed the entrance with only a quick, sideways glance at the door. It wasn't the kind of place in which people would ever stay if they had any other options. The folks who called the Middlebrook home were on one of the last rungs of their downward, spiraling life. Whether it was poverty, drugs, alcoholism, mental illness or a combination of these that landed them in a room at the Middlebrook, it wouldn't have been the first choice of any of the tenants.

The dispatcher had said that the victim, Myrtle Vehar, lived in room 305 and she would be waiting for the officers to arrive. Libby stopped at the front desk to ask the manager if Mrs. Vehar had reported any sort of criminal activity to him or if he had seen or heard anything out of the ordinary earlier this evening. She was actually hoping the manager would give her some hint about how lucid this woman was and any history of bizarre behavior with which she could plan her approach to the complainant. The night manager was surprised to see her there which probably meant Mrs. Vehar had used the pay phone in the hall to call police rather than the phone at the front desk.

This could mean the call was a fake or it could mean the woman wanted some privacy when discussing details of the incident with the dispatcher. The night manager hadn't heard any unusual sounds from the third floor and didn't seem to know why she was there.

A grizzled and bent man in a red plaid flannel shirt and yellow and black striped polyester pants that stopped mid calf was hunched over a game of solitaire at one of the tables in the lobby when Libby and Nate made their way to the front desk. He volunteered the information that he thought he may have seen a couple of teenage boys ("thugs" was the word he used) brush by him in a hurry to get to the stairwell an hour or so ago. He said he was pretty sure they were coming from the direction of Myrtle's room but could give no better description than that they were "thugs" and he knew they were up to no good.

Libby and Nate mounted the rickety stairs taking care not to run their hands along the banister or touch the filthy walls while trying to keep their imaginations from suggesting what the various stains might be. Focusing on the case at hand they found the door with a #3 and a #5 on it. The zero was missing but there was a space in the middle of the other two numbers. They exchanged looks indicating "let's give it a try" then stood off to the sides of the door and knocked quietly.

Listening intently to the reactive sounds from inside the door they heard a shuffling noise and a quiet woman's voice mumbling "who is it?" Libby chose to respond, figuring a woman's voice might be less threatening and more likely to get them let inside. "Police officers, Mrs. Vehar." Another minute or two, more sounds like furniture being dragged across the floor and finally the all too familiar sound of the chain being disengaged from the other side of the door. Libby chuckled to herself as she often did when she encountered people who really believed that a chain could possibly stop an intruder bent on getting through the door, especially a door as rickety as this one appeared to be.

Finally, Myrtle Vehar appeared. She looked like she was in her sixties but it was hard to tell, really. Her face was lined but it was the lifeless look in her eyes that added the look of age. Her hair was short and stuck out from her head in every direction. It was probably gray but had some reddish hints of previous attempts at covering the gray. She appeared to have been wearing that same pink nightie for well over a month perhaps both day and night. The nightgown was falling off her bony shoulders and wrinkled far beyond what a cotton nightie could possibly be when only slept in at night. Libby recognized that the odor emanating from Mrs. Vehar meant it had probably been two weeks, maybe three the woman had been without a shower. Using her years of experience to size up this woman as to the possibility of drug or alcohol addiction she surmised that she probably was not a substance abuser. Mrs. Vehar didn't appear to have been eating well. She wondered just what sort of income this woman could be receiving and how she was paying for even this ramshackle room.

The room matched the woman perfectly. Furniture was scarce and what was there was in ill repair. There was a small indented area with a hot plate, tiny refrigerator and three or four stained cups and crusty dishes. A four drawer dresser with the third drawer missing completely sat in the corner furthest from the door. An old chair that had definitely seen better days was halfway between the "kitchen" area and the "bedroom" area. It had a few pieces of clothing and a pair of hose hanging over it that appeared to have been pressed into the back of the chair by someone sitting on them. There was a single bed with the head against the wall and the bed jutting out into the center of the room. Libby thought it odd that the bed seemed to take the center focus of the room as if it thought nothing else mattered in this woman's life. The bed was unmade and the white sheets were cleaner than Libby expected them to be judging by the disheveled look of Myrtle and her surroundings.

Mrs. Vehar was quite agitated. She immediately began to complain about how long it had taken the two officers to arrive. Nate stiffened slightly and took a breath as Myrtle started into the all-too-common tirade. Libby sensed his reaction and what he was going to say and jumped in to avert an argument. "We are sorry you had to wait, Mrs. Vehar, and we know how important it is to you to be able to tell us what happened so please tell us how this all started?"

Mrs. Vehar was caught slightly off guard as Libby sidestepped her anger and redirected it toward the situation at hand. She stuttered briefly, then blinked a couple of times before she haltingly explained.

"Well, I was asleep... here... on the bed... and they came in and... well, they... they... raped me!"

Libby immediately removed her notebook from her shirtpocket and started to take notes. "How many were there, Mrs. Vehar?"

Myrtle stopped looking at either of them, instead looking down and around the room alternately while her breathing came faster and faster. She quickly grew even more exasperated than when the officers had first arrived. "I don't know, three... maybe, or four. I think there were three, but it was dark and they had my face covered with the pillow case so I couldn't see..."

Nate remained quiet and appeared to be slightly uncomfortable with the situation and the excited state Myrtle was exhibiting. Libby was concerned with determining who the suspects were quickly so their descriptions could be disseminated to other officers. She was hopeful someone could locate them before they were able to get too far away. "Mrs. Vehar, do you have any idea who they were... had you ever seen them around or heard their voices before?"

Myrtle stopped suddenly, staring at Libby and Nate as if shocked to realize they had heard nothing she'd been telling them. She lowered her voice to a confidently, conspiratorial tone as she told Libby "no, I'd never seen them before... because... they were aliens !"

Without the slightest hint of surprise or disbelief, Libby asked Mrs. Vehar how she knew the suspects were aliens. Myrtle became quite indignant at having to explain such an obvious thing to her. She turned, pointing to the disheveled sheets on the bed and angrily said to both of them "Well if you'd look at the bed you'd know!" Libby stole a quick glance at Nate to see if, in fact, he could see anything on the bed she had missed. Seeing the puzzled look on his face she realized she hadn't missed anything and that they were obviously dealing with something Myrtle could see and they couldn't.

Libby was afraid that if she admitted to Myrtle that she couldn't see anything on the bed sheets, Myrtle would become so exasperated she would throw them both out of the room. In addition to the professionalism and tenacity that kept Libby from ever leaving a call before she had done her best for the citizen, she had to admit she was intensely curious as to just what it was there in "plain view" on the bedsheets that had Myrtle Vehar convinced she had just been raped by aliens.

"I'm sorry, Mrs. Vehar, I still can't see what you're asking us to look at." Libby said as gently as possible.

Angrily Myrtle pointed again at the bed and shouted, "Well, it's right there in front of you! If you'd open your eyes!"

"I... I'm sorry, Mrs. Vehar. I just can't see anything there. Please tell me what I'm looking for." Libby was desperately trying to think of a way to find out what Myrtle saw on the bed without upsetting her any further.

"Girl, are you blind? There are alien feces all over that bed!" Myrtle said with exasperation.

As Myrtle turned away from them as if to indicate she now realized they couldn't help her, Nate looked at Libby with his eyes wide in a sort of "can you believe this?" look. Libby knew it would be a fatal error if she were to allow herself to even think how humorous this was becoming so she quickly looked away from Nate and focused on Myrtle.

"Do you have any idea how they got into your room, Mrs. Vehar?" Libby inquired, keeping her eyes on her notepad.

"Well, of course I do! They came in through that window there!" Myrtle said as she pointed to a small window in the corner of the room.

Libby walked over to the window and examined the layers of paint that had likely cemented the moveable portion of the window to the outer frame for years. It was instantly apparent that this window hadn't been opened in at least the last 25 years by anyone, even alien rapists. Even the glass was painted over with several layers of paint, presumably for privacy, but Libby shuddered to think of living in such a depressing room without even sunlight for cheer. The view from the window, however, would only be the brick wall of the building right next to the Middlebrook so there probably wouldn't be much sunlight to see even if the glass weren't painted over.

Libby now knew this case did not warrant taking this woman to the emergency room for an examination or starting a full rape investigation. The woman wasn't injured and alien rapes were always tough to prove in any court of law.

Still, she was aware that even if Myrtle had imagined this incident or perhaps dreamed it while sleeping, Libby had to do something to elleviate her fear and make her feel as though the police had helped her or she would never again call even if some real crime was committed against her.

Libby asked Mrs. Vehar if she had any aluminum foil. The question seemed to catch the old woman off guard. She nodded mutely toward the "kitchen." Libby went into detail as to how she should cover the entire window with foil taking care to make certain that the shiny side faced outwards. She assured Myrtle with complete confidence that aliens couldn't see her through the foil and that as long as the shiny side faced outwards it would make it absolutely impossible for them to get into the room day or night.

Libby held her breath as she waited for a response from Myrtle. For the first time since they had been there Myrtle's face relaxed and even hinted at a smile. She seemed genuinely pleased with the simplicity of those instructions and Libby realized, with relief, that she had bought into her solution. Nate and Libby left after Myrtle assured them she could manage the window project by herself and didn't need them to stay and help.

They were quiet all the way past the front desk as they assured the night manager everything seemed to be OK with Mrs. Vehar and that there weren't "bad guys" lurking in the corridors or closets of the third floor.

Once back in the patrol car Nate looked at Libby as they both burst into laughter. "I can't believe you, Libby! Aluminum foil!"

"Well, what was I supposed to do? I couldn't laugh at her! Do you want to be called back here tomorrow for another alien rape call? That poor woman needs some rest!" She chuckled.

"No, it was ingenious... really! I wouldn't have had any clue what to say to her! But where do you come up with this stuff, anyway?"

Libby buckled her seat belt, grabbed the radio microphone and stopped short of putting it up to her mouth to tell dispatch they were clear of the call. She looked Nate right in the eye and with a deadpan expression she told him, "Years of experience in dealing with alien rape, Nate. " ★

LEAVING THE JOB

THE TAILMAN
By Ed Dee

Guys like me need to get shot at once in awhile. Just a sudden blast, but close enough see the muzzle flash, inhale that burnt metallic smell. It's a wake-up call. Slow down, it says. Slow down like the next guy, the cautious soul who white-knuckles the steering wheel as he creeps past a grisly highway scene of twisted metal and crushed bodies. But guys like me are different, we fly past those scenes because grisly is second nature. Guys like me are talking about lunch or women...because we've been there, seen it all... lived our lives in the worst ten minutes of that other guy's life. The next guy. And the guy after him.

I spent thirty-two years in the NYPD and I was thinking about all this while sitting on the front bumper of my '73 VW in section B104 of this mall-in-the-desert parking lot at four o'clock in the afternoon, the heat around one hundred and fifteen degrees. I'm also thinking: Why the hell am I living in Arizona?

My wife is in the goddamn mall and no way was I going to join her...wind up sitting on a bench with a bunch of old men, chewing on toothpicks, staring into space. My wife tells me: So stay out here and roast. Off she goes; a regular comedian, that lady. Leaves me here, another retired cop... pissed-off in the hot sun.

It wouldn't kill them to plant a few trees out here, I was thinking, when I saw the little girl. She was about eight or nine years old, but don't quote me, I can't tell kids' ages anymore. A man was pulling her by the arm across the desert parking lot. Her face was slack, mouth open, numb with fear. Not the Daddy's-going-to-spank-me fear, but that pale, sweaty look you see in hospital corridors and the morgue waiting room. I got behind the wheel of my VW.

The girl wore tan shorts and a white Minnie Mouse T-shirt, and looked ready to bawl. The guy was big, six-three, a fleshy two-twenty, dark brown hair moussed back. Well dressed. He was yanking her by the arm, hustling down the line of cars. Moving fast, but I knew he wanted to go faster.

It was the look on her face that struck me. Not that she was crying, some kids don't cry. And maybe I'm not college educated, or even as sharp as I used to be. But I know fear. I fished through a box of pens near the gear shift, trying to find one that hadn't dried out in the goddamn heat.

The man put her into a brand new white T-Bird, Hertz rental sticker in the window. He took time strapping her in. I found a space on my sun visor and wrote down his plate number. The sun visors on every car I have ever owned were covered with license plate numbers – that's how this argument started. That's how I came to be sitting and sweating in this bake-oven of a parking lot in the first place.

About an hour before this we had stopped at a Seven-Eleven where I bought a can of Bud and walked outside. My wife stayed in the store, leaning on a stack of Coke twelve packs going through her weekly lottery ritual: a formula of our grandchildren's birthdays that never comes out the same way twice. I'm enjoying my brew, watching her through the window, when three scuzz balls pull-up in a beat-up black Camaro. Instantly, I know they're trouble. Instantly, I know these guys are only currently unincarcerated. The situation reeks of stick-up.

You think I'm overreacting or prejudiced, right? Listen to this: all three are sporting Hell's Angels wardrobes; they park the Camaro sideways blocking all the other cars. Two get out, one stays behind the wheel. Motor running. They slither into the store. And you know how these sleazeballs slither. Scuffing along in slippers or sandals, doing the institution shuffle, clearly escapees from something. Stick-up is the only conclusion. Who could think otherwise?

So I stroll back to the Camaro, scope out the back seat for shotguns, maybe a shooter prone across the backseat. I see nothing but the one mook behind the wheel. By the time my wife comes out of the store I'm back in the car writing the Camaro's license plate on my car's sun visor. She says: Aren't you ever going to stop being a cop? I'm about to explain the situation when the two geeks saunter out with nothing but forty-four ounce Big Gulps. So okay, I say to myself. No harm, no foul.

I don't say anything more to the wife. I back the VW out and head for our next exciting destination. On the way there, God only knows why, I decide to explain it to her.

"Are you crazy," she yells. "You have no gun, no authority, nothing." I say, "You're missing the point." Although I know she hasn't missed anything.

I drive to the mall while she stares off into space. She was thinking hard, probably for another reason why I should like retirement in the goddamn hot sun. She waits maybe ten full minutes, then says, "Let's eat Mexican tonight." That's it. Case closed. She is truly a piece of work.

I admit I'm not adjusting well to retirement. But some things you can't get out of your blood that easily. Like getting back to that kid. I kept thinking that the guy never looked back over his shoulder; a kidnapper would check back over his shoulder. This guy didn't. All he took was one glance at me, an overweight, white haired guy sitting on the bumper of a rusted VW. In fact, he looked through me, like I wasn't even there. It's these little gestures that mean everything.

I told myself it's nothing. My wife is right: I still have cop paranoia. After all, this alleged kidnapper is out of a Dean Witter commercial: grey slacks creased stiletto sharp, a blue button down oxford shirt wrinkled in the lower back like he's been sitting, green and blue rep tie, brown tassel loafers. But what about the earring...small diamond stud? What does that say about Mr. Young Republican? What about the look on the little girl's face? I don't know about you, but that's enough for me. I started the car and followed them.

I didn't say this before but I was one of the best tail men in the history of the NYPD. I'd crawl over broken glass to keep from losing my man. I made a tire-screeching, horn-blaring, wild left out of the mall, against the light. A big-haired blonde in a Beemer convertible held her middle finger high, like a rude golfer checking the wind. I threw her a kiss-my-ass smile.

As soon as I cleared the intersection it was a hard left then slam on the brakes. Blinking orange construction signs funneled us into one lane. Dean Witter was already beyond the construction, six cars in front. I saw the T-Bird dip right onto the freeway ramp, so I swung around the blinking barriers, spraying pebbles like buck shot. At times like this you can't sit with your balls taped to your leg. I gunned the VW onto the freeway begging for all the guts it had.

It took me three miles to catch the T-Bird. I moved into safe tail position, same lane, four cars between us. I put my Arizona State hat on to change his rearview silhouette. Perfect. My heart beat steady, quiet and powerful, like a Rolls Royce sealed engine.

My wife says that what I miss most is the drinking and carousing with my friends. True, I do miss that, but it's the chase I long for, the romance of the chase. The black rainy nights, three a.m. parked on the edge of a garbage filled alley, radio crackling, waiting for a move, a pass of drugs or money...then the adrenaline-pumping, all-out chaotic strike. Or laying on your stomach on a Harlem rooftop, sipping coffee from a paper cup, and staring through binoculars at the lips of an olive-skinned man in a black cashmere overcoat as he whispers the right words into a puff of steam in the air.

I won't bore you with the details of this tail. Tailing on a freeway is so easy it's an insult. All you need is car with some punch that doesn't have a pink pig on the roof. No experience necessary. All this sunlight takes the cloak out of crime, new technology steals the dagger. I know how the Swiss watchmakers felt when they invented digital. In fact everything is so easy now, computerized and cloned, craftsmanship means nothing.

My wife says I'm always looking for something to bitch about these days. My wife is stranded at the mall.

The T-Bird swings onto I-10. We cruise a couple of miles when he makes a move to the right. Airport exit. I know it's not a kidnapping, but it's close. It's a custody snatch.

I hang back a little, not wanting to go directly on his bumper. But Dean Witter gooses the T-Bird and leaves me trapped behind a dripping cement truck. He's flying now, jumping from lane to lane, missing bumpers by the skin of his ass. The guy isn't a half-bad wheelman, but I catch him at the airport entrance – he's a dozen cars in front.

The arrow goes green for him, then red for me. It's crunch time. I jump into the oncoming lane, the VW screaming in second gear as I pull abreast of a shocked white haired lady in a four-cylinder Caddy. I should be six cars behind Dean Witter but he's floored it on the straightaway. He's gone.

Ten minutes later I spot the T-Bird abandoned at the America West arrivals gate. I double park the VW, blocking in the T-Bird. Inside the terminal it takes only thirty seconds of my dead-leg trot for the crowd to open a wide path.

Maybe the Mets T-shirt helps, with the enchilada sauce spills that appear to be bloodstains. I head for the All-Gates sign telling myself I'm in good shape for my age. I'm trying to spot a cop as I run up the escalator stairs squeezing past people who must think you just ride these things. I wedge between two smiling stewardesses all hair and bone. I'm homesick for sincere, overweight obnoxiousness when I attempt a long stride up and over a Nogales shopping bag and its owner jams her experienced elbow into my ribs in the true spirit of mass transit.

Then I see Dean Witter. He's riding the down escalator, coming toward me, carrying a small piece of luggage. The little girl is with him. Her face is buried in the skirt of a pretty dark-haired woman. At the top of the stairs I swing over to the down side and grin at the faces of those I'd just bulldozed. Fraternity stunt, I say. I follow the trio out to the street.

Outside, a female cop is putting a ticket on my windshield. I look at my watch, slap my forehead in apology, and graciously accept the ticket. Dean Witter glances over at me as he tosses the luggage into the T-Bird's trunk. The little girl is calling the dark haired woman "Mommy." This is okay. No harm, no foul. I'm a guy who loves a happy ending.

The sun is beginning to set as I head back home. I snap in a Sinatra tape. He's midway through "Here's That Rainy Day." I listen to this voice, the voice of a man who understands pain and loss. I think about the look on that little girl's face. Something is still wrong there.

I stop at the first Seven-Eleven and call home. I know she's home. This isn't the first time we've gone through this. Where the hell did you go, she says? But she doesn't need an answer. I tell her I met a guy I knew, retired cop from Bronx Homicide. We went for a couple of beers, and time flew by. Bullshit story, she knows it. Are you okay, she says? She also knows all my rowdy friends are dead or dying.

Our entire thirty year married life I have put her through different versions of this same scenario. I lean back and listen while she tells me the cab home cost nineteen bucks and if I'm not home immediately, forget about it. I'm half listening, because I know she's right. But I'm also watching a guy with greasy long hair and a tattoo on his bicep. The tattoo looks like a dagger going through an angel. He's parked off to the side, facing the street. He keeps adjusting his rear view mirror.

My wife says, "With or without you I'm going out for Mexican food."
"Where?" I say.
"You'll find me," she says.

Tattoo starts his Grenada and falls in behind a girl in a BMW. I'm on the case. I pull down the visor and start to laugh as I write the license plates. I'm laughing out loud now. Laughing, shifting, talking to myself. You'll find me, she says. What a piece of work my wife is.

They are going in my direction, so I follow. Palm trees are moving in a soft evening breeze. The sun is sliding past grey puffy clouds and down behind the mountain. It has that pink glow you only see in the west. I am in place behind my tattooed quarry, as he is in place behind his.

She leads us through a left on the arrow, her head bopping to a tune I'll never know. She has a young face, but it has that pale sweet beauty of someone I do know. I grab my Yankee hat from the clothes stash on the back seat. I pull a Hawaiian shirt with it; you can't change silhouette too often. I snap Sinatra back on. The light ahead turns green and we float through. The breeze is lovely and we all have our left arms out the window. Tires hum under our little convoy.

There is a rhythm that is different now, like a new song you have to learn. I'm thinking that maybe romance is where you find it. ★

| LEAVING THE JOB |

BLUE IS THE COLOR OF DEATH
By Philip Bulone

In April 1980, I received transfer orders to the 110 Precinct in Elmhurst, Queens, New York. It was a depressing day as I walked down the steps from the locker room on my last tour of duty and passed the large oak desk for the last time. It was going to be difficult saying good-bye to all the friends I made in the 88.

Police Officers Joe Maccone and Walter Wiclzar were going to give me the traditional last ride around the streets that made up the 88 Precinct neighborhood I patrolled for the last five years. As Joe drove up and down those streets, my head filled with both good and bad memories.

As we passed Willoughby Street and Franklin Avenue, I clearly remembered the cold midnight-to-eight tour in November the year before. Billy Preston and Tommy DeVagno were radio car partners in the 79 Precinct. Their steady sector, Adam, bordered on the 88 and we spent many hours with our cars parked alongside each other talking as we passed time during a slow tour.

Billy Preston was a stocky cop who worked the steady midnight shift as a way of earning extra overtime by making a lot of arrests. He was a thirteen-year veteran of the NYPD. He had been the number one overtime earner in the Brooklyn North Area for two straight years. He lived in Babylon, Long Island with his wife and three daughters. Tommy DeVagno on the other hand, only had three years on "the job" and was a newlywed of four months. Tommy worked the midnight to eight shift while he pursued his college degree at John Jay College of Criminal Justice during the day. He aspired to someday become a lawyer.

My partner Frankie and I were parked on Flushing Avenue where it intersected with Carlton Avenue. It was about two-thirty in the morning and the radio was very quiet. It was a weekday tour and both the 88 and 79 precincts were operating with skeleton crews. As we sipped hot coffee, I heard Billy Preston advise the central dispatcher that he and Tommy had a car stopped at Willoughby Street and Franklin Avenue. Tommy's voice came over the radio, "79 Adam to Central K." "9 Adam," Central acknowledged. "Central," Tommy said, "10-15 New Jersey registration, UCR 197, K." The radio fell silent as the central dispatcher ran the license tag number through the Department of Motor Vehicle computer located in Headquarters.

Car stops on the late tour are a common practice for police officers. A good stop could result in an arrest for a suspended driver's license, or a few moving violation tickets. A great car stop could result in arresting someone for possession of a stolen automobile or drugs and turn the extra overtime hours into some good dollars. I finished my coffee, rolled down my window and tossed the empty cup onto the sidewalk where the cold wind caught it, bouncing it down Flushing Avenue. "79 Adam K," Central called over the radio. "79 Adam, acknowledge Central K," the dispatcher demanded. 79 Adam didn't respond. "88 Sergeant," Central requested. "8 Sergeant standing by, Central." Sergeant Rocky Miller answered. "Sergeant," Central said, "Be advised on 79 Adam's New Jersey Registration, UCR 197, I show that tag as stolen out of Paramus. I get no acknowledgment from 79 Adam. Are you covering the 79 this tour, 8 Sergeant?" Rocky Miller answered, "That's affirmative, Central. Give me the location of the car stop. 8 Sergeant will respond." Central advised, "Willoughby Street and Franklin Avenue, Sergeant." Central then requested, "Units to back up 88 Sergeant and 79 Adam, K." I grabbed the transmitter and informed Central, "8 Henry responding, Central." Other units from the 88 and 79 also announced they were responding.

Willoughby Street and Franklin Avenue were at the far end of the 79 and it would take a few minutes for the 79 units to arrive. As Frankie turned our unit onto Franklin Avenue, I could see the turret lights on top of 79 Adam's vehicle, lighting up the darkness. I looked into the side view mirror on the passenger's side of my unit and saw Sergeant Miller's vehicle directly behind us. As we approached the intersection of Franklin Avenue and Willoughby Street, I got this eerie feeling that something wasn't right.

79 patrol unit number 1497 was approximately fifty feet off of Franklin Avenue parked on Willoughby Street. Both the driver and passenger doors were opened. There was no other vehicle in front of the police unit. As I approached the front of the police car, I saw a leg protruding from in front of the driver's side of the unit's tire. As I walked closer, I saw Billy Preston lying face down in a puddle of blood. I looked up on the sidewalk and there was Tommy DeVagno lying on his back with only half a face. The two cops were dead. Each shot several times a close range with a 9mm automatic pistol. The street was quiet. Not a single light shone from the buildings that lined Willoughby Street. Not one person came outside to help either of the men in the blood-soaked uniforms. To these people living on Franklin Avenue and Willoughby Street, it was just another night of surviving in the ghetto. To the children of Police Officer Billy Preston, yesterday was the last time they saw their father alive. To the unborn child in the womb of Janet DeVagno, he or she would never know its father. For me, it was the first time I saw a dead cop on the street, killed in the line of duty.

These dead cop bodies didn't look like the others I'd seen at the many funerals I attended for other cops killed while working the streets of New York City. No, these weren't cleaned bodies whose wounds were patched and not visible from the coffin. Here, there were no flowers or mass cards. No Inspectors or other police brass talking about what heroes these officers were.

No, here there were no decorations and accolades. This was the real thing. The scene of two cops just murdered. Two men executed in the street because they wore a blue uniform. Murdered because they represented good, not evil. It would not matter to a cop killer if his victim had black or white, red or yellow skin. Cop killers see only one color and that is blue.

The blue uniform that Billy Preston and Tommy DeVagno put on every day they went out on patrol was the only reason they now lay dead on a Brooklyn, New York street. Seeing those two men lying dead in their own blood made me realize that being a cop is a dangerous job. It's a job that requires you to respond to situations which most people run away from. A job, where you laugh off near death experiences and the other horrors you encounter because if you don't laugh them off, you might eat your own gun. It's a job where you don't think about dying because dying is a real part of the job.

The morning after Police Officers Preston and DeVagno were brutally executed on Franklin Avenue and Willoughby Street, a telephone call to the New York Post was placed by a male who identified himself as a member of a new radical group claiming credit for the execution of the two officers. In his claim of responsibility, he also told the editor, "more cops will die."

Joe Maccone turned the police cruiser back onto Classon Avenue. He and Walter helped me load up my trunk. We hugged each other good-bye. I headed for the Brooklyn-Queens Expressway wiping the tears from my eyes as I drove home from the 88 for the last time. ★

LEAVING THE JOB

IRON WILL
by Will Cordes

"I'm dying," the old man said softly, his words barely making it across the narrow table in the restaurant booth.

The news made D. W. Smith look up from his coffee, and, perhaps for the first time, he could see just what the old man meant. Leonard Golden had been Smith's friend for more than twenty-five years, but the younger man had never noticed how Golden had aged during that time. It was obvious now, though.

The lines in Golden's face. The age spots. The yellowing of the eyes, now watery with tears. Smith had just ignored the signs.

"What's wrong?" was all Smith could think to ask.

"Pancreatic cancer," Golden replied with a slight squinting of the eyes. "My doctor says I've only got a couple of months."

"Nothing they can do?" Smith asked, raising his eyebrows hopefully.

"I waited too long, D. W.," the old man said in an apologetic tone. "I'd been feeling bad for the past year, but I didn't want to admit I was sick."

"Are they giving you anything?"

"Just something for the pain. I haven't been taking it, though."

Smith continued to stare into the eyes of his old friend, and he sensed there was more to be told. He'd never seen Golden this worried.

"What can I do?" asked Smith.

"I'm scared," Golden admitted, his eyes dropping. "Since I've never known you to be afraid of anything, I wanted to ask you how you do it."

"How do you know I've never been afraid?" Smith asked with an easy smile.

"Remember when I caught you with the other kids in that new subdivision?" Golden replied, looking back across the table once again. "I used to pride myself at scaring the hell out of little squirts like you, but you never had the look of fear in your eyes. I've never seen it in you since then, either."

Smith smiled at the memory, and he was surprised at the old man's ability to recall such an obscure event. Smith and his equally bored friends were no more than twelve years old when they'd gone to the new housing development on a warm weekend afternoon. They'd done no damage – vandalism had never entered into their minds, but they were technically trespassing in the houses under construction. Golden was a beat-cop back then, and he'd surprised them while they were trying to light the remnants of a cigar. One of his friends –

Smith couldn't remember the boy's name – had wet his pants in fright.

"You slipped up when you threatened to tell my dad," Smith confessed. "My pop was a big man, but he was easy going. Now my mom was another story. She was only five feet tall, but she could put a whipping on my bottom like no other."

Golden laughed at the thought. He remembered how the little Smith woman had once dressed down an elementary school principal. The man had called her to get permission to paddle one of D.W.'s sisters and Mrs. Smith had called the police on him. When Golden had arrived at the school, the little woman had the principal backed into a corner and she was waving her index finger in front of him like a foil. Golden had actually rescued the man, but the best part came when Mrs. Smith turned her attention to her misbehaving daughter. The girl got a much worse walluping from her mom.

"What I meant to ask," said Golden, "is how do you do it now? You've faced death so many times – much more than I ever dreamed of during my police career. How can you do it without the fear showing?"

"Leonard," Smith replied thoughtfully, "policing has changed one heck of a lot since you were a cop. The crooks are so much meaner – and so much less remorseful. You never had street gangs to worry about. Me and my pants-wetting buddies were the worst kids you ever dealt with. If I've got a secret, it's that I've always considered myself just a little tougher than the opposition. I always remind myself that they're the ones who're scared of me."

"What about God?" Golden asked. "Do you think he's got anything to do with our living and dying?"

"Well, I haven't really given it much thought, lately, but I'm sure God has almost everything to do with how we live or die."

"That's what's got me worried," Golden said, looking down at his hands clasped on the edge of the table. "When I got the news from my doctor, I cursed God for it."

"Now, Leonard," Smith said with a laugh. "I cursed God when my dog died. I'd prayed for Him to save the dog, and I felt God had let me down. But God made us what we are, and He can't hold that against us now, can He?"

"You prayed to God to save your dog?" Golden asked in surprise.

"I loved my dog, Leonard. He was the one constant in my life at the time, and when he died I really felt the emptiness in my house."

"I'm sorry. You've just never impressed me as the praying type."

"Oh, I don't go to church, but I still have a relationship with God. I have way too many sins to answer for, and no one needs the grace of God more than I do."

"Is that what gives you your strength?" Golden asked. "Is that what makes you 'Iron Will'?"

"The nickname came from those jerks at the local press corps, Leonard," Smith sighed. "I guess it had a better ring to it than 'Kevlar Will,' but the bullet-proof vest – and maybe some bad shooting on the part of my many adversaries – deserves some of the credit.

"You've known me since I was a kid, Leonard. Back then, everybody called me Junior, since my dad was Dave Smith, Senior. When I went to college, I started calling myself D.Wilson Smith, just to have a little identity of my own. And then came the police career. Like every rookie cop, I went by my initials, D.W. Only the press calls me 'Iron Will.' Them and maybe a few inmates-in-training."

"I've heard some of your detectives refer to you that way," Golden said with a knowing smile.

"But never when I'm around," Smith replied with a wink.

"Is eleven the correct number?" Golden asked pensively.

"Only if you don't count the one I ran over with the patrol car," Smith replied, stirring his coffee. "He was standing over Shirley Hathaway – taking careful aim at her head, and I didn't think I'd have time to park, get out of the car, and take a shot at him."

"Needless to say, the grand jury went nuts over that one, but I got no-billed on the second and third votes."

"When do you need to be back in court?" Golden asked, glancing down at his watch. "I shouldn't be keeping you like this."

"No sweat, old man. I don't have to be back until one o'clock. We can stay for lunch if you like."

"I'd like to, if it's all right with you."

Smith waived at the waitress who came running with the coffeepot. After refilling the two cups, the girl took lunch orders.

"Have you ever given any thought about what happens when we die?" Golden asked, his eyes fixed on the bubbles in his coffee cup.

"Is that what's really worrying you?" asked Smith.

"In a way," Golden replied reflectively. "I mean, it's not like we never expected it, you know. I guess we've been preparing for death our whole lives, but now it's so much... closer..."

"Well, for starters, let's take a look at the life you've had, then," said Smith. "Before you were a cop, you were a soldier, weren't you?"

"82nd Airborne," Golden said, nodding. "I parachuted into France with the D-Day Invasion. Got myself shot twice, and I broke both ankles in a jump, too."

"They gave you a Silver Star and a couple of Purple Hearts as I recall."

"I was lucky, when you consider the magnitude of a war."

"That's exactly my point," Smith said firmly. "I'm sure luck has something to do with it, but somebody up there was on your side."

"But I lost so many good friends," Golden argued. "Why wasn't God on their side, too? Why did so many fine young men have to die?"

"If only the vanquished had died, would the victory have seemed as sweet?"

Golden rubbed at his eyes. He'd never heard Smith talk in such a philosophical tone. He was seeing the younger man in a new light.

"And what about your kids?" Smith went on. "I've never heard you complain about them."

"That's because they're all good children. My three daughters took after their mother. Good cooks, all of them. And my son, well he's the best foreman the plant's ever had."

"Nine grandchildren, and not a cull in the bunch. Did I tell you Justin's been accepted to MIT?"

"Only about ten times," Smith said with a chuckle.

"I've got a lot to be thankful for," Golden admitted.

"And don't stop there," said Smith. "You were one heck of a cop, as I recall. Eighteen years as a patrol sergeant. The steadiest man on the watch."

"It didn't take a young squirt like you too long to pass me by."

"I darn well had to! You were too much of a stickler on the reports, and I wanted to get away from you. Can I help it if they threw me back to patrol after my lieutenant's promotion?"

"I enjoyed working for you," Golden said, biting his lower lip.

"Yeah, right," Smith replied with a gleam in his eye. "You still had to baby-sit me until I could break my detective's ways."

"It's a good thing you never lost the knack, Captain Smith."

"I was trained well, Leonard. You – more than anybody – should know."

"So, how's the trial going?" Golden asked, changing the subject as their food arrived.

"It's a lose-lose situation," Smith signed. "Four murdered kids and an equal number of young defendants. There's nothing worse than street gangs, Leonard. I'd rather deal with a well-armed robbery crew any day."

"Is the DA asking for the death penalty this time?"

"I think we can forget about a sentence like that. These juries nowadays are no better at making decisions than the folks on trial."

"You sound like you're getting disgusted with the job."

"Oh, you can bet on it. I've got my twenty-five in, but I'm still two years away from fifty, so I'm just counting the months."

"You'd really retire at fifty?" Golden asked in surprise.

"Why not? It's not like the days when you cashed in. A sixty-year-old could still be a cop back then because people had some respect for the law. Not any more. Our public is no more appreciative than our criminal element, these days. Cops are just a necessary evil."

"I suppose I've seen that in my own neighborhood. I just didn't want to admit it, though."

"That's why I've got a nice little spot picked out in western Montana," Smith said, leaning back and taking a deep breath. "Clean air, nice scenery, and no traffic to speak of, either."

"Sounds like paradise," Golden said absently, closing his eyes.

The old man flinched slightly when his friend reached across the table to gently take his hand.

"I'd expect paradise to be even better," Smith said with a wink.

"I hope you're right."

"You'll know I'm right," said Smith, dipping a spoon into his soup. "Paradise was made for people like you. Now, me..."

"You don't think you'll go to heaven?" Golden asked, the concern showing in his furrowed brow.

"I'm not like you, Leonard," Smith replied. "It's going to take one heck of a forgiving God to let me through those pearly gates."

"What do you think it's really like?"

"What do you want it to be like?"

"I'd like to see my folks again. And my friends," Golden replied.

"And, I'm sure you will," said Smith, testing the warmth of the soup. "I want to see my dog again, so that's my idea of heaven."

"But how can that be?" Golden asked, shaking his head. "How can that all be in one place. Will I be in your version of heaven? Will you eventually arrive in mine?"

"If I'm in yours," Smith said with a broad grin, "you'd better take a look around, 'cause it might not be heaven."

Golden chuckled at the remark, and Smith soon joined him. The levity allowed them a moment to finish their meal, and Smith motioned for the check.

"Will you be able to meet me for coffee tomorrow?" Golden asked, as Smith paid the tab.

"Better make it a little later. I may still be testifying, so the 10:30 recess might work. I can call you tonight, just to be sure."

The two men rose from the booth, and they walked toward the bright afternoon sun. The sidewalk, once wet from an early morning shower, was now sending up heat waves.

Golden offered Smith his hand, and the younger man took it with a firm grasp. They held the handshake for several seconds.

"Tomorrow, then," Golden said, releasing his friend's hand.

As Smith turned to leave, three young men – not more than teenagers – spread out across the sidewalk, blocking his path. Golden froze in place, he saw the shotgun in the hands of one of the youths.

"Do I know you guys?" Smith asked softly, unbuttoning his suit coat and stepping farther away from Golden.

"It don't much matter," one of the young men replied, producing a small revolver from his baggy pants. "We know you, Iron Will."

Before Golden could take another breath, Smith was brushing his coat aside. The detective captain's hand fell upon the smooth stocks of his Smith & Wesson .357 Magnum, as the youth with the pump shotgun racked a round into the chamber. Smith's revolver came up as the shotgun wielder fired the first shot.

Seven of the nine pellets of 00 buckshot tore through the right side of Smith's abdomen, perforating his liver, intestines, and a kidney. The experienced cop was well into gunfighter mode, however, and he put his first two shots into the 12-gauge shooter. A second pair of .357 shots followed, and the youth with the revolver began to fall along with his better-armed companion.

The third punk had a nickel-plated automatic, and it seemed to spew lead in every direction but the space occupied by Smith. One round hit the window glass of the diner, while another narrowly missed Golden, striking the sidewalk behind him. Smith centered the remaining assailant's chest with his front sight, and the young man was dropped by a pair of well-placed Winchester SilverTips.

Only then did Smith slump back against a parked car and slide down to a sitting position on the sidewalk.

It took several moments for Golden to make his feet move and then he was only reacting to the wails and moans of the gunshot trio. Golden walked slowly to his fallen friend's side. The old man knelt in an ever-growing pool of Smith's blood, as onlookers came running from the nearby courthouse grounds.

"What better proof do you need of God's grace?" Smith asked absently, his eyes fixed on the writing gang members.

"What are you talking about, D.W.?" Golden asked incredulously. "They've gut-shot you."

"They've killed me, Leonard," Smith said, gingerly fingering his damp clothes. "You never think to wear a vest to court... but that's not what I mean. Can't you hear it?"

Golden glanced about, trying to pinpoint what Smith had heard. The old man could hear running footsteps on the sidewalk, but most of the sounds were drowned out by the cries of the dying youths. He turned back to Smith with a questioning stare.

"The Lord has allowed me to hear their fearful cries of agony," Smith said, taking a halting breath, "but He's denied them mine. It's truly amazing."

"Let me put some pressure on it, D.W.," Golden offered, his hands shaking with fright. There was more than a quart of Smith's blood on the concrete.

"No," Smith said softly. "I'm leakin' outa both sides, Leonard. There's no stoppin' it. I wish my mom hadn't made me give up cussin' for New Year's though. I could sure stand to make a nasty comment right about now."

"Somebody went to call an ambulance. Just hang on," Golden tried to say firmly.

"Given a choice," Smith said, glancing about at the warm sidewalk. "I'd just as soon die here as in the back of some runaway meat wagon."

"You're not gonna die, D. W.," Golden growled, in a voice much more convincing than before.

"Yes I am, Leonard," Smith said evenly, his eyes confirming the issue. The fallen assailants had grown silent in death, and the bystanders were venturing ever closer.

"Is there someone I can call?" Golden asked, the tears returning.

Smith smiled at the offer, and he licked his parched lips in thought.

"Just tell all our friends," the dying man whispered, "that I've had one heck of a life... and leave it at that."

Golden took a deep breath, as his fallen friend's eyelids lowered. The old man took one of Smith's bloody hands, and he felt Smith's fingers clamp down on him.

"I've got a final thought for you, too, my friend," Smith said, his eyes fluttering.

Golden waited in silence, not even daring to breathe.

"I'm not... afraid of it," Smith said, as his last breath slipped away. ★

OFF THE BEATEN PATH

IT WASN'T PERJURY, IT WAS ONLY A LITTLE WHITE LIE
By Keith J. Bettinger

The cops saw some of it coming, but never did they expect what actually happened. Officers had been indicted and tried. Some were convicted for performing their duty. It was not that they did anything wrong. It was just that innocence, as an outcome at a trial, would not be popular with the public. The powers that be found it was more efficient to sacrifice a cop here and there rather than see the public take its outrage to the streets and the news cameras.

As the Apocalypse approached, some officers felt a strange foreboding. Many were fans of cop novels. They had cut their reading teeth on works by Wambaugh, whose first novel was The New Centurions. The "old" Centurions were the soldiers of the Roman Empire. The Centurions were the troops that enforced the laws and upheld order in the Roman Empire. The Centurions were the last defense as the Roman Empire fell to the invading hordes, the plunderers and anarchists, intent on overthrowing centuries of growth, prosperity, education and government.

The "new" Centurions were the soldiers of the street, the police. They kept today's communities from falling into chaos. Some officers began to wonder if they, the "New Centurions," would face an ending similar to the "old" Centurions.

It started before the impeachment, but the President and his lies made all the puzzle parts fall into place. The impeachment proceedings did little to find the truth or deal with the high crime of perjury. It was a beauty contest. It was about protecting one's own interests and seat in government. The politicians claimed they were just doing what their public wanted. The politicians swept away duty and obligation, the constitution be damned. They created new definitions for crimes, and made excuses to justify aberrant behavior. They excused the President's abhorrent behavior, and put the blame for embarrassing the President on others. They claimed it was nothing more than partisan politics. However, the partisan politics they practiced were to protect what was important to themselves, not what was correct under the Constitution. It was what the magicians call smoke and mirrors.

Militias soon destroyed government buildings. They did not hide their acts, but took credit for what they did. They claimed the government was trampling their constitutional rights. A number of government employees were injured and maimed. Some citizens cheered. After all, the government lies and cheats. Therefore, the government and its representatives had to pay. The government employees should have expected to be injured and maimed. It was part of their job. They represented the lying oppressor. The oppressor, who sends the little guy to jail for doing the same thing for which the president was acquitted.

Feminist groups started to fall apart. Their cries for justice, equal rights and equal pay fell on deaf ears. They had not picked their battles well and had now lost their war. They chose the wrong side. They picked the fair haired boy with the smile and shining eyes. They picked him over the "trailer trash" who demanded their day in court and just compensation for being wronged. The public who really listened and cared, cared for the victim, not the predator and those that supported him. By supporting him, the feminists trampled on the rights of their own gender. Citizens were no longer sympathetic to the feminist cause.

The late night news shows were filled with interviews with the President's former friends. Former, because they now realized they had been used as cannon fodder in his battle to stay on top of the mountain. In order to protect their friend and leader, they refused to testify at hearings and trials. For their loyalty, they went to prison. Prison for being loyal and refusing to testify in a courtroom. They suddenly realized that if they had lied, they probably would have been as free as their former friend. As free as the person who told the public, "I lied – but I had to lie." They were on the inside, sullenly looking out. They wanted and needed to tell their stories. He was on the outside, laughing at how gullible people really were. For those former friends on the inside, the truth was too little, too late.

Cheating scandals took place at the country's educational institutions. Scholarships were worthless. Everyone had high grades. Cheating took place openly in the classrooms and the professors looked the other way. Honesty and integrity no longer mattered. Now the attitude of faculty and students had simply become "what is in it for me."

The military academies, institutions that were once bastions of honor, now had to deal with cheating on large scales. This dumbfounded the military leaders. The cadet honor courts were accepting this conduct. They turned around the fact that they would not tolerate lying and cheating or those that did. The student honor courts said they had integrated their military training into dealing with academic problems. If a point or two lost on a test would cause a cadet to be educationally inferior, then the cadet had to overcome and adapt to see that the situation did not deteriorate to the point of expulsion. Lying and cheating were seen as forms of overcoming obstacles and adapting answers to situations. After all, if the President could overcome and adapt, and he was the commander-in-chief, shouldn't his subordinates be entitled to the same considerations?

Violence against correction officers in the prisons was an everyday affair. Cries of injustice were heard echoing down the hallways of steel barred doors. Everyone was framed. Everyone within told the truth. The prisoners were just victims of society, a society that played partisan politics from the top of the food chain down to the bottom feeders in their cells.

The police officers on the street were trying to do their jobs. Cases that took many hours of hard work fell apart in court. Not because the officers did anything wrong, but, because they represented the government and the public found the government corrupt. If the President could lie and get away with it, why would you trust any branch of government? Especially a branch that could take away your rights and incarcerate you? If a President could get away with lying, why should others be punished for wrong doing? Furthermore, who has a civic duty to work for the government as a juror? Jurors simply made their discontent known by throwing court cases.

Riots in the streets became commonplace. Any act by the government, especially those by the police that did not please the public, spilled onto the streets. This was the same public that never did anything to improve the community. This was the public that was made up of the users and abusers of the system.

The soapbox of discontent was replaced with rocks and broken store windows. Riots were not about outrage, they were excuses for looting. Storeowners collected money. Included in the money were taxes. Taxes represented all forms of government. It did not matter that lives and businesses were being ruined by outrageous criminal behavior. If the storeowners did not like the new rules of the street, they could take their complaints to their governmental representatives. The problem was, the government representatives were too busy placing blame on others for what was taking place. They were hiding behind their walls of partisan politics.

In the middle of a deserted downtown area, officers were huddled in groups behind patrol cars. The cars were drawn in a circle. The sight was reminiscent of the Conestoga wagons with pioneers hiding behind them to fend off attacks. For some officers, students of history, it was a reminder of history and its great sieges. For some officers who were veterans, it was deja vu and Khe Sahn. The officers, the Centurions of the city, were wondering what would become of them? They hid behind cars trying to protect one another, while society collapsed around them. Their city was dark except for the burning buildings on both sides of the street. At each intersection were invading hordes plundering the city of all its financial and moral values.

The officers ducked behind the cars for protection from rocks and gunfire. There was little they could do but band together for their own protection. They no longer saw themselves as Centurions – protectors of the Republic. Those days were gone. That image had marched off forever with the merchandise stolen from the stores. They saw themselves as losers in a war. A war they had no control over. They did not know how the Centurions felt as Rome fell. However, as they huddled together, trying to protect one another as the violence increased, they suddenly knew how Custer and his troops felt just before the end. ★

OFF THE BEATEN PATH

CAFE MIDNIGHT
By Penny James

The frowsy blonde took a long drag on her unfiltered cigarette. "How's my favorite copper?" she asked, blue smoke wrapping around her words.

Joe McGwire stared at her. He'd never been in this joint before. How could she have known he was a cop? As he studied her eyes, he realized that this was a woman who really had seen it all.

"Fine, ma'am," he finally answered.

"Jewel," she said, pointing to the name tag pinned to her rumpled uniform.

The blonde poured him a cup of coffee and slid a pitcher of cream and a sugar shaker his way. She sauntered into the back and Joe could hear snatches of muffled conversation.

"Thank you, young man," a cultured, feminine voice whispered at his elbow. Startled, Joe turned to his left. A demure woman in her seventies, wearing a cloche hat and wool coat, reached for the cream pitcher. "A spot of cream always makes my tea," she added, her English accent self-evident.

Joe glanced around the diner. He and the prim septuagenarian were the only occupants. "Isn't it a bit late for you to be out by yourself in this neighborhood?" he asked.

"Nonsense," she answered brusquely. "So, Mr. McGwire, tell me about this murder case you are working on."

Making a conscious effort to close his gaping mouth, Joe stared at the woman. He was speechless.

"Miss Marple," another cultured voice, this time male, called from the shadowy recesses of the diner. "Leave the lad alone. When he wants our assistance, he will ask for our advice."

Joe shook his head, then sniffed his coffee suspiciously. A dapper man in an old-fashioned white suit motioned for the old woman to join him in a booth. His neatly trimmed moustache twitched above his full-lipped mouth.

"Oh, posh," Miss Marple replied. "Monsieur Poirot, he is too young to know when he needs our help."

Despite her words, the woman glided across the black and white tiles checkerboarding the diner's floor and joined her Belgian companion.

Joe sniffed his coffee again. Then he took a big gulp, hoping the shot of caffeine would clear his head.

"Don't mind that old biddy," a gruff voice growled at his right elbow. Joe almost broke his neck turning to see the man sitting next to him. "Spade," the man introduced himself. "Sam Spade."

Joe's mind was reeling and the only coherent thought he could pull out found its way to his larynx. "You sound like Bogie," the young cop stuttered.

"Naw," the grizzled man said, a chuckle lurking just below his words. "Bogie sounds like me."

Joe was now convinced that he was dreaming. Or sleepwalking. Or maybe, as the department's shrink suspected, he really had gone over the edge. His pager beeped at him. Joe glanced at its digital readout then looked around for a pay phone.

"You'll need a nickel," the man on his right growled, pointing to an old-fashioned pay phone hanging by the front door. "Damn thing only takes correct change."

Joe dug into his pocket looking for a nickel as he walked across the checkerboard floor. This was the damnedest dream he'd ever had.

Sure enough, the phone only had one slot and it would only take nickels. Joe pushed his into the slot and listened to the mechanical clicks as the antique ate his money. He dialed the precinct desk sergeant's number and listened to the annoying rings for a full two minutes before someone picked up the other end.

"We got a DOA down on the west side," the sergeant barked at him. "The LT wants you there yesterday."

Joe fumbled for his notebook and pen and wrote down the address. "I'm on my way," he signed off.

Turning back to the counter, Joe wasn't too surprised to find himself alone. He threw a couple of ones on the counter and hollered toward the back, "Thanks, Jewel."

"See ya, sweet cheeks," Jewel called, her voice raspy from the unfiltered cigarettes she smoked.

Joe could see the scene from a couple of blocks away. The lights on the squad cars and other emergency vehicles cast lazy rainbows across the scene. He pulled in behind a squad car and as he climbed out of his car, the damp, midnight air hit him like a bucket of cold water. Joe buttoned his sport coat and wished he had thought to bring his overcoat.

Yellow scene tape cordoned off an alley and shadowy figures swam through the darkness on the fringes of Joe's vision. A lone street light painted a paltry pool of light at the mouth of the alley. Joe noticed five figures huddled near the edge of that meager glow. The man stretched out on the wet pavement was obviously the DOA. Another figure was taking photos while a third stood writing on a clipboard. Joe recognized the man with the clipboard as Dr. Quincy, the medical examiner. He knew better than to crack a joke about the ME's television namesake. There had always been a legend floating around the department about the rookie who hadn't been able to resist a comment while attending an autopsy. Rumor had it that the rookie was never seen again and that there was a crypt at the morgue that was welded shut. Joe had never felt the urge to test the story's veracity.

All of this aside, the other two people held Joe's attention. A portly man

167

wearing a bowler knelt next to the body. The tall, angular man at his shoulder wore a cape-shouldered coat and a deerstalker cap. Joe rubbed his eyes. The two figures were still there, although the photographer and the ME were ignoring them.

"Ah, Watson," the gaunt man said to the kneeling figure. "Young McGwire has finally arrived. Will you be so kind as to impart our conclusions to him?"

The man in the bowler looked up, squinting against the flashing lights that framed Joe's body. He adjusted his glasses on the end of his nose then motioned for Joe to come closer. Joe leaned over to look at the body's chest where Dr. Watson was pointing.

Watson cleared his throat. "The victim appears to be an Oriental male..."

"Chinese," Holmes clarified. "From the Houshang district."

Watson glared at his colleague. Holmes ignored the look, waiving his hand imperially for Watson to continue. "In his early twenties..."

"Twenty-two," Holmes interrupted.

Watson sighed. "There are six stab wounds..."

"Seven," Holmes amended. "The large hole in the middle is actually two wounds."

Joe peered at the victim's chest. "How can you tell?" he asked.

"How can I tell what?" Quincy, the ME barked.

"That the big hole is actually two wounds," Joe explained.

"I can't," Quincy. "Not until I get him onto the table."

Joe glanced at Holmes. His lips were pursed as he held up two long, bony fingers, the gesture explicit. "Double check that big hole, Doc," Joe said.

"Who died and made you a medical examiner," Quincy muttered darkly.

"Just a hunch, Doc," Joe added, hoping to placate the crusty M.E.

"Notice the ritualistic positioning of the body," Holmes added, walking around the body, his head cocked at an angle.

Joe noticed. The victim's arms and legs had been positioned to resemble the classic "dead body" pose: the arms bent at the elbows, right arm up, left arm down, and the legs splayed to look like the victim was a running stick figure. Joe couldn't wait to see the chalk outline the forensic team left behind in this case.

"The victim has been dead about an hour," Quincy and Holmes stated simultaneously. Joe choked back a chuckle as both men glared at him. He glanced at Dr. Watson but was ignored as the doctor was still studying the body.

Before Joe could respond, a uniformed officer approached. "Body was found by a lady walking her dog," he told Joe, nodding toward a silhouette in the back of a squad car. "Said she'd never seen him around before and she says she's lived here all her life."

Joe nodded. "Get her information. I'll give her call in the morning. Any other witnesses?"

The cop shook his head. "I'm surprised the babe was out in this neighborhood so late. After dark, this area isn't exactly Grand Central Station."

That fact wasn't going to make Joe's job any easier. He watched as the cop opened the back door of the car and leaned in to talk to the woman. He couldn't hear the conversation over the vociferous yaps emanating from the woman's little dog. The cop backed away and the dog hopped out, quickly followed by his mistress. Long, lithe legs unwound from the back seat and stretched into the street. A body built for a bikini followed. She was beautiful. Joe gulped. He'd barely noticed the opposite sex since his wife had moved out and filed for divorce. This member of the female gender was a definite reminder of why men looked at women.

"Ahem," Holmes cleared his throat. "Now that the burlesque show is over, we have work to do. Mr. McGwire, you will go back to your office and wait for me there. I have a few inquiries to make before I can conclude my investigation."

"Whoa, now," Joe interjected. "Your investigation? This is my investigation and don't you forget it."

"I won't, Detective," a new voice said.

Joe whirled around. A cop was looking around to see who, besides himself, Joe might have been talking to. Joe gave the cop a lame smile and shrugged. The cop walked away, shaking his head. Maybe the stories about McGwire were true.

"If you do not want nor appreciate my assistance, Detective McGwire, I will not trouble you with my presence forthwith. Come, Watson. There are others who need our services."

"Now just hold on a minute," Joe countered. "Look. I'm really confused."

"So am I, McGwire," Dr. Quincy replied, "but I'm not staying here another minute if I don't have to. You through with my corpse?"

Joe glanced at Holmes and Watson. Holmes nodded curtly. "Yeah. Thanks, Doc. I'll stop by tomorrow."

"He should look for a pattern in the stab wounds," Holmes ordered.

Joe called to the doctor's retreating back, "Hey, Doc?" Quincy turned, looking impatient. "When you get a good look at the wounds, see if they form some kind of pattern."

Quincy looked pained. "You think we got a serial here or something?"

Joe shrugged. "It's just a hunch."

Quincy shuffled to his van, shaking his head. Within a few minutes, a black body bag was placed in the back of the coroner's van and the doctor drove away.

Joe quickly wrapped up his end of things at the scene and prepared to leave. Holmes was waiting by his car. Watson was no where to be seen. "Can I give you a ride, Mr. Holmes?" Joe asked.

Lost in reverie, it took Holmes several moments to answer. "Ride? No. I have never been comfortable with infernal combustion engines. As I said earlier, go back to your office and await me there. As soon as I have some news, I will seek you out."

Joe stared at the famed detective. "Excuse me, Mr. Holmes, but what do you know about this case that I don't?"

Holmes choked back a sarcastic snort. "Volumes, my dear boy, volumes. But be that as it may, this is, as you so succinctly reminded me, your case. I am just here to lend whatever humble expertise I have."

Joe didn't have to be a genius to figure out that Holmes was chiding him for his earlier assertion. "Forgive me, Mr. Holmes, but I'm not really sure just where you came from or why you are here."

"All in due time, my boy. All will be revealed in due time." Holmes turned on his heel and strode away, his coat flapping behind him.

Joe watched him fade into the darkness before climbing into his car. He pinched himself, hoping that he would wake up in his own rumpled bed. He had no such luck. Starting the car, he put it in drive and pulled away from the murder scene.

A sergeant and two street cops watched him leave. The captain shook his head sadly. "Poor McGwire," he muttered. "Ever since Eddy was killed, that kid hasn't been the same and now he's talking to himself."

"What are you talking about, Sarge?" one cop asked.

"Eddy Queen and Joe McGwire were partners. Remember that big shoot out? Eddy was killed. Joe almost was. Joe blames himself. His wife left him. He went a little nuts. The captain almost pulled his badge. He was getting it back together but after tonight, I'm not so sure."

Joe thought about going home but the sun was just beginning to paint the eastern horizon with a pale brush. Instead, he headed to the police station. The department shrink had suggested that Joe have his own office, rather than having to rough it out in the bull pen with the other detectives. Though the office was glass on three sides, Venetian blinds could shield him from prying eyes. He was grateful for that as he twisted them closed. Having the squad watch as Dr. Watson snored contentedly in his desk chair just wouldn't do. Joe considered waking the good doctor so that he himself could catch some z's.

"He's wrong, Joe," a gravelly voice said.

Joe whirled. Sam Spade was leaning against the wall behind the door.

"Who's wrong?" he asked the gumshoe.

"That pretentious prig who calls himself a PI," Sam replied.

Joe chuckled, knowing just who Spade was referring to. "Pretentious prig? I think he's rubbing off on you, Mr. Spade. But what is he wrong about?"

"You aren't dealin' with no serial killer. That murder tonight was a hit plain and simple."

"It didn't look like any hit I've ever seen, Mr. Spade."

"It was. Johnny Ling has been a stooge in the Asian gangs since he was a punk kid. He spilled his guts to the wrong guy and he got paid in spades."

"How'd you know his name?" Joe asked. Spade cocked a disdainful eyebrow. Joe shrugged. "How do any of you know anything?" he mumbled. "Okay. So it's Asian gangs. Drugs? Turf? What was the motive?"

"Take your pick."

"Ahem," someone coughed. "My American colleague is partially correct," Holmes said brusquely. Joe didn't miss the sarcastic emphasis placed on the term "colleague." Holmes continued. "Mr. Ling was involved with the Triad Tong, a particularly nasty group immersed in all manner of the illicit activities. However, his executioner is a most peculiar assassin. Have you reviewed the autopsy report?"

William Vernon, captain of detectives, watched the shadows move across the Venetian blinds covering Joe's windows. "Who's in there with him?" he asked a nearby detective.

The man shrugged. "No one," he answered without looking up.

Captain Vernon walked to Joe's office, shaking his head. He'd gotten several calls from cops at the murder scene, all worried about McGwire. He tapped on the door. "You alone?" he asked, opening the door and sticking in his head.

Joe glanced around his office. "Un, yeah, Captain. Sort of." Holmes and Spade stood in one corner arguing quietly while Dr. Watson continued to snore contentedly in Joe's desk chair.

"You got anything on this murder?" the captain asked.

"Victim's name is Johnny Ling. He was a member of the Triad Tong," Joe began, well aware that Holmes and Spade were hanging on his every word. "I suspect it was a hit, but there are some unusual circumstances that I want to follow up on."

Captain Vernon nodded. "Good work, McGwire. Keep me posted." He started to shut the door behind him, "Oh," he added. "Quincy wants to see you ASAP." He returned to his own office feeling much better about Joe's mental health.

Spade and Holmes both drew breath to start their renewed assault on Joe's investigation. He held up his hand. "Enough. You heard the captain. The ME wants to see me. We'll continue this discussion later."

Down at the morgue, Quincy met Joe at the door wearing a blood-splattered, disposable gown. "You were right," Quincy allowed. "There were seven wounds." Joe nodded, trotting to keep up with the other man. "And, you were right about them forming some sort of pattern."

"I told you so," Holmes said, appearing at Joe's side as they turned a corner. His long legs had no trouble keeping up.

"Here," Quincy said, ducking into an autopsy room. "I'll show you."

Ling's body was laid out on a stainless steel table, covered with a disposable sheet. Quincy pulled back the sheet, exposing the corpse's chest and abdomen. Five slashes surrounded an irregular shaped hole.

Quincy bent over the area. "You were right. A second object was forced through the center cut, giving it a rounder shape. Any one of a hundred knives could have made the cuts. There's no telling what was used in that seventh one."

"A Du's hiki," Holmes said, peering over Quincy's shoulder.

"A doohickey?" Joe asked.

"No," Holmes chided. "A Du's hiki. This was done by a member of the Dusun tribe of northern Borneo. A hiki is a ceremonial staff representing the Pillar of the Sky."

"You can call it whatever you want," Quincy said.

"No," Joe said. "A Du's hiki made that wound."

Quincy peered over his reading glasses at the young detective. "What in the world is a Du's hickey?" the ME growled.

"According to the Dusun religion, a human's soul can only get to the first heaven by climbing up the Pillar of the Sky. There are seven heavens all together," Holmes pontificated. "In order to start the soul on its journey, a

Dusun shaman would mark the position of the heavens on the deceased's body. The first heaven would also be pierced by the Pillar of the Sky as represented by the shaman's staff, his hiki."

Joe stared at Holmes, astounded by the wealth of this inexhaustible information.

Holmes barely paused for a breath as he continued, "H. Ling Roth gave a most interesting dissertation on the subject at the Royal Academy in London back in 1896. You may want to read his two volume treatise entitled The Natives of Sarawak and British North Borneo."

"So what are you talking about?" the ME demanded.

"I'm not sure," Joe replied. "It's what he said."

"He who?" the ME asked, looking around.

"It all has to do with some obscure religion in northern Borneo. A hiki is a religious staff used in a funeral ceremony," Joe began explaining. The look on the ME's face made him falter. "Never mind," Joe added. "It's too complicated to explain. I'll just put it in my report."

"Good," Quincy muttered. "You do that." Louder, he added, "Since you seem to know more about this than I do, you tell me."

"His name is Johnny Ling. He's in his twenties... "

"Twenty-two," Holmes interjected.

"Twenty-two," Joe amended. "He belonged to the Triad Tong."

"That explains the tattoo on his butt," Quincy added.

"This was probably a hit. Ling was supposed to be a stooge."

"But... ?" Quincy prompted.

"There are certain aspects of this that make me wonder if it's not a serial killer." Quincy waited. "Well, the wound pattern. Using the hiki. The way the body was laid out. It just doesn't add up to a simple hit."

Quincy snorted. "Since when has a hit ever been simple?"

"Good point," Joe allowed. "But deep down, isn't a hit man just a serial killer who gets paid?"

"When did you become the pop psychologist?" the ME asked. "I don't care who or why. I know the how and now so do you. Get out and let me get on the next one." As Joe started to leave, Quincy called after him. "A Du's hiki? How do you know this stuff?"

Joe shrugged. "I read a lot?" he answered lamely.

Joe hurried out of the room. Once in the long hallway, he slowed down to mull over his flash of insight.

"You are correct, Mr. McGwire," Holmes complimented him. "Serial killers murder for free. Think how happy they would be if they were paid to do what comes so naturally to them."

Joe nodded. "Yeah, you'd have the perfect executioner. But, don't serial killers really want to be caught? Don't they leave behind clues that a professional hit man wouldn't?"

"Precisely."

"So now you have a hit man leaving clues to make it look like a serial killing."

"By Jove, I think you have it."

"Maybe the Brit ain't so bad after all," Spade growled from Joe's blind side. Joe didn't even jump this time. He was getting used to these two popping up out of nowhere, a scary thought in and of itself. "Okay, so it was a hit made to look like a serial killing. So who contracted the hit?"

"Precisely," Holmes chimed in.

"Not who," Spade growled. "Wu."

Joe stopped. "What?"

"Wu," Spade said. "Victor Wu, one of the enforcers for the Triad. He put the contract out on the kid."

"Why?" Joe's brain was reeling. This was worse than first year journalism in school. Who, what, where, when, why and how in the world was he going to explain this to the captain?

"Why do you think?" Holmes asked.

"Oh give the kid a break," Spade interrupted. "That punk Ling was selling out information to the mob."

"Mob? As in Mafia?" Joe asked, not really wanting the answer.

"Syndicate. Cosa Nostra. Organized crime. You call it," Spade replied.

"Let me see if I've got this straight. The Italian mob wants to move in on the Chinese Tong's action. Johnny Ling is selling information to the mob so the Tong has him killed by a hit man parading as a Borneo shaman who's actually a serial killer?"

"Or, Ling may have reneged on the deal with the Cosa Nostra," Holmes interjected.

Joe shook his head. "So you're saying that the mob hired a Borneo shaman to hit a Chinese stool pigeon who didn't stool and the shaman may or may not be a serial killer or a hit man? I need an aspirin."

Engrossed in the conversation, Joe had no idea of where the three of them had traveled. He looked up to discover they were standing in front of the Café Midnight.

Spade clapped Joe on the shoulder. "You'll feel better after a shot of Jewel's coffee."

Once again, Joe found himself sitting at the counter looking into Jewel's impossibly mascara'd eyes.

"The boys keeping you busy, sweet cheeks?" the waitress purred as she poured him a cup of coffee.

"Hmpf," Miss Marple sniffed from her table in the corner. "Boys indeed. What he needs is a good, clear female head to straighten him out."

"Why me?" he implored of the waitress.

"Just lucky, I guess," she laughed.

"Am I nuts?" he asked her, hoping she was sane.

"No more than any of the rest of us," Jewel replied.

That was not a particularly comforting thought to leave with Joe. As he drank the stale coffee in his cup, he mulled over the idea of quitting the force and becoming a bus driver... or a shoe salesman.

"Excuse me, please," a voice with an oriental accent interrupted Joe's reverie. "Number one son has brought a message. Victor Wu wishes to meet with you."

Joe swivelled on his bar stool to stare at the round little man standing behind him. "Let me guess, Charlie Chan?"

"Most astute, Detective McGwire," the man complimented. "My esteemed colleague, Mr. Sherlock Holmes, was correct in so highly recommending you."

"Chan knows Chinatown," Spade said. "Ask him if Wu is involved."

Joe cocked an eyebrow at the Oriental detective, who answered, "He says he is not but I will leave that judgement to you, Detective McGwire. Please, Wu waits."

Joe dug in his pocket but his hand came out empty. "Go on," Spade said. "This cup's on me."

Joe stumbled out into the bright afternoon sun. A black sedan rolled to a smooth stop in front of him. "You Joe McGwire?" the passenger asked. Before Joe could reply, the back door opened. "Get in," the man ordered.

Joe kept his mouth shut, studying the two thugs in the front seat. Both of them were Oriental. The passenger could have once been a Sumo wrestler. In comparison, the driver was tiny. After a short ride, the car stopped in front of a Chinese restaurant. Joe decided his life was playing out like some Grade B movie. All he needed now was a long-legged dame to complicate matters. What he got was Victor Wu, one of the most vicious enforcers in the dominant Chinese tong.

Joe stood in front of Wu's table, since his host hadn't asked him to sit. He waited for Wu to begin.

"Heard you were looking for me," Wu stated.

"Johnny Ling is dead," Joe said coldly.

"This is of concern to me?" Wu countered.

"Word on the street is that Ling worked for you," Joe stated.

"Lots of people work for me." Wu shrugged.

"I also heard that Ling might be part-timing somewhere else." Joe was digging now.

"That is always a young man's prerogative, though not always a wise decision."

Joe looked around the room. A little man with a shaggy haircut looked out of place in a booth at the back of the restaurant. Joe decided to take a chance. "Dusun?" he asked, nodding toward the back.

"What would an underpaid public servant like you know about the Dusun?" Wu blurted.

"I know they have a very special way of killing people," Joe countered.

Wu regained his composure. "I have other business," he said curtly, dismissing Joe. "You are on the wrong track, Detective."

"Maybe. Maybe not," Joe said softly. "Don't leave town, Wu."

Joe finally got back to his apartment just as the full moon rose, hanging above the city like some monstrous Chinese lantern. As he walked through the door, Spade coughed in the shadows.

"You got company, copper," the gumshoe growled.

Joe reached for his hip, wanting the cold comfort of his .45.

"No need for that, Detective," a well-oiled voice greeted him calmly. "Mr. Piazza would like the pleasure of your company."

Joe rooted around in his memory. He knew the thug in the $500.00 suit didn't mean the baseball player. "Tony the Duke Piazza?" Joe asked.

The next thing he knew, he was bundled into the back of a black Lincoln and stuffed between two large Mafia henchmen. One smelled of garlic, the other Old English aftershave. Joe stifled the urge to giggle at how ludicrous his situation had become.

As the big car rolled to a smooth stop and the back door opened, Joe knew immediately where they were. Angelo's Italian Restaurant was a legend but when Joe was thrust through the front doors, he felt like he had walked into a scene from the "The Godfather."

All the tables were covered with red and white checked table cloths. A bottle of extra virgin olive oil, a glass of long, crispy bread sticks and a block of real Parmesan cheese adorned each table as a centerpiece. Tony the Duke sat at a back table, surrounded by various thugs, mugs, and big lugs.

When Tony opened his mouth to speak, Joe was almost disappointed that the Mafia don didn't have a voice like Brando, especially since the man sounded more like Mike Tyson.

"I would ask you to join me," the don squeaked. "But you won't be here long enough to enjoy even a glass of vino." Joe cocked an eyebrow, waiting for the man to clarify his meaning. Joe didn't want to consider all the alternatives. "I lost a soldier last night," the don continued. "An expensive soldier. I want the people responsible. I spent a lot of money on this soldier and now have nothing to show for my investment. My ears at City Hall tell me you're the man who's going to solve this crime."

"I assume you are talking about Johnny Ling's murder?" Joe asked.

"Don't assume nothing," the don growled. "That only makes an ass out of you and me."

"Then I don't have the foggiest idea of what you are talking about," Joe asserted.

"My nephew," the don hinted. Joe gave him a blank stare. "Little Tony Domino," Piazza finally told him.

Joe fervently swore to himself that if he ever woke up from this nightmare he would never eat anchovies on his pizza again. "So what happened to Little Tony?" Joe asked, afraid of what the answer would be.

"I send the boy to the best schools. I send him to law school. And this is how he repays me... " the don's voice drifted off. Joe waited, slightly impatient. "He wants to be a writer," Tony finally sighed. "He wants to write crime stories."

Joe screwed his eyes shut willing away the headache that was playing the "1812 Overture" on his temples. "What's that got to do with me?" he asked.

"This murder. The one on the west side. Little Tony wants to write about it. I want you to babysit Little Tony. Make sure he gets the inside scoop. His mother, my sister, God rest her soul, would never forgive me if Little Tony doesn't make good."

Joe started to protest when Spade whispered in his ear. "Don't sweat the kid," Spade said. "We'll take care of him. Just say okay so we can get your hide out of here in one piece. Tell 'em to have the kid meet you at the café first thing in the morning."

With the date made, Joe was driven home and unceremoniously dumped in front of his building. He dusted himself off and glared after the retreating taillights. Then he glared at Sam Spade.

"What were you thinking?" Joe demanded.

"Relax, kid. You won't have to worry about that snivel-nosed wannabe," Spade assured him

"And why not?"

"It's elementary, my dear McGwire," Holmes interjected. "We will have the crime solved before tomorrow morning. Hence, young Tony will have no chance to travel on your coattails to literary fame and fortune."

"Did you just say what I think you did?" Joe looked at Holmes in amazement. "I've read about every one of your cases. Not once did you ever say, 'it's elementary'."

Holmes flashed a brief, rare smile. "You are correct, Mr. McGwire. However, I have always wanted to say it."

Joe looked at his watch. "It's eight o'clock. I have exactly twelve hours before this kid shows up at the café wanting a guided tour of this investigation. What am I going to tell him? A bunch of dime novel detectives are solving the crime for me?"

"I beg your pardon, young man," Miss Marple sharply remanded him. "Not even my fifth editions sold for a dime. Gentlemen, I feel we are wasting our time with this young hooligan. He obviously does not appreciate our assistance."

"I give up," Joe muttered.

He headed toward his apartment. Inside, he found the mustachioed Poirot sitting at his desk staring at the screen saver swirling across the computer monitor. "This is the most amazing display," Poirot sighed. "This is so much faster and simpler than my card file system. Please, Monsieur McGwire, will you show me how it works?"

Joe shrugged then took the chair Poirot had just vacated. He touched the mouse and the screen cleared of its dazzling colors. Joe moved the mouse, touched some buttons, and with a series of electronic beeps, he was connected to the Internet.

"Fascinating," Holmes allowed.

"You can say that again, brother," Spade added.

"May I make a suggestion?" Miss Marple chimed in. Joe looked at her, waiting. "Mr. Holmes seems to think the unfortunate young man was murdered for the sake of ritual. Although he has expounded upon the subject to the point of tedium, perhaps you should check out this Dusun tribe for yourself."

Miss Marple's suggestion made sense. Joe's fingers danced across his keyboard. Only two entries appeared on the search engine he was using. The first was the 1896 study mentioned earlier by Holmes. The second was a more recent study done by an anthropologist from Harvard. Joe accessed Harvard's archives and started reading, screen by screen, the study by Linus Macauley, Ph.D.

Essentially, Holmes had been correct about the funeral rites for deceased

Dusuns. Nowhere did either treatise mention human sacrifice or murder. Joe's next stop on the electronic highway was the Immigration and Naturalization Service web page. That had been Poirot's suggestion. The Dusun tribe was not mentioned specifically, but there had been three natives of Borneo admitted on visas within the past few months.

"Talk about a needle in a haystack," Joe groused.

Miss Marple had appropriated his easy chair and was matter-of-factly sipping tea. "Perhaps we aren't really looking for a Dusun," she mused. "Looking for that proverbial needle would be much like a wild goose chase, would it not, Mr. McGwire?" Joe nodded, waiting for her to continue. "Perhaps we are looking for someone who is impersonating a Dusun shaman."

Holmes, Spade, and Poirot all exchanged glances. Holmes looked over at Watson, who was comfortably snoring in Joe's other living room chair. "I say, Watson. Wake up, old chap. We need your medical expertise."

Watson, coughing and sputtering, came fully awake. "Roth died in the late twenties," he said. "I'm not familiar with that other chap. Macauley, wasn't it?"

Joe went back to the computer. Dr. Linus Macauley was still listed as a Harvard professor in the anthropology department. Joe pulled up his biography to read. He yawned, blinked, rubbed his eyes, and started reading some more.

"No way," he gasped quite some time later. As the group of erstwhile detectives gathered around to see, Joe suddenly switched off the computer. "I need some sleep," he said smugly.

Bright and early the next morning, Joe occupied his favorite stool at Café Midnight. Jewel had served him up a big breakfast with all the trimmings. Spade sat at the far end of the counter, muttering under his breath. The English contingent sat at their customary booth. All of them were pointedly ignoring the young cop. He was working on his third cup of coffee when Little Tony Domino came through the door. Dapper in his tailored suit, Little Tony glanced around then sauntered over to Joe at the counter.

Joe stood up with his cup and gestured toward a booth. "Over there," he indicated. "We'll be more comfortable."

Jewel appeared with a second cup for Domino and the pot to refill Joe's cup. Once she'd departed, Joe opened the conversation with reference to Domino's literary aspirations. Little Tony launched into a discourse on his chosen field. Joe listened for about fifteen minutes and then interrupted.

"Seen your old college roommate lately?" he asked innocently.

Little Tony stopped in mid-sentence. "Linus? No."

Joe realized that he had the entire diner's attention now. "When's the last time you talked to him?"

A thin sheen of sweat glistened on Domino's upper lip. "I don't recall. Years probably."

Joe nodded sagely. "Now, he was getting his Ph.D. while you were in law school at Harvard, right?"

Domino nodded. "What are you getting at, Detective?"

Joe smiled. The sweat had spread to the man's forehead. "Really into lost tribes and that sort of stuff, wasn't he?" Little Tony nodded mutely. "Did you ever read any of his stuff?" Tony's eyes grew round. "I really liked his treatise on the Dusun funeral rites." Tony choked on his coffee. Watson pounded him between the shoulder blades.

"Thanks," Tony wheezed, looking around to see his savior. His mouth gaped. "Hey, what is this?" he growled.

Watson tipped his hat. "Dr. Watson at your service, sir."

Spade was leaning over Joe's shoulder. "Way to go, kid. I'd never figure this punk for the perp."

Little Tony barely stammered out, "Who are you people?"

Joe smiled. "Allow me to introduce you to some of the most famous detectives in literature."

Miss Marple and Holmes both sniffed at Joe's use of the word some, but like the rest, greeted Domino politely when introduced. By the time Joe finished, Domino's face had paled to a pasty white.

"How?" he muttered. "How did they know?"

"We didn't," Spade allowed. "My boy Joey had it all figured out. This is his bust." Everyone nodded in agreement.

"I figured nobody could get it. I was going to write about it. Show Uncle Tony the Duke. Get rich. Do the 'Today Show' and get interviewed by Katie Couric. How?" he asked no one in particular.

"Pure, dumb luck," Joe replied. "But why Johnny Ling?"

"Uncle Tony wanted some of Wu's action. Wu's new squeeze has this weird bodyguard. When I found out he was from Borneo, I remembered Linus' paper. I figured you'd go after Wu."

Joe looked up. "Did you get all that?" he asked the uniformed officer who'd slipped in the door. The cop nodded, pulling out his handcuffs.

Standing in the door, Joe watched the squad car and its passenger pull away. When he turned back inside, only Spade was present. Joe slid onto the stool next to the grizzled veteran. "Thanks, Mr. Spade," he said.

"Call me Sam," the gumshoe allowed. "And don't thank us. You did it all by yourself. See ya around, kid."

"Refill, sweet cheeks?" Jewel asked.

Joe looked up at her and shook his head. "Naw. I gotta go downtown and book Little Tony." When Joe looked back, Spade was gone. Joe shook his head and rubbed his eyes. He and Jewel were the only ones in the diner.

"You come back, copper," Jewel told him, lighting a cigarette. "We'll all be here for the next one."

Joe stopped in the doorway to look back. Jewel had disappeared into the back but Joe could hear a muffled conversation. Blue smoke curled up and formed a cloud around those faint words. Joe smiled. "See you guys," he whispered.

As Joe came out of Café Midnight, a wire-haired terrier fell into step with him. "Well hello there, pup," Joe greeted him. The pooch suddenly went for Joe's ankle, snagging his cuff and shaking the material for all the little animal was worth.

A sleek, cream-colored car with bulbous orange fenders and lots of chrome rolled to a stop at the corner. The driver tried to soothe his passenger's ruffled feathers. "Don't fret, sweets," he told her.

"It's not fair, Nicky. You're just as good as that lot," she pouted.

The man's mouth twitched below his pencil thin moustache. "Know what I love about you, pet," he cooed. "Not only are you rich and beautiful but you have brains, too."

"Oh, Nicky," the woman laughed. "You are incorrigible."

The man glanced down the street toward Joe, who was still trying to shake off the tenacious terrier. "I suppose we'd better rescue Detective McGwire," he hinted.

"Oh pooh. Since he didn't let us help, I think he deserves a good chewing, especially since Asta found the body," she countered.

"Trust me, pet," the man assured. "Joe McGwire has a lot of sleuthing in his future. He'll call us the next time. There's more than enough crime to go around."

The woman pouted a moment then threw her arms around the man, giving him a quick peck on the lips. "I always trust you, Nick," she purred. She opened the door and whistled. The little dog's ears pricked but he didn't let go of Joe's pant leg. "Come here, you bad dog," the woman called. The dog gave Joe's leg another shake. "Asta, come here."

At that, the little dog turned loose and ran up the street. He hopped into the woman's lap and she closed the door. Joe stood staring as the long car slid out of sight behind the row of buildings. He recognized those legs from somewhere.

"Asta?" he mouthed silently. Joe shook his head. "Naw," he said out loud. "It couldn't be." ★

HUMOR

A HEINOUS CRIME ON STATEN ISLAND
By Keith J. Bettinger

My name is Day, Bob Day. As soon as I come on the job, some idiot sergeant nicknamed me Some. Now I'm a boss. I get to pick the nicknames. I also get to read and correct little people's reports. My partner is Lenny Birnbaum. We're cops!

It was a hot, sticky, summer night in the wilds of Staten Island. We were working the graveyard shift in the major case squad. On Staten Island every shift is the graveyard shift and any case is a major case.

The phone rang. I answered it. It was a cop. He said he had a case for us. I asked him where. He told me. I asked what happened. He said I wouldn't believe him, we should come to the scene. We decided we would.

Lenny drove. I don't drive. I'm a boss. We arrived at the scene. It was right across the street from the hospital. The crime scene was the front lawn of God's Little Waiting Room Nursing Home. Someone had stolen all the sprinkler heads out of the lawn sprinkler system. I couldn't believe such a heinous crime had been committed on my shift. All Lenny could say was, "Oy vey! It looks like a good day at my cousin Murray, the urologist's, office." It's criminal that crime can still upset such tough cops like Lenny. I tried to keep it all in perspective.

I asked the reporting officer if I could see his report. He gave me his clipboard. There was nothing there to read. The gushing water had washed it all away. The ink looked like blue tears. It looked just like the mascara running down the face of the nursing home owner. She was insured for everything. Broken hips, missing and swallowed false teeth, slipping on gruel. But no one thought to insure the 25 eight-dollar sprinkler heads. She wanted to know if we could find the perp. That's what cops like us call the bad guy.

We asked the cop at the scene did he see anything suspicious. He said when he pulled up he noticed a guy in a raincoat, but he thought he was just a flasher. He should have been taught at the academy, not everything is as simple as it seems. Sometimes you have to look at the whole picture.

Lenny followed a trail of wet footprints down the street. Lenny's a good detective. That's why I have him as a partner. He was hot on the trail, following the tracks, then the trail went dead. Lenny met up with a Great Dane and its owner out for their evening walk. The Dane just flooded away any hope we had of tracking our suspect.

In the morning we were still on the case. We weren't going off duty until this case was solved. We owed it to our citizens. They pay our salary. We had another reason for solving the case. The commissioner's mother was a guest at the nursing home.

When we got back to the office there was a message. Report to the commissioner's office. Lenny didn't want to go. I told him we had to, the commissioner's the boss. Lenny just doesn't understand kissing up to the bosses. It's a game we all have to play. We drove into the big part of the city. Manhattan. We were on our way to the big building, 1PP. Police Plaza, the heart and soul of our department.

Lenny was driving slow. Traffic was terrible and Lenny was worried about the commissioner. I wasn't worried. I understand command and all the stress of being at the top.

We were on our way downtown when Lenny suddenly interrupted me while I was reading someone else's report. Lenny said, "So, there's a flasher on the corner. You vant ve should stop and maybe make an arrest?"

I told Lenny, "A flasher can wait. We have a real crime to solve!"

As we rode by I suddenly noticed something large sticking out of his raincoat. I heard Lenny gasp, "Mine Gott!"

There was the flasher going "PsssPsss" to all the commuters trying to get to work. When they looked his way, he would open his raincoat and flash a look at sprinkler heads hidden in his coat.

We stopped and jumped out of the car and grabbed him. Lenny asked, "You vant I should cuff him?" It's tough being the boss and having to make all the decisions for other people.

We threw him in the car and took him to 1PP. We booked him just like Danno always did, right from the boss' office. We showed the commissioner no one messes with his old lady's plumbing.

All the bad guy kept asking was, "How did you know it was me?"

I told him, "It's hard to believe anyone as streetwise as a crook from the wilds of Staten Island would be so stupid as to try and fence sprinkler heads in Manhattan. Everyone knows there's no lawn to water in the concrete jungle."

He just hung his head and shook it from side to side. He knew his crime spree was over.

We went back to Staten Island and Lenny wrote the reports. I read the reports that Lenny wrote. Some days we get the bad guys, some days we don't. Today was one of those days. Today was lawn sprinklers. Who knows, tomorrow could be someone's birdbath. Now it was time for us to solve some more major cases on Staten Island. ★

NOVELLA

THE GRINCH WHO E-STOLE CHRISTMAS
by Sergeant Laurick Ingram

Christine

It was October 1997 when Christine Wilfing of Virginia was "surfing the Net" – the World Wide Web – and happened upon an enticing advertisement: "PENTIUM COMPUTERS $499." Because it was such a good deal – $100 to $500 below what they normally sold for – prudence dictated she thoroughly investigate the ad before buying one.

She e-mailed the seller and asked for more information about the computers. He e-mailed her back a lengthy letter detailing the specs on the machines, Pentium processors; 300 MHz; 32 megs of RAM; one-gig hard drives, basically a darn good deal. He further explained who he was and because he built the machines himself, he could offer such great prices. The letter was punctuated with catch phrases like: "I burn them in for 100 hours to make sure they work." "Satisfaction guaranteed." "References available." "Free software programs for churches and charities." "A 15% discount if you pay in advance by cashier's check or postal money order."

Knowing a little more about the items for sale, she proceeded to check the references offered from whom she received glowing endorsements. That coupled with the fact he was dealing in postal money orders made the deal even more credible, because mail fraud would be a federal crime.

Convinced this was a legitimate offer and considering these would make excellent Christmas gifts, Christine not only ordered one, but she also informed her friends and associates of the great deal she had happened upon. Within a few days, postal money orders totaling more than $8,000 were funneled through Christine to the seller. The ad said the computers would be delivered in four to six weeks, which meant in plenty of time before the holiday rush.

When the first computer was not delivered within the six weeks, it was possible the seller was just running a little behind. Christine shot him a brief e-mail inquiring about the delay to which he immediately responded explaining he had been sick and running a little behind on his orders.

Two weeks and several e-mail inquiries later, not one computer had been delivered and Christmas was fast approaching. Christine's friends and associates were now pelting her with e-mails requesting the status of their orders. In turn, she had stepped up her efforts from e-mails, to registered mail, to faxes, and phone calls all of which were met with excuse upon excuse: "I've been sick… but thank you for your prayers, I'm better now." "United Parcel Service is running behind." "They're on their way."

Two days before Christmas, when the computers still had not arrived, it was unlikely they would make it on time, if ever, but since this was the season of miracles, Christine hoped on.

One good/bad thing about doing business in Cyberspace is that buyers and sellers from all around the world are only a few keystrokes and a mouse click away from one another: the good. In real time and space, however, buyers and sellers may be a few miles or an entire country away. In Christine's case, her money and her friends' money – the money orders had long since been cashed – were more than a thousand miles away somewhere in South Florida and the computers that should have been under her Christmas tree in Virginia were nowhere to be found: the bad. At 11:59 p.m. Christmas Eve, 1997, it was painfully obvious that somewhere in a cave in Cyberspace was the Grinch who had e-stolen Christine's Christmas.

I was ripe for change when Lieutenant Ed Petow approached me and asked if I wanted to come work for him again, but running the Hi-Tech Crimes Squad this time. Three years ago when I was still a detective, I helped him develop the CATS, Cargo Anti-Theft Squad, from four detectives and one sergeant to its current status of a twenty-five-member multi-agency task force. When I made sergeant, I was transferred out of the CATS and back to patrol. This was not a punishment, simply routine career pathing for a rookie sergeant. I did a year in patrol then was offered an assignment in Robbery supervising RID-E, Robbery Intervention Detail – Enhanced, where I had been for the last twelve months.

RID-E was the intensively proactive arm of the robbery bureau tasked with seeking out and apprehending suspected robbers and other violent felons. The team had been formed in the wake of the horrific robbery/murder of Tosca Dieperink, a Dutch tourist visiting Miami-Dade. Tosca and Gerrit-Jan, her husband, were lost and stopped to ask directions at the Shell gas station on the corner of 79th Street and 22nd Avenue. They felt safe because Shell was a Dutch owned company. Crime is motive and opportunity and the motive, greed, met the opportunity, a lost couple, at 9:40 a.m. Friday, February 23, 1997. When the gun toting robbers approached the car, the Deiperinks locked their doors. When Tosca would not open hers, the gunman shot through the window, striking her in the chest and killing her right before Gerrit-Jan's terrified, disbelieving eyes. The brutal murder sent shockwaves throughout America and Europe and the Miami-Dade Police Department (MDPD) responded quickly and with purpose. The robbers were apprehended and within weeks the Robbery Intervention Detail concept was born.

Over the next twelve months the stepped up efforts of robbery investigations coupled with the prolific arrests and contacts of RID-E drove the robbery rate down more than 50%. During my twelve months, March 1997 to 1998, in RID-E there were 852 fewer robberies throughout the county, but – there is always a but in these cases.

But during that same year the team had been involved in five car crashes –

eight, if we included the time that subject stole Erroll's car and crashed into three civilian's cars while fleeing from us. Another subject was suing us because he alleged my detectives used excessive force taking him into custody. And in September of last year, while on a "routine" traffic stop, yet another subject dropped his car into reverse and rammed my car as I was getting out to approach him. Frightfully opposed to becoming police road kill, I reacted appropriately. Now, six months later – even though the subject, having recovered from his gunshot wound, had pleaded guilty to aggravated assault on a police officer and the state ruled that my actions were legal and justified, a departmental shooting review panel was still mulling over whether firing into the car at the man who was trying to kill me violated the Department's policy against shooting into moving vehicles.

Work notwithstanding, my personal life was headed toward a different kind of crisis. In two weeks my wife was due to be promoted to sergeant, so like me a year ago she would be transferred from her current assignment in the Basic Training Unit back to road patrol. Her schedule would more than likely go from four/tens (Tuesdays through Fridays 7:00 a.m. to 5:00 p.m. with Saturdays, Sundays, and Mondays off) to midnights with Tuesdays and Wednesdays off. RID-E already worked flexible schedules because their hours were tied to the robbery trends. One week we would work 10:00 a.m. to 6:00 p.m., the following week could be 9:00 p.m. to 5:00 a.m. and every other week we worked a sixth overtime day. Shift work, in and of itself, is an enormous stressor on home life, but when we added to the equation our two small boys, four-year-old Joshua and one-year-old Jawanza, it became three times as hard. Daytime was pretty much covered with Joshua in preschool and Jawanza at the care givers, but evenings and weekends were woefully lacking of a reliable and trustworthy babysitter. It did not take a child psychiatrist to conclude that small children, unpredictable schedules and catch-as-catch-can babysitters was a fertile mix for disaster. Somewhere there had to be stability.

Let me get this straight. Eight car crashes. I am being sued. If the shooting panel rules against me, I could be suspended. In less than two weeks, I will have a thirty-six hour per week child care deficit. And you, Lieutenant Petow, are offering me days with weekends off; a corner office instead of working out of my car and an opportunity to investigate white collar computer nerds who almost never try to run you over. I counted my blessings and asked the lieutenant, "Hi-Tech Crimes Squad, when can I start?"

Two weeks later, I was in the lieutenant's office remembering how much I liked the man. His was a proud second generation Irish-American who, after being transplanted from Boston to South Florida over twenty years ago, still carried around those extra h's Bostonians used whenever they pahrked their cahrs. On his desk sat a paperweight that read "Deadlines Amuse Me" and hanging on his wall was an antique sign, "HELP WANTED, Irish need not apply."

"Laurick," he began. "With the advent of digital technology, the incidences of cloning cellular phones is down about eighty percent over this time last year when South Florida was losing about $250,000 per week. The industry seems to have enough of a handle on it that they can keep it down to an acceptable loss. So what I want to do is change your squad's name and enlarge its mission to include Hi-Tech Crimes."

"I can go for that, but what exactly are high-tech crimes?"

"That's what I want you to tell me."

Like I said, I liked the man, but more importantly he trusted me. I talked with him a little more and learned the definition that had been kicked around so far was: Crimes that by their natures require highly technical equipment or knowledge to commit. Which is a lot like telling someone that to make a cake all you need are eggs, flour, milk, shortening, and sugar. It is technically accurate and of no use whatsoever. So I knew one priority would be defining "What exactly are high-tech crimes?"

It is axiomatic that before you know where you are going you should know where you are. My second priority would be getting to know my squad members and what our talents were as well as where we needed to improve. Strangely enough, I knew the lieutenant had not sought me out for my extensive knowledge of computers. I mean I knew my way around WordPerfect, balanced my checkbook in Quicken, was vaguely familiar with Lotus spreadsheets, and knew my ASCII from a hole-in-the-ground, but by no means did I rate the coveted titles of "techno-nerd, geek, hacker." My three main talents were my ability to investigate and successfully build huge conspiracy cases, to organize and plan enforcement initiatives and to work with almost anybody – officers in my department, officers from other departments, citizens, news reporters and even the feds. The basic two-part philosophy upon which the third one rested was, first, I had learned the hard way whenever undertaking multi-agency investigations only 50% of my time was spent on the actual investigation. The remainder of the time had to be used clearing up misunderstandings. In theory, when departments combined efforts, the result should be more talent, more money, more cars. In reality it was more arguments about things that had nothing to do with core crimes in question. Things like how asset forfeitures will be divided, who pays for the cellular telephones, whose media relations department will handle the press release, who gets the biggest desk or who gets the office by the window? The way I dealt with most of these issues was by remembering part two of my philosophy: Focus on who gets caught, not who gets credit.

After my meeting with Lieutenant Petow, I walked down the hall to meet my new squad of three detectives. On paper, I showed having four detectives, but only three were working. The fourth was currently under indictment for perjury. Even though the case against her was strong, the department still had to hold her position until the trial was over. Something to do with that bothersome little phrase, "innocent until proven guilty." But three detectives were better than two.

My most senior detective, Steve White, was a 22-year veteran of police work with seventeen of those years spent as an investigator, with about ten years as a narc. He sported a ponytail, was partial to faded jeans, and played lead guitar, for Reunion, a top 40's band he managed on the weekends.

My number two detective, Greg Darling, was a towering, broad-shouldered Bahamian father of four and commissioner for the South Kendall Optimist

Football League. I knew him from my narcotics days. While I was working the north end, he was working the south. He had a slow and steady style and, like me, an eye for conspiracies.

Now if my first two detectives were the point, number three was the counterpoint. Marie Duboulay was a cappuccino complexioned, auburn haired, bi-lingual Haitian woman with a bachelors degree in public administration, who unlike us, had not been jaded by long stints as undercover narcs, and could be counted on to disagree with almost any suggestions the first two made. This type of healthy disagreement was absolutely essential if this team was to be successful. In my thirteen years as an officer, the absolute worst trouble I have seen police officers in – especially in narcotics – came when there was a group of them that all thought alike and no one had the courage to dissent.

In our current assignment, Steve, Greg, and Marie's germane strengths were knowledge of the Internet and cellular telephones, ability to assemble and disassemble computers, and knowledge of collecting and organizing evidence, respectively.

Once I knew what my personnel talent pool was, I took an inventory of my other tangible assets. I was okay in this component. Because the squad had already been operating, albeit in a different way, they already had cars, phones, desks, and other capital items as well as supplies necessary for a squad to function. We were a little deficient on computer hardware and software, but with a tweak here, a memo there, and a favor or two called in, within a month the squad had Pentium computers. We now had literature from other departments (particularly the FBI's Computer Investigations Squad) who were looking at how to approach high-tech crimes. Also, we had begun reading various magazines and newspaper articles, as well as the Internet for Dummies book and calendar. Culling information from these various sources, we took another stab at defining high-tech crimes, specifically as they related to computers. The new working definition went, "an offense in which the computer is a primary instrument in the commission of the crime."

The immediate problem with this definition would be Johnny Cochran. I could hear him now. "So, Sergeant Ingram, going by your definition, if Molly had had her fill of her boss Bob's snide remarks regarding women in the workplace and whacked him several times across his head with her keyboard, it would be by definition a 'computer crime.'"

"Well, Mr. Cochran, I never said it was a 'perfect' definition, I said it was a 'working' definition."

But rather than risk embarrassment on national television we just refined the definition one step further to read: "a crime committed, in which a computer is an essential primary instrument, in that the crime could not have been committed with any other tools." Viola! We had an answer for the question: "What exactly are high-tech crimes?"

Noah's Ark

Honesty engenders loyalty, so I try to be honest with the people who work for me. I had been with the squad for a little more than three months and I told them honestly that in pecking order of the Economic Crimes Bureau, we were "bottom feeders."

In my initial assessment of the squad to Lieutenant Petow, I told him the squad would require at least six months of training before they would have the technical capability of putting together computer cases. This was brought into sharp focus for me when one of our first cases involved a pimple-faced high school student with a "C" average. The little miscreant not only hacked into three Web Pages belonging to a government agency, another country, and a local radio station, he and his cohorts used the Internet to order up more than thirty-thousand dollars in electronic merchandise using credit card numbers they generated on their computers. A "C" student, no less. I knew immediately if a fifteen-year-old could do that kind of damage, there was no telling how much damage a disgruntled computer programmer could do.

Lieutenant Petow understood this and as such was not pressing me to build or handle cases at the same rate as squads in other bureaus. But the Fates were unkind to us and the good lieutenant and his cargo CATS were moved out of the Economic Crimes Bureau and over to the Robbery Bureau.

My new lieutenant, Rafael Fernandez, was a handsome Cuban-American man with jet black hair and dark Castillian features. He too understood the need for training, but he also understood that our police department was operating under the management style known as Compstat, short for computer comparison statistics. Compstat was what NYPD Police Commissioner Bratton had used to lower crime in New York. Simply put, computer statistics were quickly crunched and analyzed to determine what particular crimes were most being committed in a particular area. Once a week in a joint meeting, the NY precinct commanders were grilled regarding problems in their areas and what they were doing to solve them. The plan was being hailed as cutting-edge community policing and profoundly reduced crimes across the board, but – there's that but again – 70% of the precinct commanders did not survive Compstat. Armed with that daunting statistic, our police commanders were zealously questioning their lieutenants about problems and solutions in lieutenants' spheres of control. Because everyone knows what rolls downhill, Lieutenant Fernandez was constantly questioning me about what I had done that could be reported in the weekly Compstat meeting.

I am a visionary, but also a realist and have been around police work long enough to know how to survive. Until we had enough cases to be taken seriously, I instructed my crew to take anything that could possibly be considered a computer crime. Even if Molly whacked Bob with a keyboard. I would deal with Mr. Cochran later. For now, keeping the squad alive was paramount. So we took any and every case that came our way, which were usually the cases that other investigators or agents had no use for. Like I said, "bottom feeders."

Keeping the squad alive was important to me, first off, for personal survival. That is, it meant I had a job. Second, I truly admired Lieutenant Petow's foresight. RID-E was a good but reactive concept that grew out of a horrific murder. The cargo CATS were a good but reactive concept that grew out of the freight forwarding industry losing over a million dollars a week to thieves.

My squad was being formed because a crime wave was looming on the horizon and for once we had a chance to get ahold of it before it got ahold of us. But Ed Petow was one visionary versus the many nearsighted investigators and supervisors whose actions were dictated by the "Tyranny of the Urgent." I was constantly being asked by other supervisors and officers, "What exactly does the HTCS do?" When I would tell them part of our mission was investigating Internet crimes, their response was, "Is there a need for that, yet?" I heard it so much that on the door to my office I posted, "It wasn't raining when Noah built the ark."

The Cybercrime Triad

The crime of robbery is easy to quantify and venue contain, that is, you can easily measure how many robberies are occurring and assign a value to the property taken. The property, victim and subject all had to be in the same place for it to happen.

Cargo theft is easily quantified but a problem we ran into with this crime was that sometime it was not venue contained. To illustrate: Grandma Griswold wants to give the entire Griswold clan – there are 114 of them – fruit cakes for Christmas. Grandma lives here in Miami-Dade in the Marlin Garden Condominiums. She phones Claxton, Georgia, the fruit cake capital of the United States, and orders 115 fruitcakes – the extra one is for her and grandpa. So the Claxton Fruitcake Company rents a 40-foot container – no refrigeration necessary, because their fruitcakes can outlast plutonium. They load the container with the cakes, close the doors, place a number-engraved seal on the hasp, and place the container on a chassis to be picked up by a trucker tomorrow.

The next day the trucker hooks up the container-loaded-chassis, hops on I-95 and trucks south to Grandma's condo. Along the way, the driver makes a few stops where she snags a bite and fuels her rig. She arrives in Miami-Dade a little past midnight when she dares not wake Grandma. She parks her truck in the Holiday Inn overflow lot, gets a room, and grabs forty winks. The next morning, Christmas Eve, she delivers the container to Grandma's condo, but when they open it, lo and behold, there is only one partially eaten fruitcake in the container. Grandma clutches her pained breast, realizing that for the first time in twenty years the Griswolds will not have their fruitcakes under their trees. Immediately, Grandma phones the police and we arrive. A quick inspection of the trucker's paperwork indicates the serial number on the container's seal does not match the serial number on the trucker's bill of lading.

After telephoning the Claxton Fruitcake Company, we learn that they swear the 115 cakes were in the container when they sealed it. The driver swears she never removed the seal. And Grandma just swears.

As police officers of Miami-Dade County, we are charged with investigating crimes occurring in our jurisdiction, but this crime is not "venue contained." We do not know if the fruitcakes were stolen in Claxton or in any one of hundred jurisdictions I-95 goes through or if they were stolen here in Miami-Dade. The jurisdiction that the crime is contained in is the federal venue, because we do know the truck never left the country. Not to say the FBI does not care that the Griswolds' holiday cheer has been stolen, but when they consider their limited resources to deal with such issues as nuclear secrets being sold to China or the Atlanta bombing, Granny's lost fruitcakes are rock bottom on the list of their priorities. Although we also have our heinous crimes, because we service a much smaller area versus the entire country, we have a much closer relationship with our citizenry. And doggone it we can't have 116 unhappy Griswolds running around, so granny can rest assured we are either going to catch that varmint or get him caught.

The way my department overcame this jurisdictional black hole was to form partnerships with other local, state, and federal agencies. Wherever the crime was first discovered was the jumping off point for the investigation. And wherever the subject or evidence was found, the case could be indicted. In 1998, the CATS recovered more than 19 million dollars in stolen property. I tailored this policy to my investigations. If any portion of the crime occurred in MDPD jurisdiction, we would at the very least take a look at the case. Hopefully, down the pike I could get some other agencies to come on board.

The reason Internet fraud behaves like Interstate theft is the similarity of the information superhighway to real highways. The Interstate was built by the federal government in the 1950's. In the event of a war, the military would be able to move heavy equipment from state to state, hence the term, Interstate highway. The Internet, constructed by the DOD in around 1970, mirrors this idea but for information instead of heavy equipment. It was a way for the DOD to quickly transmit information from place to place, hence the terms Internet or information superhighway.

Just as the Internet mirrors the Interstate, Internet fraud mirrors Interstate theft and in many instances the fraud is not venue contained. I call this nuance the "Cybercrime Triad." The three major components of an Internet fraud are the perpetrator, the victim, the evidence. Either all three, or any permutation, thereof could be in different venues. Let's say Granny Griswold had an e-mail address, "grannyrules@aol.com" and logged onto the Internet where she found a web page for the Claxton Fruitcake Company. She orders her 115 cakes and sends the company a money order for $1,150, but never gets the cakes. Later, she learns there is no such company. The money order went to a post office box, where the subject picked it up and cashed it. The post office box shows as the business's address of record, but the Internet provider's office that manages the web page is in Austin, Texas. So I have a victim in Miami-Dade, Florida, electronic evidence in Austin, Texas and a subject who cashed the check in Claxton – a triad.

Schettino

Most people who log on to the Internet do so primarily to e-chat, e-mail, or e-trade. These activities do not concern me so much as do their dark counterparts: e-hacking, e-stalking, e-stealing. The incidents of latter are commensurate with the amounts of the former occurring online. By the end of 1997, ten million people had purchased a product or service online. Projected sales by the year 2000 are in the billions when 900 million users are expected to be online. Slick Willie Sutton, a notorious bank robber was once asked, "Why do you rob banks?" His answer: "Because that's where the money is."

Today, where the money is, is on the Net.

By July 2, the squad's chances of survival were bleak. Without Lieutenant Petow in our corner we were losing ground on a daily basis. We had survived two internal administrative restructurings, but a third one was looming nigh, and even with the steady stream of bargain basement cases we were managing, it still did not look good for us.

One of the first things we did when we were building the CATS was to send a countywide memorandum, explaining who we were and what we did. Since the crime was new, many officers and citizens had no idea who to call or how to report it. Miming the CATS concept I drafted a memorandum to be distributed countywide detailing the existence and purpose of the team. That memo quickly became a bureaucratic tennis ball being volleyed up and down the chain-of-command. Actually, I was not too surprised by this, because it had actually taken three months before everyone concerned agreed on how the cargo theft squad's memo was supposed to read. The big difference here was that the cargo theft memo was eventually circulated, whereas the HTCS memo wound up in the circular file. I never understood the decision but had been around long enough to choose my battles wisely. In the trash it lay, in the trash it stay. Without entities being properly informed of the nature of our cases, how to document them and how to contact us, we were getting an average of one computer case per week, that was until Barbara called.

Barbara Moser was not only my federal counterpart, but my physical and mental counterpart as well. She was lead administrative agent for the Miami Division of the FBI's Computer Investigations Squad with whom my team was developing a good working relationship. Her career path had lead her through FCI–foreign counter intelligence–and primarily administrative assignments. With the exception of twelve months as a school resource officer, my career path had led me to primarily enforcement oriented assignments from patrol to crime suppression team to narcotics to cargo theft, back to patrol (as a sergeant) then to RID-E.

Barbara's style was "Give it to me in triplicate, I'll check with D.C., and let you know in two weeks." Mine was, "If it's a crime and we know who did it, let's lock him up, this minute." In her entire career Barbara probably had not actually arrested ten people. By 1994 I had arrested over a thousand. The part of investigations that required undercover, surveillances and take downs was my bailiwick. The part that required analyzing voluminous amounts of evidence and dissecting crime scenes was hers. Our proactive, reactive styles blended well together. We had developed a reasonable degree of trust and even though I was sure we were still feeling each other out, we shared a kindred spirit. She was experiencing many of the same headaches and heartbreaks building her team as was I.

July 2, 1999, she phoned me to tell me that a Broward (the next county north of us) robbery detective had called her regarding an Internet fraud he did not know what to do with. She had given him my number and was giving me a heads up that he might call, which he did as soon as she hung up.

"Sergeant Ingram, Hi-Tech Crimes Squad."

"Hello, I'm Vince Schettino. I work robbery in Broward."

"Yeah, Barbara told me to expect your call. What can I do you for?"

"This lady, Tirzah Krayl, from Naperville, Illinois, telephoned me today. It seems back in September she ordered a computer over the Internet. She sent $1,345 in money orders to an address here in Broward, but the guy never sent her the computers. She said she made reports everywhere, but everybody she's talked with either says the case is too small, it's not their jurisdiction, or they don't know who handles this. I told her I didn't know either, but I'd check around. Do you handle something like this?"

"Something like this is exactly what we handle, but if the money orders went to Broward, it's out of our jurisdiction."

"Well, this lady said she did some checking of her own and the guy lives in Miami-Dade and cashed the money orders there."

"Are you sure?"

"I'm sure that's what she told me."

"Okay, I'll give Mrs. Krayl a call."

"Something else about this call that's strange, is I could swear I heard it dispatched before."

"I don't follow you."

"I seem to remember similar calls involving some kind of Internet fraud being dispatched to District Two. I'll check it out and get back to you. In the meantime, here's Mrs. Krayl's number."

I phoned Mrs. Krayl in Naperville and boy, was she glad to hear from me. She was at her wits end with trying to get some help on this case. She recounted how a few weeks before Christmas she had seen an ad on the Internet offering Pentium computers for $499. A Mr. Glen Wayne Steagal, selling the computers offered references, an extensive essay on his reliability and knowledge of computers, as well as a 15% discount if you paid with postal money orders. After sending the money orders, she waited the allotted six weeks, but the computers never came. Her numerous e-mail contacts were replied to with a litany of excuses. Using the Internet and with the help of some friends, she had tracked the seller down to Miami-Dade County, reported the crime to any and everybody, but so far nobody knew what to do about it. She said she had also spoken with an agent from the Florida Department of Law Enforcement, FDLE, who said Mr. Steagal had done this before, but when she wanted to arrest him the state said it was a civil case.

"No kidding. Well I'm not saying it's not, but let me take a look at it. Coincidentally, how many other cases did FDLE have?"

"Fourteen."

"No kidding."

"Another agency I called was the Postal Inspectors, since I purchased postal money orders and sent them express mail."

"And?"

"They took a report, but I don't know what they plan to do with it."

"Okay, we'll take the case." I finished collecting her information and hung up, but before my hot little fingers could dial FDLE, Schettino had called me back.

"Sergeant Ingram, Hi-Tech Crimes Squad."

"Ingram, it's Schettino. I called District Two. Detective Cindy Adamsky over there says she's holding six more cases for a total of about ten grand."

"Whoa!"

"Here's her number."

Rather than phone Detective Adamsky, I drove up to Dania to the District Two station. There, she gave me copies of her reports and the name of a Miami Herald reporter who was getting ready to do a piece on the caper. The reporter routinely read the weekly police reports and thought the Internet angle would make an interesting story. Adamsky did not give her a statement but gave me her number in case I wanted to talk with her.

The next morning back in my office, I telephoned the reporter, Hannah Sampson, who answered the telephone.

"This is Hah-Nah."

I fought off the impulse to ask her if she was related to Ed Petow and instead asked her what she knew about the Internet case. She told me that in addition to the cases I picked up from Broward, there was another man named Phil Bigner who had been swindled for $25,000. In fact, Mr. Steagal had caused Mr. Bigner's business to fold.

"How soon were you planning to write this story?" I asked.

"In the next week or so."

"Now Ms. Sampson, I have no authority to tell the press what to or not to print, but if you could hold off on this story it would help me greatly. It looks like this Steagal character has been doing this for a while, but I haven't had time to build a case against him. If you wait, you may find there's an even bigger story here than you have now."

"Okay, I'll wait."

After I hung up, I placed another call. I needed to thank someone who was not too busy to listen to a lady then direct her to me. "Hello, this is Sergeant Ingram. May I speak to Vince Schettino?"

It's raining

I phoned FDLE and Mrs. Krayl was right. They had had fourteen cases on him. The complaints began in 1996. Back then he was sending computers to his customers, but the computers either were of lower quality than advertised, used, or broken. The state attorney's opinion was that since he was sending some merchandise, it was civil. The agent agreed to drop me off a copy of her files.

Next, I telephoned the United States Postal Inspectors – incidentally, the oldest law enforcement organization in the country. I spoke with the group supervisor, Jim Pinorsky. "Agent Pinorsky, I'm Sergeant Ingram with the Miami-Dade Hi-Tech Crimes Squad investigating a case involving Internet fraud."

"Is the subject Glen Steagal?"

"You know him?"

"I don't know him, but I have at least a half-dozen complaints on him."

"And what are you doing with the cases?"

"Right now, we're just collecting information, but as of yet the cases do not meet out guidelines. The US Attorney won't file on them."

"Would you mind if I took a look at them?"

"Be my guest."

I told him I would get the cases from him later, but first I had to go see a man in Coral Springs.

In less than two weeks I had gone from one to thirty-two victims and my instincts were telling me there were more yet to be found. Phil Bigner would be a critical witness in this case, because I already knew one hurdle to be jumped would be putting the subject at the keyboard. Because the crime was occurring in Cyberspace, none of the victims – none except Phil Bigner, that is – had actually seen Glen Steagal. Using the information Mrs. Krayl had given me I had already ordered a drivers license photograph of Steagal. He was a thick-faced, white male with gray hair. According to his driver's license he was six-feet-two-inches tall and born in 1939. In the few cases my squad had done thus far, the geeks, hackers, and crackers we would run into were mostly from the MTV generation. This guy was pushing 60 so I suspected it was either his son or grandson actually surfing the net. Not that I thought him uninvolved, because the cashed money orders were endorsed by him and he had been arrested for grand theft before, though he wasn't convicted. Nonetheless, I could see a plausible hypothesis of innocence emerging.

"Sergeant Ingram, it's my son's business. He does the advertising, deliveries, and customer contacts; all I do is deposit the checks." It would fly.

I had called before I came, so Phil Bigner was expecting me. Bigner, a purposeful looking, slightly graying man, with a distance runner's physique, lived in a second floor apartment near Coral Springs Boulevard. To date, he had sustained the biggest loss. After inviting me in and supplying me with a cup of strong coffee – cream, no sugar is how I take it – he proceeded to tell me how he met Mr. Steagal at a marketing conference. He had seen Steagal's ads online, but was dubious about the low prices. Because he was only thirty miles north of Steagal, he wanted to meet him in person, which he did at this conference. He questioned the host of the conference about Steagal's reliability and the host vouched for him. Because he had faith in the host by proxy he now had confidence in Steagal. But that is what con men are good at, engendering confidence.

Bigner's plan was to purchase the computers at $499 then mark them up and resell them. He could sell them for as much as $750 while still competing with the going prices. Being a smart businessman, Bigner first tested the waters by advertising the computers. In about a month-and-a-half, he had taken in more than $20,000 in orders, but the first few customers who ordered were calling him complaining that their computers never arrived. An uneasy feeling settled in the pit of his stomach and he immediately stopped taking any more orders. The first few e-mails he sent were replied to with excuses about being sick and backlogged. But fifty e-mails, faxes, and phone calls later no computers had been delivered. Being a fair man, he reimbursed his customers their money and took it upon himself to collect from Steagal. He went down to an address he had found on Steagal and waited there all day. As Steagal was pulling up in a white van, Bigner got out of his car and walked toward him. No sooner than they made eye contact, Steagal gunned the engine and sped off. Right then Bigner knew there would be no computers.

Several months later, the purposeful Mr. Bigner was now the purposeful and pissed Mr. Bigner. Going one step further than Mrs. Krayl, he not only had lodged complaints to any law enforcement or regulatory agency that would listen, he scoured the Internet for others who had been duped by the charlatan. He collected statements, copies of e-mails, and copies of money orders from the various victims and put everything together in organized package–heck, he did a better job than some cops I know would have. He found more than a dozen other victims, one of whom was a lady in Virginia named Christine Wilfing who told him a sad story of a stolen Christmas.

The Paper Panther

Once Mrs. Krayl expressed how frustrating it had been I assured her from this point forward, I was responsible for whatever happened. She was still free to call and complain to whomever she chose, but something could and would be done about this man. The same assurance I offered her I offered Mr. Bigner and every victim in between. By now the victims numbered fifty, the losses had exceeded $100,000, and complaints had been lodged with more than a dozen federal, state, and local agencies. Once it was clear that we had the case, victims started falling out of the atmosphere. Almost all of them had a similar story and similar frustrations regarding getting someone to do something about this man – who, by the way, was still operating on the Net.

The case was quickly becoming a procedural, technological and legal paper panther and in a few short weeks, the HTCS went from under feeders to overwhelmed. I needed help. Procedurally, we had to find a way to give ourselves enough time to organize our case against Steagal, while at the same time keeping him from victimizing any more unsuspecting people. We also had to find a way to organize the voluminous paper work already being generated by this case. Between e-mails, case reports, canceled checks, and purchase orders there was more than 5,000 pages of evidence so far. Technologically, I needed someone who could contact our various victims over the World Wide Web and let them know what we were doing, but tell them not to inform Steagal. I also needed someone who could shadow Steagal on the Web and give us a heads up if he was stalking new victims. Legally, I needed a sharpshooter who could keep up with the mountains of paperwork, understand the technical nuances, and present it all in such a way that six disinterested jurors who may, or may not, have a clue what Internet fraud is, could still understand that a crime had been committed. What I needed were the two Karens.

Karen Number One was Karen "Kata" Austin, a freckled face, red head partial to Virginia Slims cigarettes. Back when I was helping Ed Petow get the CATS organized, I knew even less about computers than I knew now. I went to Kata who helped set up the database that kept track of $50 million dollars in stolen property, and innumerable tags, serial numbers, names and dates of birth. She had just finished working on a case involving a 138-count indictment against an Israeli organized crime family and was bristling for a new challenge. When I told her what I needed, she jumped in with both feet. Karen Number Two was Karen Gilbert, a petite dark-haired woman with Semitic features who had a legal mind like a laser – focused, penetrating, intense. Karen and I had worked together first on cocaine trafficking cases, then on cargo theft cases. She was constantly seeking out new legal challenges and boy, did this one qualify. Most of our subpoenas, search warrants, and indictments would be prototypes because this would be the one of the first cases of its kind to be filed and tried in the eleventh judicial circuit. Like me, Karen immediately recognized that it would be problematic to put the subject behind the keyboard at the time of the thefts. What she instructed us to do was to go up on his four telephone lines. (We knew he had four from subpoenas, and by go up she meant pen registers to record the numbers he called and the numbers that called him. The pens were not as intrusive as wiretaps, which required a lot more probable cause.) Surveillances had to be conducted in tandem with the pens, so we could at least put him in the house at the time of the calls. Also, we could monitor his online times. Those were our marching orders. But before I did anything, I walked back to my office door and beneath my Noah's ark saying posted, "It's raining."

Divine Favor

The pens were installed in about two weeks and boy, were they humming. He was making and receiving calls on all four lines and spending more than fifty hours a week on line. My eyes ache just thinking about staring at a computer screen that much. Kata was doing a superb job getting our files organized while Karen Number Two was bringing herself up to speed on the case. My squad was burning up their keyboards typing reports. When they were not typing reports they were watching Steagal's condominium. But so far Steagal still had not poked his head out of his cave.

One day in Lieutenant Fernandez's office, he and I started theorizing that maybe he had an automated dialer and was actually phoning in from another site. When my team had checked him for cars we could not find any registered to his name, so we did not know which, if any, car in the lot was his. "I'm starting to get nervous," Fernandez said. "Are we going to catch this guy?"

"Of course," I said, with a lot more confidence than I felt. By now, new victims were contacting us on a daily basis. The total losses now hovered around a quarter-million dollars and the bosses were starting to pressure Fernandez as to why we had not yet arrested Mr. Steagal.

I left Fernandez's office tired, frustrated, and scared. For the amount of personnel, money, and resources I had sunk into this case, if Steagal got away it would signal certain doom for my squad. I went back to my office and tried to work, but my mind would not focus. Screw it! I grabbed my briefcase and decided to head home early for a change. I was just about to go through the Golden Glades interchange when I considered driving by Steagal's condo, but I thought better of it. The team has been on this guy for hours upon hours and he had not come out yet. What are the chances I will see him on a drive-by? One hundred percent better than if you don't drive by, a small voice in my head said. So I tooled on down North Miami Beach Boulevard to northeast Tenth

Avenue where I hung a left. Four blocks ahead, a white van was pulling out of the condominiums underground parking lot. From that distance, I could not see the driver, but I knew, I just knew, it was him. I followed the van up to Miami Gardens drive where it made a left and gave me a beautiful broadside view of the thick-faced man I had seen in the driver's license photograph. Thank you, Lord!

Quickly as I could, I telephoned Fernandez on my cellular.

"Lieutenant Fernandez."

"Better to be lucky than good," I said.

"You got him."

"I got him."

"Do you need help?"

"Take too long for them to get here, we are already northbound on I-95, but I am going to call Cindy Adamsky in Broward and see if she can send me somebody."

"You're the man."

"Thank you, boss."

It used to crack me up when I would watch Miami Vice and Crockett would tail subjects in the $150,000 Testarrosa and never get made. In reality, you need five nondescript cars to do an effective moving surveillance and even then if the subject is anticipating a tail, it is hard as the dickens keep up with him. But since I was living under divine favor anyway, I gave it a shot. Incredibly, in rush hour traffic, I tailed him more than twenty miles all the way from his condo in Miami-Dade County to the post office box on Griffin where all the checks were going. I watched him take a package in, come out, then leave.

By then I had called Cindy and we had a uniformed Broward deputy standing by to stop him a few blocks down the street. I did not want him arrested, but I did need to be sure it was him and not his look-alike brother. It was him.

I returned to work the following morning with renewed vigor. The end was in reach. I borrowed the Israeli Organized Crime Squad and put both squads on him from sunrise to sunset. They were able to follow him from the condo, to the post office box, to a few other places and the Uleta Branch Post Office where a detective actually witnessed him cashing a postal money order. From there they followed him back to the condo.

When I brought Karen up to speed, she was satisfied that we had enough to get a search warrant for the condo. We had already served his Internet provider with a search warrant permitting us to raid his e-mail, so the condo would be the next to last step before arrest.

On Friday, September 11, 1998, at 5:00 p.m., I had in hand a search warrant for the residence on one Glen Wayne Steagal. Lieutenant Fernandez and I were hammering out the last minute details for Monday morning. I had spoken to investigators from other agencies, who had tried to speak with Steagal on past occasions and they all agreed he will not let you in. A couple of other victims had tried to sue him and the process servers could not get him to come to the door either. At the last minute, Lieutenant Fernandez decided we should use the department's special response team. Another way television shows differ from reality is that on TV, detectives love to go charging through doors. In reality, if you do not practice, practice, and practice, you would do well to never, never barge through a door. It is a good way to get shot. If we needed to do a dynamic entry, SRT would have to be the ones.

So Friday, at 5:45 p.m., when I should have been picking out a video for my five-year-old, I was sitting in front of an SRT lieutenant being lectured on why Economic Crimes Bureau detectives do not know how to write search warrants. Condescendingly, the lieutenant was explaining why my description of the premises was not sufficient for SRT. One line, according to the lieutenant should not have been written to read "Unit XXX is the westernmost unit on the third level of the south section and its front door faces north." Rather it should have read "The front door to the unit is the westernmost door on the level of the south section and the door faces north."

"Okay, so let me get this straight, it is Friday afternoon and the courts are closed until Monday morning at nine. Since we want to serve this warrant Monday morning at five a.m., you want me to have the shift commander notify an on-call judge, and you want me to go to his or her house over the weekend and explain why we will not serve a perfectly legal warrant that describes where we want to search but doesn't read exactly how you would have preferred."

"Yes, and I know you guys in economic crimes don't do these often, so you wouldn't know that we review the warrants before the judge ever signs them."

I did not bother to tell the SRT lieutenant that I knew better, because I had written over twenty-seven search warrants, twenty-four of which were drug warrants executed by SRT. I would have understood if the lieutenant had simply said, "I'm a lieutenant. You're a sergeant. I don't want to do the warrant." I could respect that and would have replied. "You are a lieutenant. I am a sergeant. Show me en route to Blockbuster Video Store, and I'm outta here." But to have to listen to this specious double speak about the insufficiency of a search warrant that had been approved all the way up the chain-of-command to my major was like hosing me down and telling me it was raining. All I could think was Laurick, if you open your mouth you're going to get suspended. I gritted my teeth and said, "Thank you, I'll be going, now." I phoned Fernandez, told him what had happened and headed home.

Sunday morning in church is when the idea hit me. I go to a Baptist church and the services run about three hours which gives my mind a lot of time to wander. The idea was this. Steagal lived in a community primarily populated with older Jewish couples. We were going to handcuff Greg Darling, and have one North Miami Beach uniformed officer go to the condo manager and say he caught Greg trying to break into the white van downstairs. The officer would ask the manager if he or she knew who owned the van. Of course, the manager would know and then go and get Mr. Steagal for us.

Monday morning at five a.m., members of my squad and six other agencies were all huddled in the shadows of the underground parking lot beneath the condos. From downstairs I could hear what was going on. The manager, an older lady, did know who owned the van and walked the officer to the door but no matter how hard she knocked, no one would open the door. That simply

197

would not do. Someone had tried to burglarize Mr. and Mrs. Steagal's van and they had to be told. The landlady, went back to her apartment and faxed the Steagal's a letter, saying "Someone tried to break into your van." When that didn't work she came back out got a stick and began banging on the side window.

From downstairs, I could hear this whole thing and it was taking everything I have to keep my team from falling apart with laughter and giving away our positions. Persistence and purpose paid off and a thick-faced, white haired, bearded man slowly opened the door. With blinding speed, Steve White rounded the corner and stepped in the door way announcing: "Miami-Dade Police, Hi-Tech Crimes Squad. We have a warrant to search these premises!"

Downstairs, I fell to my knees, "Thank you, Lord!" Cindy Adamsky just smiled and said, "You're the man."

By the time I got upstairs to the unit, Steagal was handcuffed and seated on his couch, holding his head down, trying to look penitent. "Mr. Steagal, I'm Sergeant Ingram, do you know what this is about?"

"No."

"Do you know a lady named Christine Wilfing?"

"I don't want to say anything until I talk to my lawyer."

"And you're going to need a lawyer, Mr. Steagal. Believe that."

Glen Steagal lived like a hermit in a cave. File cabinets, bookshelves, desks, everything was stuffed to-the-max with reams of advertisements, tomes of e-mail, and files upon files all covered with a thick layer of dust.

Ironically, seeing Steagal close up, hearing him speak, and seeing how he lived was not at all what I had expected. I realized that this was no techno-wizard, nor geek, nor hacker. This was an ordinary con man with an extraordinary power at his fingertips. The awesome power of the Internet, where if someone has just a little Grinch in them, there is no telling how much Christmas they can e-steal.

Note: With the exception of the Deiperinks, the victims' names have been changed to respect their privacy.

The High-Tech Crimes Squad did survive. ★

NOVELLA

DERRINGER
A BLUE MACKENZIE STORY
By Paul Bishop

When the end of your life stares at you from the business end of a gun, the barrel opening appears bigger than creation. If you expect to survive, you have to get beyond the fear of death. You have to tear your attention away from the tunnel size opening and focus on the real threat, the finger on the trigger. If you neutralize the threat on the trigger then the gun is useless. It is something only a professional can do, but then I've survived being on the wrong side of a gun enough times to be considered a pro.

This time, however, it was going to be a tough call. The threat with his finger on the trigger was an amateur and looked about as stable as a lemming heading for the nearest cliff.

Three days earlier I had been throwing the heavy iron around when Lacy called across the gym floor and told me Max Venables was on the phone. I finished the set of dead lifts I was working on and picked up a towel to wipe the sweat out of my eyes.

"Tell him I'll call him back," I groused, upset at the break in concentration.

"He said it was important," Lacy persisted.

Max is an entertainment lawyer and a close friend. Whenever he has a chance, he sends a client in my direction. In the entertainment business everything is important. Even bowel movements can become media events.

"I'll still call him back," I said.

Lacy shrugged her shoulders in resignation and glided back to the phone on the reception desk. I noticed the gains she was making with her calves. Lacy hasn't been pushing iron long, but she's blessed with a natural, physical aptitude.

She turned up at Derringer's Gym, which I own, about a year ago. Since then, she's turned into one of the sport's fastest rising stars, and has become an irreplaceable assistant. Her business and managerial abilities make it possible for me to help people, such as Max's clients, when the mood takes me.

I hit the weights again, blitzing my back muscles, isolating each one and really blasting it with weight, striving to obtain maximum geometric development. I did twelve reps of dead-lifts with a 445 pound bar, and then flowed straight into two sets of hypertensions. For the next hour, I worked my lats, my traps, and the small muscles across the top of the shoulders. I finished off with a set of ultra shrugs that had me seeing stars. I was so wasted I could barely keep my head up, but my erectors felt like two steel pythons running up either side of my spine.

I showered in my small apartment over the gym, and changed into an old pair of Levi 501s, a plaid work shirt, and Tony Lamas. I slipped my two inch Derringer into the holster sewn inside my left boot and called Max. We agreed to meet in an hour at Yesterdays. Lacy stuffed some checks and order forms under my nose. I signed them while watching two dozen sweaty bodies battle with their pain threshold on the main floor. I told Lacy where I was headed, and bobbed out the door for the fifteen minute drive to the restaurant.

I'd started lifting weights when I was fifteen. At seventeen, I won the title of Mr. Junior Universe. At eighteen, my weightlifting career was curtailed when Uncle Sam sent me to Viet Nam and introduced me to something else at which I was good – killing.

Two tours and uncountable LURP missions later, the war ended and the CIA picked up my option. For the next five years, I plied my violent trade throughout the Pacific until the stress caught up with me and brought on a total physical and mental breakdown.

I can talk about it now, but at the time I thought it was the end of my life. I was pulled out of the field, given a small pension for services rendered, and stuck back into the real world of civilian life, a life I had forgotten existed. At twenty-five, I was a burned out shell with nothing inside.

Somehow, I found a solitary spark buried somewhere and began to put myself back together using the only thing that meant anything to me – bodybuilding. For a while I was as happy as a pig in poop. I bought Derringer's and found escape pumping up my 6'3" frame with a 58" chest, 23" arms, 29" thighs, 20" calves, 34" waist, and 275 pounds of various other muscles. After a year, though, I began to feel something was missing.

The need for the hunt had come alive again. I fought it until, with the help of a psychiatrist, I came to accept it as a part of me and realized I might be able to use it for the right reasons for a change.

The CIA sniffed around for a bit, but I sent them packing in no uncertain terms. Instead, I posted a twenty-five-hundred dollar bond, passed a civil service exam, and hung a private investigators license behind the door of my bathroom.

I didn't advertise my services, but picked up work from old contacts who still operated in areas that provided a need for an independent investigator. Since then word-of-mouth has brought more than one client around to drop his troubles on my door step.

The LA weather was acting as if it had no idea it was winter. I had the top down on my Mustang and found the short drive to meet Max invigorating. Yesterdays is one of my favorite watering holes. It has a dozen or so tables on its second floor balcony that overlook the Westwood street scene. When I entered, I found Max and another man already sitting in the far corner.

"Hello, Blue." Max stood up and extended his hand. Tall and rapier thin, he was dapper in the pinstripe of his conservative dark blue suit. Before taking over his father's law firm, Max had been my field control for two years in the

South Pacific. On occasion, I wondered just how completely he'd put away his cloak and dagger.

He gestured to the man sitting next to him. "Blue, meet Harry Stein, owner of Nightsong Records." Ever the gentleman, he gestured back towards me, "Harry – Blue MacKenzie."

Stein stood and I shook his hand. He seemed impressed by my size, which I don't like to see happen. It makes clients think you're going to break heads rather than use one. At one time Stein had probably been in fair shape himself, but there were too many businessman's lunches and not enough workouts under his belt now.

"Harry has a problem you might be able to help him solve." Max came right to the point after we were seated and I had a sweating bottle of Harps in front of me.

"Have you ever heard of Nightsong Records, Mr. MacKenzie?" Stein asked. When I shook my head, he looked at Max as if to say I should have at least made out as if I'd heard of his company, if only to soothe his ego. I didn't tell him to call me Blue.

Max covered smoothly as always. "Have you ever heard any recordings by Charity Ross?"

"Sure," I replied. "She has a current country-rock crossover hit called Moonwatch. The critics are having a field day calling her the new Crystal Gayle." I rapidly made the mental connections. "I take it Nightsong Records is Charity's recording label."

Stein smiled, revealing two gold teeth. "That's right. Charity has been with Nightsong since the start of her career. She's now the mainstay of our catalogue." Stein suddenly looked uncomfortable.

"The fact of the matter is," Max cut through the garbage, "after twenty years in Nashville, if it wasn't for Charity Ross, Nightsong Records would have to close the studio doors."

Stein turned a bit purple at Max's bluntness, but didn't deny the observation.

I waited a beat, sipping beer. When Stein didn't offer anything further, I pressed on. "Aside from having all your eggs in one basket, and that egg being number three with a bullet on both the country and rock charts, what other problems do you have?"

"She's gone," Stein said morosely. He was staring at his half empty glass, and idly making wet rings on the table.

"Gone?" I looked at Max, and then back at Stein. He finally raised his eyes to meet mine.

"She disappeared over a month ago with her next CD only half finished. A week later, I received a letter from her asking me to forward her mail and her residuals to a post office box in Los Angeles. I sent her several letters imploring her to get in touch with me and let me know what was going on. The only reply I received was a short note telling me not to worry and again asking for me to forward her checks."

"Wouldn't her checks go through her agent?"

"I'm her agent as well as her producer. And if I don't get her new CD in the stores before Christmas, I might as well forget being around to celebrate New Years. I held back her residuals, but didn't get any response. Last week, I decided to fly out to find her, but I don't really know where to start. The post office says she hasn't picked up her mail in two weeks, and that was my only lead."

I thought for a moment. "Does she have any other money that she can access?"

"An accountant handles her cash flow and the movement of money within her investments. It was one of the reasons I was surprised she asked for her residual checks to be forwarded directly to her. Normal procedure is for everything to be handled through her accountant. In day to day life, she really has no need to handle paper money."

I tried to conceive of that kind of existence.

"Frankly, I'm at my wit's end, so I've had to resort to something I dislike. I'm taking Charity to court to get her to honor her contract and finish her CD."

I looked at Stein in amazement. "You can't be naive enough to think you can get a civil case through the courts in time to get a CD on the stands for Christmas."

"No, I'm not that naive, but I'm not without influence. With a little string pulling, I've arranged for a preliminary hearing of the case in Nashville next week. I want you to find Charity and serve her a subpoena. I don't expect the court to resolve anything, but if I can talk to Charity face-to-face, I know I can get her to come back willingly. Max handles some of my west coast dealings. He seems to have faith that you can help."

I glared at Max. This wasn't my kind of thing. However, I owed Max several favors. "Does Charity have any friends in L.A.?" I asked.

"A few friends in the business, naturally, but I've checked with them."

"How about relatives?"

"Her mother and sister are back in Nashville. Her father left the family a long time ago, before Charity started singing. All her other relatives are still in Texas where I discovered her." The last declaration was said with a touch of pride.

"Did she say anything to anyone before she left?"

"Not word one. She left the studio late on a Friday night after a really good session. Saturday, we had dinner with friends and she was full of enthusiasm for how the CD was coming along. I called her Sunday night, but there was no answer. On Monday, she just didn't show up for the studio session."

"How about a boyfriend or a lover?"

To my surprise Stein actually blushed. "Charity and I have been close for quite a while. There was no one else for either of us. It's one of the reasons I can't understand her taking off. I'm worried sick."

The blush made me like him a bit more, but I still couldn't help wondering if he was more worried about his lover or his nest egg.

"My fee is five hundred dollars a day plus all expenses. You'll get an itemized list. I'll want a week's retainer, refundable if my fee doesn't run that high. If that's agreeable, Max will write up a contract for you to sign."

"Thank you," said Stein. Max smiled weakly at me.

"I also want the P.O. box number Charity gave you, a copy of the subpoena, a stack of publicity stills, and a number where I can reach you."

Max had anticipated me and handed over a thick manila envelope.

"Please hurry, Mr. MacKenzie," Stein implored me as I stood up.

I didn't bother replying.

On the way home, I picked up a copy of charity's Moonwatch CD at the local music mart. Upstairs in my room, I put it on the stereo, and a throaty voice began to drift softly from my speakers. I dug into my small collection of CDs. My personal taste runs more to Tom Waites or Jimmy Buffett, but I had been given a copy of one of Charity's earlier CDs as a gift. I finally found it and pulled it out.

The picture on the cover showed a blossoming young girl with rose petal skin wearing a full length skirt topped with a peasant blouse. A yellow ribbon weaved through her waist length, blond hair, which was blowing wildly in the wind.

The photo on the current CD was a shocking contrast. Charity's hair was now bobbed in a short, almost punkish style, her body had become a woman's and was poured into a skin tight, black jumpsuit. Her eyes were filled with a kind of hollow hunger, which she hadn't known existed when the first photo was taken.

Her voice had changed too. The new sound reaching my ears was rougher, sexier, even a bit cynical, but also seemed to be struggling to meet the demands of her new image. It had happened to countless others before her. Charity was just another victim of fame, demand, adulation, and manipulation. I thought again about a lifestyle where you never handled any of your own money.

I waited until the CD ended before picking up the phone and jabbing in the number for the Postal Inspectors, the security branch of the mail service.

There is really nothing mysterious about detective work. All it requires is a simple recipe of two parts common sense blended with equal measures of perseverance and luck. While simmering the basic ingredients over a world-weary flame, you add a pinch of cynicism and a dash of toughness. The most important step comes just prior to serving when the whole concoction is stuffed into a wrapper of intelligence and sprinkled liberally with contacts – the one ingredient you can't leave out when baking a detective. Knowing where to go and who to talk to is what separates the detective from his employer. It's what he gets paid for. It's the reason Harry Stein had no idea where to start, but I did.

When the phone connected, I asked for Sally Swain and was placed on ignore while somebody tried to find her. I'd met Sally at a bodybuilding contest six months earlier. Since that time, she had changed from a voyeur to an actual fan of the sport.

"Howdy, stranger. Staying hard?" she asked when she came on the line.

"I'm still throwing the iron around if that's what you mean."

"You know it isn't."

"Does your mother know you talk dirty?"

"Who do you think taught me?"

"It's more than my life is worth to answer that one. Listen, I need a favor."

"I'll be right over."

"Whoa, girl. Cool your jets. I only want you to find out the owner information on a P.O. box number."

"What's in it for me?"

"Dinner at Milano's?"

"Followed by a session of pumping iron back at your place?"

"We'll see what develops."

"You are so wishy-washy sometimes. Okay, okay, give me the box number."

I did so and Sally returned me to the ignore button while she looked up the information on the office computer. After ten minutes of listening to elevator Montavani, her sunny voice came back on the line.

"This sounds like something right up your alley. The box is registered to Barbarians Inc. in Westlake." She rattled off a street address almost quicker than I could copy it down. "Remember," she said. "Drinks, dinner, champagne, dancing, more champagne, and then back to your place to see what comes up." The itinerary appeared to have expanded somewhat.

"I'll call you."

"Sure you will – next time you need a favor."

When I hung up the phone the receiver was smoking. Sally scares me to death.

I'd heard of Barbarians Inc. before. Instead of advertising in reputable muscle magazines, they promoted themselves on the back pages of comic books, true detective tabloids, and soldier-of-fortune rags. They promised instant muscles if you used their miracle protein powders, gimmick exercise machines, and wonder workout courses. They were part of the dark stigma that has given bodybuilding a bad name over the years – suckering kids and young adults into thinking there is an easy way to achieve the body beautiful without the agonizing hours of work.

I was a bit surprised to have the investigation lead back to my own doorstep, but then again, Max Venables is a crafty bastard and probably knew the direction things would take when he recommended me to Harry Stein.

Even when Max was acting as my control – when we were playing the game – he often wouldn't tell everything he knew. It was his way of double checking his own information. If I independently uncovered facts that coincided with intelligence already in Max's files, then chances were the information was reliable. It was also a system that allowed Max to pick the right agent for a job. If he believed Charity Ross' disappearance was somehow connected with the world of bodybuilding, even if it was the sleazy side of the game, it was no wonder he had steered things in my direction.

If I remembered correctly, Barbarians Inc. had recently been the subject of an investigation by a television news magazine. Claims were made that Barbarian exercise machines and equipment were worthless and could not possibly live up to the declarations made by the manufacturers. Even more damaging were the allegations that the protein powders sold by Barbarians were laced with illegal steroids – fat soluble compounds used to increase muscle mass at a high risk to the users health. Logic dictated a trip out to the home base of Barbarians to see what crawled out when I turned it over.

Westwood to Westlake is a thirty minute trip across the San Fernando Valley and into the environs of Ventura County. Christmas tree lots were staked out along the route, but were not yet stocked. I pulled off the freeway at Hampshire road and stopped in the parking lot of a K-Mart to check my map. Another two minutes of driving through a tangle of side streets brought me to a small industrial complex where I found Barbarians Inc. sandwiched between an Adidas shoe warehouse and a clothing manufacturer's sweatshop.

When I tried Barbarians' front door, I found I should have saved myself the trip. The door was locked down tight and the interior of the office was as dark as the whale's belly after Jonah's candle went out. There were some deep gouges around the lock area of the door frame. It looked as if someone had tried to break in. I walked around to the back of the building, but found the warehouse type sliding metal door was also secured. There were no emergency numbers posted.

I was about to leave when a security guard came around the corner and approached me. "Can I help you sir?" Even though he was looking back at middle-age, the guard was in fair shape, no pot belly or overflowing love handles. His uniform was crisply pressed and his leather gear was not only clean, but shiny.

"I'm looking for somebody connected with Barbarians Inc."

"You and half the rest of the world," he spoke with a smile. "Don't tell me they sucked somebody like you in with their ads," he said taking in my size. "If they did, you're probably their only success story."

I grinned a grin. "No, I don't use their products. I'm just trying to get in touch with the owner or his representative."

"You're not a cop or a reporter," the guard said, giving me the eye. "What are you, private heat?"

I nodded confirmation

"Thought so," he said. "I was an LA cop for thirty years, and I can still spot a keyhole peeper a mile away. No offense intended."

"None taken. What did you mean when you said me and half the rest of the world?"

"Well, two days after that TV news magazine, Contrast, aired its story about Barbarians, investigators from the Federal Food and Drug Administration showed up here and started making noises about court cases and legal suits. As soon as they left, Barbarians closed their doors, and I haven't seen the staff since." The guard paused to adjust his leather gear slightly. "The following evening someone broke into the offices and threw the files all over the place. It was impossible to tell if anything was taken."

"Any idea who did it?"

"A few. The day before it happened I caught a tall, skinny kid with dark, curly hair snooping around. He claimed he'd ordered some items from Barbarians, was dissatisfied with them, and wanted to get his money back. It's my guess he came back later to try and recoup his losses somehow."

I took one of Charity's publicity photos out of my jacket pocket and flashed it face forward. "Have you ever seen this girl around?"

The guard's eyes flicked to the photo for an instant and then switched back

205

to me. I wouldn't have wanted him hunting me while he was still on the force. I wouldn't want him hunting me now.

"I saw her go into Barbarians the day before they closed shop. She left a few hours later with the owner, Alex Rivers."

"You have a home address for Rivers?"

"Nope. And I wouldn't give you one if I did."

I spent a second wondering how far some long green might go. He seemed to read my mind.

"Don't bother reaching for your wallet. I wasn't on the pad with the force, and I'm not about to jump on now."

I grinned another grin. Had I really found an honest man? "Okay, thanks for your help. If the girl or anybody else shows up, I'd appreciate a call." I handed him a card.

I drove back to the K-Mart and parked next to a pay phone. I was still burping Halloween candy, but the windows of the discount store were ready for Santa. I used the phone to call a television writer I knew from the gym. When I told him what I wanted, he quickly agreed to find out who wrote the Barbarians' segment for Contrast and set up an interview for me along with a screening of the segment. It was exactly what I wanted to hear.

The following morning, a brisk wind had cleared the hills and I was on the road with the top down again by nine. I presented myself at the Contrast studio doors in Burbank. I was clean shaven, and nattily dressed in brown slacks, a yellow Polo shirt, and a tweed jacket. My loafers were highly polished, but didn't sport any tassels.

I'd already put in ten miles of dawn road work. Exercise is my version of Holmes' cocaine habit. When the jagged edge of depression rears up, I turn to pumping iron and workout with a vengeance, to the point where nothing can penetrate my self-imposed wall of weight and pain. When I take on a case, though, my dormant instincts run rampant, keeping depression at bay, and for a while I feel like a live wire again. But I still had to do something physical every day.

Inside the lobby, I asked for Toby Wainwright, the writer of the Barbarians segment. I was told to wait and took a seat on a too-soft couch along one wall. Out of the corner of my eye, I watched the female receptionist struggle between being repulsed by my muscles or slipping me her phone number. Repulsion won.

After a couple of long minutes, a tall woman with long, well-shaped legs stepped out of the elevator and walked toward me on red high heels. Thick auburn hair tumbled down her back, and even across the lobby I could see light flashing off her jade green eyes. Her knee length, cream colored dress was made of a soft silk that flattered her curves and accentuated the upturned tilt of her breasts. The left side of the dress was slit high enough to catch my breath in my throat.

I remembered a friend who, when asked if he had ever slept with a redhead replied, "Not a wink." I knew what I was putting on my Christmas list. I certainly hoped I'd been good enough.

"Mr. MacKenzie?" she asked, extending the long fingers of her right hand toward me. "I'm Toby Wainwright."

I was caught off guard and almost stammered. I'd figured her for Wainwright's secretary and my pass to the inner sanctum.

"Your male chauvinism is showing, Mr. MacKenzie." The twinkle in her eye let me know she was used to my kind of response.

"Don't tell me, you have a brother whose name is Sue."

"His name is Leslie, actually. But he's learned to live with it." She smiled nicely, and I released her hand, which had been firm and cool.

She asked me if I wanted to screen the Contrast segment first and talk after. I agreed, and quickly found myself ensconced in a screening room with a cup of lukewarm coffee. The fifteen minute piece of film which flashed across the screen was the standard type of TV journalism which leaves you feeling you know all the answers, but are a little foggy on what the questions were.

The main thrust of the segment seemed to focus on two points – the unknown and shady background of Barbarians' owner Alex Rivers, and the allegations claiming Barbarians' protein powders were full of illegal drugs while their vitamin supplements were nothing more than gelatin based placebos. When the film ended, Toby brought me another cup of coffee and sat down in the seat next to mine. I could just sense the barest whiff of her perfume.

I asked the obvious question first. "What brought Barbarians to your attention?"

"Contrast's producers were looking to do a series of segments on consumer rip-offs. It's the popular thing right now, and I was assigned to check into the chain of health spas you see doing a lot of advertising. In the process, I came across numerous get-fit-quick schemes – the type of things designed to appeal to a person's initial enthusiasm in the hopes that, after paying their money, the consumer will stop following the program, diet, exercise or gimmick long before they realize it isn't working." She stopped talking for a moment to sip her coffee and rearrange her legs. The movements pulled her dress tight across her body.

She noticed me watching her and returned my gaze with a mischievous look. Bodybuilders thrive on being looked at, so I've never understood why some women get upset if you visually appreciate them. Toby's acceptance of my lecherousness made a nice change.

"I singled Barbarians out of the pack," she continued, "because their ads seemed designed to appeal more to the youth market. I was also able to come up with a few juicy horror stories, like the one in the film about the boy's liver failure which was blamed on the steroids in Barbarians protein powder." She looked a little sheepish. "I know it sounds callous, but you have to have something to use as a hook in this business."

I smiled reassuringly, and she continued.

"After the chemical analysis of Barbarians' products started coming back, I knew I was on to a good fraud story. I started a background check on Alex Rivers, but ran into a brick wall. Rivers didn't have a past, and it took my sources until the segment was written and taped before they could uncover any reliable info."

"They find anything interesting?"

207

"There's still not much, but apparently Rivers was a nickel-and-dime conman kicking around the midwest until he hooked up with a kindred spirit named John Vreeling. Together they went into a legitimate machinery rental/supply business in Texas.

"Surprisingly, the business boomed for about ten years before Rivers forced it to the verge of bankruptcy by fiddling the books. There was a big scandal and Rivers skipped town, leaving his family to the welfare rolls, and his partner, Vreeling, so desperate he committed suicide.

"Rivers moved around quite a bit after that, always one step ahead of the law and his creditors. He made some good money by running several medium-size mail-order scams, which gave him the backing to open Barbarians three years ago."

"Where does he get his supplies from?" I asked, mesmerized as she recrossed her legs.

"The body building gimmicks are made up and shipped from a warehouse in the midwest, but the protein powders, diet supplements, and vitamins are all manufactured in Mexico. He has a small hideaway somewhere down there."

I drank some more of the tepid coffee. "How did Rivers react when you started snooping around?"

"To say the least, he was uncooperative. Byron Owens, who set up all of Barbarians' exercise programs, was more helpful until Rivers found out he was talking to us. I think Owens really believed everything was on the up and up."

I knew Owens. He was a second-rate bodybuilder with the physical potential to become a champion, but he didn't have what it takes between the ears or in the heart. Unfortunately, Owens was a walking stereotype of the musclebound oaf.

"You know, of course, what happened to Stella Constantine?" Toby asked me earnestly.

Bells jangled in the back of my head. "A couple of weeks ago, in the newspapers, they were reporting her murder. I remember the details as being pretty graphic, involving rape and torture. The police listed it as a S/M session gone bad when they recovered all the whips and chains from her house. Witnesses stated they'd seen her that night at a local club with a new man on her arm who nobody knew. Description was vague, tall, dark, slender, no further. What does she have to do with Barbarians?"

"She was Barbarians' nutritionist, and Rivers' on-again-off-again mistress. He didn't even show up for the funeral."

"I guess he was in one of the off-again stages." I paused. There was something nagging at me, but I couldn't quite capture it.

I pressed on. "What happened after the segment aired?"

"I gave all my information to the Food and Drug Administration. They started their own investigation and now want to bring Rivers up on charges. The police are also interested, having now linked Rivers to a warrant stemming from the embezzlement charges in Texas. That's all fine and dandy except Rivers is nowhere to be found."

"When did the Barbarians segment air?"

"A month ago. On the 28th to be precise."

I was definitely on a roll now. I could feel it. The 28th was the night Charity disappeared. I brought out the publicity photo of Charity. "Have you seen this girl since the segment was put on the air?"

"No, but I know who she is – Charity Ross. How is she involved?"

"She's missing, and I'm looking. The more I look, the more it seems like she's tied in with this Rivers character."

"Is she in trouble?" Toby's voice had taken on a note of urgency, and I looked at her sharply.

"Not that I know of, but she left her record company with a pile of it."

"I think I have a bomb for you, Blue. Alex Rivers' real name is Appleton Ross!"

The detective business is like swinging at a pinata – sooner or later, the bat is going to connect with the papier-mache and the goodies are going to tumble out.

I spent another hour with Toby going over her research. As we did, a pattern of events rapidly emerged, with the Contrast segment as the catalyst. The TV ratings gave Contrast a 35% share of the viewing audience for Sunday the 28th, about 64 million people tuned in. Charity Ross had only been one of that 64 million, but she was also the only one that recognized Alex Rivers as the father who had abandoned her years before. I wondered if the reunion had gone anything like she anticipated.

After the Contrast segment aired, and the FDA began poking around, Rivers had responded like a true con-man – shutting down his scam, and dropping from view. My concern was that he had taken Charity with him.

There was also something else concerning. The little feeling I hadn't been able to pin down had finally connected up the description of Stella Constantine's killer with the description of the suspect the security guard believed broke into the Barbarians' office.

I asked Toby if she had a current address for Byron Owens. She dug it out of her files and scribbled it on a slip of paper for me. When we parted company, I looked at the note and saw she had added her home phone number in bold red letters. I grinned like a naughty school boy.

Returning to my car, I drove to Woodland Hills – a bedroom community at the west end of the San Fernando Valley. The address Toby had given me for Owens was in a large group of semi-detached townhouses on Topanga Canyon just below the Warner Center. Townhouses, like condominiums, have become all the rage as an alternative to the overpriced conventional housing in LA. Their huddled masses can be found all over the city like acne on a teenager's face.

The units I was interested in were all painted a uniform dull brown. With their identical wood and stucco fronts, I felt sorry for a drunk trying to find his way home in the middle of the night. After a couple of wrong turns, I located Owens' cubicle and knocked on the front door. It was opened almost immediately by a tall effeminate looking youth with a shock of scraggly blond hair. He had a Christmas tree light earring and tinsel draped around his neck.

"My God! Are you a friend of Byron's?" he exclaimed as his eyes roamed all over my body. I suddenly understood about women and lecherous looks. I

209

gave him a hard stare and he took a step backwards.

"Sorry," he said in a more normal voice.

"It's okay. I'd like to talk to Byron if he's in."

"He's down in the recreation room," said the youth pointing a long-nailed finger towards another brown building. "That's where he keeps his weights. Sometimes I think he cares more about his body than mine."

I looked at the kid's slight, willowish frame and wondered what there was to care about. He took my look the wrong way.

"If you decide you'd rather talk to me, I'm at Whiskey Creek on Sepulveda most nights." The lisp had made a comeback.

"Thanks, but I don't go both ways."

"Shame," he said and closed the door.

As I passed the pool on the way to the recreation room, I could hear the familiar crashing of heavy metal weights which goes with weight training. I pushed open the recreation room's sliding glass door and stepped inside.

Owens was totally absorbed on a Nautilus bench press machine. He had 350 lbs held half-way up. His biceps bulged like small mountains, and his pectorals look like coils of heavy rope. I waited as he slowly pushed the weight up and then slowly brought it down again to finish his set. As he lay on the bench, sweat glistening on his skin, breathing returning to normal, I noticed a bottle of cheap vodka under the bench.

"Hi, Byron," I said with an over-accentuated lisp, which I couldn't resist.

He looked up violently, the initial anger in his eyes, however, changed to disinterest when he recognized me. We had never been close, but we had been on talking terms until now.

"I see you've met Larry," he said wearily.

"I just bet he prefers to be called Lawrence. I didn't know you were into boys."

"It isn't something I like to broadcast, and I'd appreciate it if you keep it to yourself."

That was fair enough.

With one hand he picked up the bottle from under the bench and took a long pull from its neck.

"What the hell are you doing?" I was amazed, wondering what kind of effect the alcohol was having on him during the workout let alone any bodybuilding diet.

"Don't even attempt to lecture me, MacKenzie. Especially if you want something. I'll work out my way, you work out yours."

"How did you know I want something?"

"You've got no other reason to come around here. You're just like everyone else. First that reporter bitch, then those pricks from the FDA, then some kid who I don't know from Adam, and now you. It's getting like I should open up shop and charge admission."

At the mention of the unknown kid, I felt the pot on my back burner start to boil over. I waited impatiently for Owens to finish another set on the bench.

"This kid? Was he tall, slender, curly black hair?"

"Yeah."

"What did he want?"

"Same as everyone else. He wanted to know where Alex was."

"Did you tell him?"

"Him, the police, and the FDA. That prick has brought me so much grief, it's only fair he should share some of it."

"When was the kid here? Did he tell you his name?"

Owens took another swig from his bottle. I noticed his eyes were becoming fuzzy around the edges. The pupils were beading up like a mean pig's.

"He was here about two weeks ago. If he told me his name I don't remember it."

That put the kid's visit after Stella Constantine's murder. For some reason I felt a chill run up my spine.

I tried a long shot, "Did Stella Constantine know where Alex was?"

Owens was quiet for a moment, "She loved him, you know – like I did. But when his daughter showed up after seeing that TV show, Stella became jealous. She didn't understand the girl was just a new toy for Alex – that as soon as he got tired of playing daddy, he'd dump the tyke and come back to us. But, because Stella was making such a scene, Alex didn't want her following him, so when he split, he didn't tell her anything."

Even though I didn't know her, I felt a little sick to my stomach at the thought of Stella Constantine in the hands of a torturer who was convinced she had information she didn't have. It can be a fine line between torture and murder, and the presence of the tall, curly headed kid, who was shadowing this entire case, had obviously stepped over that line.

"Where is Alex?" I asked.

"You too, huh? Well, the more the merrier, I guess. He's on his way to Mexico. He has a house there, hidden away on the south bank of Puerto Vallarta. 187 Calle de Pedregal."

"What do you mean on his way?"

"He's taking his time, sailing his boat down there. Said it would give him a chance to catch up with his daughter's life. He was really getting into the role of playing daddy, but my guess is he hoped some of her celebrity would rub off. He isn't due to dock there until tomorrow."

I sat for a few minutes watching Byron take several more slugs from the bottle. I should have been ready for it when it came, but my mind was miles away on a boat headed for Mexico with a con-man and his mixed up daughter, both being chased by an evil of which they were unaware.

I should have been ready for it, but I wasn't.

Byron shot up off the bench and tagged me on the right cheekbone with a clenched fist. I went down like a sack of bricks.

A lot of people equate a bodybuilder's large muscles with slow reflexes and no brains, but you don't ever find those people putting their money where their mouth is because deep down they know the musclebound cliche is a bunch of crap.

Byron was fast, but the alcohol in his system was throwing his balance off. I rolled when I hit the floor, hoping to get to my feet before Byron could hit me again. I wasn't that lucky and received a kick to my ribs which lifted me over to fall flat on my back again.

When the next kick came, I didn't even try to get out of the way. I just took it hard on the flexed muscles of my rib cage, and then locked the foot against its point of impact by wrapping my arm around it and capturing it in the crook of my elbow. Then I rolled inward toward my attacker.

As off balance as he was, with his foot trapped against me, Byron fell out of the sky like a giant sequoia. As he hit the hardwood floor of the recreation room with a dust raising thud, I released his foot and continued to roll until I was out from under his legs.

I bounded to my feet, ready to tear his head off, adrenaline flowing like electricity through my body, but it was all over. Byron lay on the floor, curled into a fetal position trying to gain control of a crying jag.

"I didn't know about the steroids, man, or the kids he was ripping-off." Tears rolled down his cheeks as he spoke. "I wasn't smart enough to be great like you. I was just happy to be working. I didn't ask any questions."

Neither did Hitler's henchmen, but if that was Byron's alibi I'd let him be happy with it. I rubbed the hot spot which was swelling on my cheek and walked out. On the way out of the complex, I knuckled the door of Byron's unit again. Lawrence answered.

"Oooh, look at you," he said observing my war wound.

"He needs you," I said, foregoing any smart replies.

Lawrence stared at me for a second and then took off down the path to the recreation room without another word. He'd left the door to the unit open, so I pulled it shut with enough force to damn near tear it off its hinges. All that pent up adrenaline had to go somewhere.

I checked in with Max and brought him up to date. He could pass word along to Stein. I could have talked directly to Stein, but it was easier dealing through Max. That way I didn't have to waste time being tactful with a client's feelings.

Max and I agreed that if we notified the police or the FDA of Rivers' whereabouts, they would just wait for him to come back stateside. A delay wouldn't affect their criminal case against Rivers, but it certainly wouldn't help my client get his singing star back.

There was also the specter of the tall, curly haired kid. If he had killed Stella Constantine to get to Rivers, as my gut feeling told me, he wouldn't let something like a short trip to Mexico stop him. I didn't care a damn about what happened to Rivers, but if the con-man ran true to form, he wouldn't hesitate to put Charity in the line of fire if he found himself cornered.

Max immediately authorized additional expense funds and booked me a flight to Mexico via Areonaves Airlines. It was white knight time.

The next morning, I packed my passport and my amour, mounted a silver winged stallion, and charged off in pursuit of a distressed damsel, a con-man, and a psychopathic windmill.

I rented a Jeep from the Hertz counter in Puerto Vallarta and headed down Airport Road toward town. After the movie studios had featured it as the background for the film Night of the Iguana with Liz Taylor, the once sleepy village had turned into a mecca for the garish tourists who flocked to soak in the sun and wander down the twisting cobblestone streets.

The steep hillsides, covered with dense tropical foliage, provided precarious perches for homes and shops. From a distance the many red tiled roofs looked like the beautiful blossoms of an ever climbing bougainvillaea. The natural charm and beauty of the area was helped along by the Christmas lights and decorations blooming like out of season flowers.

I drove across the Cuale River on the two lane bridge which connects Puerto Vallarta's industrial north bank with the white beaches and tourist traps of the south side. The bedlam wasn't any less than that of a big city rush hour. I dusted off my rusty Spanish, which was as passable as several other languages I'd picked up in my shady past, and received directions. I've found local residents are always surprised and flattered when you speak their language.

When the traffic eased, I picked up speed past the major shopping center along Lazaro Cardenes, refused to detour through the Zona Roja – Puerto Vallarta's red light district – and followed the river along a narrow twisting trail with perilous drops down boulder strewn ravines at every switchback.

I was beginning to think my directions were wrong when the houses clinging tenaciously to the ravine walls began to get more and more luxurious. I had entered the area the locals refer to derisively as Gringo Gulch, because of the large amount of rich Americans who maintain homes there.

If the residence at 187 Calle Pedregal was any indication, the con-game had been good to Appleton Ross, or Alex Rivers, or whatever he was calling himself in this part of the world. A more likely scenario, however, was that the house and the boat he sailed – which I had verified docked that morning by calling the harbor master's office from the airport – were all part of another elaborate scheme.

I drove passed the 187 address, a rambling, ranch style hacienda done in white stucco, and parked a hundred yards up the road. I got out of the jeep, rescued my camera bag, and removed the lead lined bag I use to get my film safely through the customs' X-ray machines. I also use it to get my derringer safely through the X-ray machines. I checked the load in the gun and tucked it safely away in its familiar holster under the lightweight windbreaker I was wearing. I locked up and headed toward the house.

The grounds were surrounded on three sides by six-foot high, white stucco walls. A wrought-iron arch spanned the gateless gap which formed the front entrance. The house was unapproachable from the rear, as it was nestled deeply into a natural cleft in the ravine wall. Across the street from the front of the house, the world fell away down a sheer drop to one of the many watery arteries which fed the cuale.

A tiled red roof capped the one story building in the traditional Mexican fashion, and white wrought-iron had been used to form a trellis for the blue jacaranda which clung to the exterior walls. Large carved, hardwood doors defined the entrance to the house, and an old bell with a wooden clanger hung silently beneath a stucco arch above the doors.

Dusk had fallen, and I caught a trace of jasmine in the breeze. I tried to think of a fancy ploy to get inside the house, but I eventually decided there was nothing to be lost by trying a direct approach.

I kept one eye on the deepening shadows as I approached the entrance, but there appeared to be nothing more sinister than a large crow who startled at my approach. I found no reassurance in finding no trace of the presence of the tall, dark, curly haired shadow who had been ahead of me the whole case.

My knock on the door was answered by a stocky Mexican woman in a flowing black gauze dress which had been enlivened with red and blue embroidery. She had a ready smile, but her carriage marked her as the housekeeper.

"Buenas noches, senora. Podria hablar con el Senor que vive en la casa, por favor?" I enquired.

"Your Spanish is very good, senor, but my English is better," she said.

"Si, senora, es muy bueno." I smiled at her.

"Who shall I tell Senor Raven is calling?" she asked, smiling back.

"My name is Blue MacKenzie." If we kept on smiling at each other someone was going to mistake us for a couple of happy-face pins.

The woman stepped back to allow me to enter the hacienda's lobby and asked me to wait while she spoke with Senor Raven. Ross, Rivers, Raven. Maybe he took a perverse pleasure in retaining his initials, some kind of private joke on the world.

I watched the maid walk down the hall and turn into a den type room on the left. I decided to forget my manners and followed her without waiting to be announced.

I didn't know what to expect, but what I found was evidence the father and daughter reunion was not all smooth sailing. Charity was there, sitting on a lumpy floral couch pushed up against the left wall where it had caused a small wear mark in the grass cloth wallpaper. Her punkish hair had grown out some. It now laid flat and lifeless across her skull. Her eyes were red and puffy from crying, and she was systematically shredding a tissue in her hands.

Raven, or Ross as I had come to think of him, was standing by a large picture window with a drink in his hand. His bulky frame was slightly stooped, his hound dog features softened by the room's dim lights.

"Who the hell are you?" he snapped when I walked in. The housekeeper turned around sharply, anger flaring across her features because I hadn't waited. I put on my best smile.

"Hello, Charity. I've been looking for you," I said gently. She looked up at me from the couch like a scared rabbit.

"I asked you a question, Mister, and I want an answer!" Ross' voice had a slightly drunken blur to it. I turned toward him.

"I've been looking for you too, Ross," I said, still ignoring his question. The use of his real name, however, put a befuddled look on his face.

"He said his name was Blue MacKenzie when he came to the door." The housekeeper's voice was full of scorn, almost as if she expected me to be a liar as well as bad mannered.

"Muchas gracias, senora," I said without turning to face her, my eyes locked onto Ross. "Would you please leave us. Senor Raven and I have business to discuss."

She didn't like being told what to do in what she obviously considered her own house. I continued to stare down Ross until he waved the woman away.

"Yes, yes. Go on, Carmella. Everything is okay. Thank you." I felt the daggers of her eyes piercing my back as I listened to her withdraw from the room with a swirl of her skirt.

I reached into my windbreaker and pulled out the subpoena Stein had given me. "Nightsong Records wants you to come home, Charity," I said handing her the paper. When she didn't take it I dropped it in her lap. "In fact they want you bad enough to subpoena you to court." She didn't say anything, but I sensed I had just kicked out the foundation from an already shaky house of cards.

"That subpoena is no good down here, MacKenzie, or whatever your name is!" Ross said gruffly, his voice rising to form the exclamation point.

"It is if she ever wants to go back to the States without a contempt of court warrant waiting for her," I said. "And as far as you're concerned, Ross, I think I'll take you back with me as well. There are a couple of organizations who want a crack at you, and I dislike your methods enough to enable them to take one."

"You're crazy! What makes you think you can walk in here and take over?"

"I guess I'm just that kind of guy. A real A-type personality. If you're thinking of giving me a bad time, I'll contact the local federales and let them know about the warrants for your arrest. You can spend Christmas in the rat pit they call a jail waiting for extradition." I was reaching, but it's easy to con a con-man because they believe it can't be done.

Ross looked like he was going to explode. I thought for a moment he was going to do something stupid like rush me, but the tension was suddenly broken by the sound of the housekeeper's scream, which was suddenly cut short.

We all turned to look at the doorway to the den we were in and I felt like I was waiting for the other shoe to drop. Framed in the door jamb was the curly headed enigma I had known in my bones would turn up like a bad penny.

He was holding Carmella in front of him, one arm around her throat. Ugly red finger marks were beginning to glow on her right cheek. He suddenly pushed her forward into the room, revealing a .357 Magnum clutched in his other hand. It looked like a sleeping giant. I spared a glance at Ross who just looked confused.

"Don't you recognize me, Appleton?"

"Who?"

"Tommy Vreeling, you bastard! I'm not surprised you don't remember me. It's been a long time, but here I am." Vreeling's voice was filled with a lunatic tremor, which was reflected in his eyes but not in his steady gun hand. In the flesh, Vreeling was as wiry and tall as my imagination had made him. He was wearing a white tee shirt tucked into stove pipe Levis, and a brown bomber jacket which was as scarred as a gnarled oak.

"What are you doing here, Tommy?" Ross seemed to have sobered instantly.

"Isn't it obvious? I've come to kill you." This was delivered in a soft monotone, like an epitaph.

"What are you talking about?" Ross was frantic. "Back in Texas, I used to bounce you on my knee when you were small. What reason could you possibly have to kill me?"

"Reasons!" Vreeling yelled and we all jumped. "My father used to bounce me on his knee too until you killed him. He thought you were a big man – as big as all Texas – and then you turned on him and killed him. So I'm going to finally kill you."

"Don't be ridiculous, Tommy," Ross' voice was beginning to crack. "Your father committed suicide."

The gun in Vreeling's hand started to jerk around like it had a life of its own. "Don't you dare call me ridiculous, Ross. My father killed himself because you milked him dry and ran out on him. You may as well have pulled the trigger yourself for all the difference it made. I've waited a long time to track you down, and then I saw you on TV in your swanky suits and executive offices – ripping other people off just like you ripped my father off when you stole the business blind and left him to hold the bag."

I could see his finger begin to whiten. "Don't do it, Tommy." Even though I spoke quietly my voice startled him, as if he had been unaware there was anyone else in the room. "He's not worth it. Let the police handle it. I know you think you've got nothing to lose after killing Stella Constantine, but I know someone who can help." I hoped Max would forgive me.

Vreeling's gun swung toward me, which wasn't what I considered an improvement.

"What are you talking about?" Tommy asked. "I didn't kill that broad. She couldn't tell me where Ross was so I dumped her. Who said I killed her?"

So much for my deductive reasoning and gut feelings.

Ross chuckled. "You're a fool, MacKenzie. Look Tommy, I'll make everything up to you somehow. Kill this ape and we can talk about it. I loved you, Tommy, you were like a son to me. You've got your facts confused is all. Give me time to explain things."

Warrants pending Stateside weren't enough for Ross to want me dead. There was another reason which had become abundantly clear.

"Maybe I'm the one with my facts confused," I said. The gun was still pointing at me, the entrance to the barrel looking like the Holland Tunnel. I tore my eyes away from it and concentrated on Tommy. Neutralize him, and the gun was useless. "If Tommy didn't kill Stella then you must have done it, Ross. What happened? Did one of your sicko sex sessions get a little out of hand? Didn't she want you to go sailing with Charity – your new toy as you called her?" Out of the corner of my eye I finally saw a reaction from Charity. She jumped as if she'd been pinched.

"Shut up, MacKenzie!" Ross yelled. "It was a mistake. She liked being beat up. She called me before I left with Charity and said she needed to talk. When I got to her apartment she threatened to call the police and turn me in unless I left Charity and brought her here instead. I hit her and she laughed at me. I hit her again and again, but she just kept laughing until she was dead. Killing Stella was a mistake, but killing you won't be. Do it, Tommy – shoot him now. I'll make everything up to you."

Tommy wavered in a state of mental confusion. I was getting ready to do something, anything. Anything but stand there and die. But Tommy had been living with his obsession too long and he finally swung his gun back toward Ross.

"How can you make up for a lifetime of being without a father? You weren't even one to your own daughter." The gun came up into a two handed grip and Tommy spread his feet into a secure stance.

A professional does all his talking with his weapons, never giving a victim a chance. A psychotic bent on revenge like Tommy Vreeling, however, needs to verbalize the deed. His pleasure comes not in the killing but in watching the victim squirm.

While Tommy talked, I had moved slightly, putting a low coffee table between us. With my right foot, I viciously shoved it across the tile floor into Tommy's shins. I followed behind the table, my entire two-hundred-and-seventy-five pound frame slamming into the potential killer like a defensive cornerback trying to destroy an offensive receiver.

Air whooshed out of Tommy's lungs and the gun flew across the room on wings. He went like a rag doll in my grasp. As we fell to the floor, I smacked my head against the door jamb. I hung onto Tommy, pinning his arms, while my head spun and I fought to remain conscious.

The sound of a shot penetrated the fog behind my eyes, and self preservation kicked in. I propelled off the floor and into the hallway, snatching my Derringer from its holster. I peered around the bottom of the door frame.

Vreeling was out cold, but it was Charity who drew my attention. She was holding the ugly Magnum out in both hands at arm's length. Smoke drifted almost nonchalantly from the barrel. I looked to where she had the gun aimed and saw her father sprawled across a wicker chair, his right shoulder a red pulsing mess.

I thought for a second, she was going to shoot again. Instead she started to cry, hysterical sobs wracking her body. The gun dropped to the floor. I crossed the room and put my arms around her.

"It's okay. It's over."

"When I was a child," she spoke through her tears, almost inaudibly because her face was pressed into my chest, "I never knew why he left. I thought it was because he didn't love me anymore because of the glass I broke the day he didn't come home. After all these years I still wanted to be forgiven. When I found him again, I was happy just to be around him. He talked of all the things we would do together to make up for the lost years.

"When he asked me to sail to Mexico with him, I couldn't believe it. It was better than I had ever imagined. I couldn't tell Harry where I was going because Daddy was in so much trouble. He convinced me that if I told anyone I was with him, they would tell the police and I would lose him again. I didn't care what he'd done. I had a father again."

"But then he ruined it. He got drunk on the boat and started to slap me around. He said all his problems were my fault because I had so much money and had never helped him. He started to scream at me and then – he – then he ripped my clothes off and... and... My own father!" She started to pummel my chest with her tiny fists. "I hate him! I hate him!" She stopped struggling

217

and began to cry steadily. All I wanted was to be forgiven.

Carmella came over and took Charity from my arms. I checked Ross. He was losing blood, but still alive. I made like Florence Nightingale and then called for an ambulance from the phone in the hall. I also called the police, but only after I had called Max who promised to contact an efficient local lawyer with enough mordida money to get Charity and me back on American soil in a hurry.

Finally, I walked back to the den and settled down to wait.

Life was not pleasant. Somehow, I doubted Harry Stein was going to get his CD on the racks in time for the Christmas rush, but that was a problem I could do nothing about.

I had done what I'd been hired to do.

I tried thinking happy thoughts.

I wasn't the one who'd been naughty.

I'd been nice.

Toby Wainwright was still at the top of my Christmas list. As I waited, I wondered if she had plans for Christmas Eve. ★

About the authors...

STORMY BARTON APGAR

Stormy spent 18 years in law enforcement as an officer with the Cheyenne, Wyoming, Police Department, a Sheriff's Deputy/Narcotics Agent in northwest Montana, and a State Trooper – her favorite job so far. She has taught at the Montana Law Enforcement Academy, the Wyoming Highway Patrol Academy, Flathead Valley Community College, Sheridan College and the University of Wyoming where she's tried to pass on her philosophy that it takes integrity, compassion and a sense of humor to be a truly professional law enforcement officer. She is currently practicing law and teaching at the University of Wyoming in Laramie. She lives near Buffalo, Wyoming, with her husband and an assortment of dogs, horses, cats, geese and wild antelope.

WILLIAM BELL

Twenty-two year veteran officer William Bell has been a university police officer, small town cop, housing authority patrolman, Kentucky state parole and probation officer, New Orleans deputy sheriff, a US Border Patrol agent in New Mexico and a US Customs agent in southern California. He has been with Customs for the past 11 years in Kentucky and Indiana and is now a supervisory inspector in Indianapolis, Indiana. He has had nearly 100 articles published in *Guns & Weapons for Law Enforcement*, *Combat Handguns*, *Glock Annual*, and *Guns of the Old West* as well as *Police*, *The Police Marksman*, *Customs Today*, the NRA's *American Guardian*, and *The Cowboy Chronicle*.

KEITH BETTINGER

Keith Bettinger and his wife Lynn live in Huntington Station, New York, with their three sons and a menagerie of pets. Keith retired as a Suffolk County, New York, police officer in 1991. During his time on the department he received numerous awards including the departmental Bravery Medal, the Silver Shield Award (Police Officer of the Year) from the Suffolk County PBA and the Police Act Award from the Suffolk County Police Conference. Keith holds a Master's Degree in Clinical Counseling. His proudest accomplishment was starting a peer support group for officers involved in shootings. He spends his retirement traveling and writing for numerous law enforcement publications.

✗ PAUL BISHOP

Paul Bishop is a 23-year veteran of the Los Angeles Police Department where he has twice been honored as Detective of the Year. He currently supervises the Sex Crimes and Major Assault Crimes units in West Los Angeles. Paul is the author of nine published novels, including *Kill Me Again*, *Twice Dead*, *Tequila Mockingbird* and *Chalk Whispers* in his current series of LAPD crime novels featuring homicide detective Fey Croaker. Paul also writes for such episodic television series as *Diagnosis: Murder*.

PHILIP BULONE

Philip V. Bulone is a retired New York City Police Department Detective and former State of Florida Tax Fraud Investigator. He operates a private investigation agency and teaches security and investigative courses in Boynton Beach, Florida. Phil has written articles on a variety of police related issues which have been published in several newspapers in South Florida and police related publications. He lives in Boynton Beach with his wife Mary and son John. Phil is working on two police related novels.

✠ ROBERT COHEN

A former US Navy officer, Bob Cohen joined the New York City Transit Police in 1985. He worked in Brooklyn, Queens and Manhattan, rising to the rank of lieutenant by the time of the merger with the New York City Police Department ten years later. He's currently a captain in the NYPD. Bob has written columns and feature articles for the *Queens Chronicle*, the *Tin Can Sailor* and the *Watersider*. He's recently completed a collection of humorous vignettes and short stories titled *War Stories: New York City Transit Police*. Bob lives in Queens, New York, with his wife and children.

WILL CORDES

Born in Springfield, Massachusetts, Will Cordes was raised in Atlanta, Georgia, where he served for 22 years with the DeKalb County Police Department and Sheriff's Office. He retired as a captain with the sheriff's office in 1996 and moved to Missoula, Montana, where he is now resident agent with the Montana Department of Justice Division of Criminal Investigation (DCI). He is a 1992 graduate of the FBI National Academy and a member of the "Possible Club." Will has written four police procedural novels and is currently working on three more. His articles have appeared in *The Single Shot Exchange, Tactical Shooter, The Police Times* and *the Georgia Gun Owner*.

ED DEE

Yonkers, New York, native Ed Dee grew up in the city's west-side projects. He spent 20 years on the NYPD walking the streets of the South Bronx and supervising detectives in the Organized Crime Control Bureau before retiring as a lieutenant with a suitcase full of stories he had to write. He left Fordham Law School to obtain an MFA in creative writing. His master's thesis became his first novel. He is the author of four novels, *14 Peck Slip, Bronx Angel, Little Boy Blue* and *Nightbird*, published in 1999 by Warner Books. Ed lives in Delaware with his wife Nancy. He has two daughters and four grandchildren.

JIM DEFILIPPI

Jim DeFilippi was born and raised in Duck Alley, New York, a small neighborhood on Long Island. He became a military policeman in 1969 and, after his discharge, went to northern Vermont to write and teach school. He is married with two grown children. He has published two novels, *Blood Sugar* and *Duck Alley*. He was nominated for "Best Short Story of the Year" at the International World Mystery Convention.

LIZ MARTÍNEZ DEFRANCO

Before Liz pursued a full-time career as a professional writer and editor, she worked as an optician and optical instructor. She has served as the executive editor of several consumer and trade magazines and is the author of *The Retail Manager's Guide to Crime Prevention*. She has also worked in the criminal justice system including pre-trial services for jail inmates and a short stint with the Bureau of Export Enforcement. However, she has industriously avoided taking a job that might require her to begin work before 10am. She has also been an Auxiliary Police Officer with NYPD where the department thoroughly trained her to dial 911 in case of an emergency.

ERNIE DORLING

Ernie Dorling was a Special Agent with the Bureau of Alcohol, Tobacco and Firearms and is now a supervisory Special Agent with the Defense Criminal Investigative Service. He was also a police officer with the Hollywood, Florida, Police Department. Ernie has written several academic articles and has recently completed his first non-fiction book, *With Consciousness of Guilt*. Ernie has worked as a federal agent since 1978 with assignments in Washington, DC and Germany where he completed his Masters Degree in Public Administration. He lives in Connecticut.

JOHN ELLER

John Eller has been in law enforcement for more than 30 years serving as the Chief of Police in Woodbury Heights, NewJersey, from 1973 through 1981. He has been the chief of police in Brookhaven, Pennsylvania, since 1981. Eller has been a certified police instructor in both New Jersey and Pennsylvania and taught at the Burlington County and New Jersey Police academies and the Delaware County and Philadelphia police academies. He writes weekly columns for local newspapers and is the police columnist for *9-1-1 Magazine*.

ARTHUR JAMES FARRAR

AJ Farrar has more than 30 years of experience in military, state and local law enforcement. Before retiring as a lieutenant from the Ventura, California, Police Department in 1993, AJ served in a variety of line and staff assignments and as both a pre-service and in-service instructor/coordinator/manager of training and educational services. AJ holds master's degrees in criminology/law enforcement and management and advanced California Police Officer (POST) certificates in supervision and management. Since his retirement, he has provided management, training and security consultation for a variety of public and private organizations and written articles on a variety of law enforcement topics.

ROGER FULTON

Roger Fulton is the president of the Police Writers Club and the editor of their newsletter, *The Police Writer*. Roger is the author of three successful books, *Common Sense Supervision*, *Common Sense Leadership* and *The Practical Police Manager*. He writes a regular column and articles on police management and training for *Law Enforcement Technology* magazine. He has also had articles published in more than a dozen other law enforcement publications, as well as providing published articles and reports on writing and getting published. Roger holds a Ph.D. in criminal justice management and is a graduate of the FBI's National Academy. He is a retired Captain with the New York State Police.

GINA GALLO

Chicago has a Great Lake, great food and great stories from its citizens. As one of the Windy City's finest, Gina Gallo has been a Chicago police officer since 1988. She has worked as a tactical officer and had assignments in the Gun Task Force, Public Housing, Mass Transit and Prostitution and Gangs. Her regular column, *Sworn Secrets*, appears in two police magazines. Gina is a frequent contributor to various publications in the US and Great Britain. Her first book, *Armed and Dangerous: Memoirs of a Chicago Cop*, will be published by Forge Books in 2000. After completing a subsequent novel about the Gangs Unit, Gina is working on her third book.

LAURICK INGRAM

Laurick Ingram was born in Opa-locka, Florida, a welfare baby and the youngest of eleven children. In his 14 years as a police officer he has worked as an expert witness in street narcotics and received 82 commendations, two medals of valor and one officer of the year award. He now specializes in cyber crime. He is a regular contributor to newsletters and trade publications, is an avid reader and graduate of the Writer's Digest School of Novel Writing. He is married, has two sons and an indefatigable drive to write, rewrite and write some more.

PENNY JAMES

Penny James is an internationally recognized forensic fire photographer who has been both the managing and a contributing editor of the Fire Photographers Journal. She also serves as the Region 6 Director for the International Fire Photographers Association and is part of a technical search and rescue team consisting of six suburban fire departments. She worked both the Murrah Federal Building bombing in Oklahoma City, Oklahoma, and the F5 tornado in May 1999. After writing many articles on various aspects of fire photography, Penny has turned to the fictional side of the literary world.

MARLENE LOOS

Marlene Loos has been a Suffolk County Police Officer in Long Island, New York, for six years. She has the dubious honor of being the first female officer shot in the line of duty in Long Island's history. Writing has been a major part of her recovery. Marlene holds a master of arts degree in Humanities from Hofstra University. She has co-authored an article accepted for publication by Mademoiselle magazine and is completing her first manuscript.

DAN MAHONEY

Novelist Dan Mahoney was born in Manhattan five minutes after Steven King was born in Maine, an omen he considers a good one. The oldest of five children, Mahoney worked as a machinist and auto mechanic before enlisting in the Marines at 17 and then joining the NYPD. During his 20-year stint as a patrolman and detective, he also received a BA in romance languages and held a part-time job as Yoko Ono's security chief. Mahoney retired from the

NYPD as a captain in 1989, signed on with a detective agency, and started writing. His first book, Detective First Grade, was published in 1993, followed by Edge of the City, Hyde and Once In, Never Out. His fifth novel, Black and White was published in 1999. He lives on Long Island with his wife Yvette, an NYPD officer, and his son Kevin. In addition to skiing and traveling, Mahoney likes to hang out with his old pals in Manhattan bars, where they spend many hours telling each other stories about what great cops they were.

MARILYN OLSEN

For the past 14 years, Marilyn Olsen has been the editor and principal writer of the 84-page quarterly magazine, Indiana's Finest, published by the Indiana State Police Alliance. In that time she has published more than 400 articles on law enforcement-related issues. She has just completed the introduction to an upcoming book on the nation's 49 state police agencies and is writing a book on the history of the Indiana State Police.

CHARLES PADIAS

Charles E. "Ed" Padias, is a retired commander from the Los Angeles County Sheriff's Department, where he had extensive experience in all phases of law enforcement including patrol, detectives, administration and internal affairs. Training Ride is a modified version of a chapter in Ed's completed novel, Drawing the Line, which is to be the first of a series. He is currently seeking an agent for his second novel. He and his wife, Nancy, live in Tehachapi, California.

LOUIS A. SAVELLI

Lou Savelli, a resident of Brooklyn, New York, is the father of a wonderful daughter, Kristiana, 9, who he says brightens his every day. He is a supervisor with NYPD's Gang Investigation Squad and the cofounder and first vice president of the East Coast Gang Investigator's Association. He has authored several law enforcement related articles and gang intelligence handbooks. He lectures extensively on law enforcement related topics and is currently working on a book on crime prevention and a book on gangs.

ROBERT SHAW

Robert B. Shaw, Chief Warrant Officer, US Army, Retired, served 35 years in Army law enforcement. His assignments took him around the world to Asia, Europe, the Caribbean and several major military installations in the US. His primary focus on conducting and supervising felony investigations for the Army's Criminal Investigation Division was interrupted for a decade-long stint in the CID's crime laboratory as one of only a few court-qualified Army forensic photographers. He lives in a dense forest at Pebble Beach, California, resolutely refusing to play golf.

PAMELIA STRATTON

Born and raised in Lexington, Kentucky, Pamelia S. Stratton received an undergraduate degree from the University of Kentucky in elementary education and kindergarten and a master's degree from the University of Tennessee in Urban Planning. She spent six years working for an aviation consulting firm in Cincinnati, Ohio, conducting environmental and economic impact statements for airport development projects and then became a Special Agent for the FBI in 1981. In the past 18 years she has served in the Cincinnati, Fort Myers, Florida and Philadelphia offices of the FBI. She is just beginning her writing and screenwriting careers.

JOSEPH TRUNCALE

Joseph J. Truncale was a career police officer for 29 years, retiring in 1995. He has more the 300 articles, essays, poems and reviews published as well as more than 35 books and manuals. A columnist for three publications, he has also been the publisher and editor of three newsletters, *The Street Warrior*, *The Samurai Heart* and *The Rational Thinker*. Only *The Samurai Heart* is still being published at this time.

JAMES WEISS

James (Jim) Weiss was a US Army military police officer in Germany and then a patrolman, sergeant and lieutenant and platoon leader with the Brook Park, Ohio, Police Department where he made more than 3,000 non-traffic arrests. He received a BA in Police Studies at Capital University and a degree from Police Executive Leadership College at Ohio State University. After retirement Jim worked as a child abuse investigator for the state of Florida. He now freelance writes for police magazines.

THE POLICE WRITERS CLUB

The Police Writers Club is open to writers of fiction and nonfiction, illustrators, photographers, cartoonists, editors and publishers of police-related publications. Both published and unpublished writers are welcome.

Membership benefits include:
- Getting Started Booklet: The 30-page Sharing Your Expertise-Writing for Law Enforcement Publications, takes you through the writing and publishing process step-by-step from idea to final payment.
- One Year Newsletter Subscription: The Police Writer, published quarterly, includes news, research, marketplace information, writing tips and tips from fellow members.
- Membership Certificate: Each member receives a formal membership certificate, suitable for framing.
- Publications List: This list includes information on more than 50 police magazines, journals, newspapers and specialty newsletters that may accept articles from free-lance police writers.
- Police Writers Directory: The PWC maintains a directory of our published writers' biographies for release to interested publishers and editors. It is sent to the top ten law enforcement publications in the US.
- Networking: Whatever your needs, you can find information, guidance and support from our multi-talented membership and staff.
- Other Resources: Access to a list of criminal justice nonfiction book publishers, trusted editorial, reader and critiquing services, criminal justice video and screenplay producers and more.
- Opportunity for corporate sponsorship. Each corporate sponsor receives a free advertising listing in each quarterly issue of The Police Writer

To join, contact
The Police Writers Club
PO Box 416
Hayes, VA 23072
or Policewriter.com.

ABOUT .38 SPECIAL PRESS

This anthology was published by .38 Special Press, a publishing house created by a group of police writers who met through the Police Writers Club. .38 Special Press helps writers, particularly those who have not had a book previously published, through the publishing process including manuscript review, editing, design, printing, distribution and marketing. We review manuscripts at no charge and then suggest ways in which the resulting book may be published in the most efficient and cost effective way possible.

If you would like more information about .38 Special Press, please contact us at:

.38 Special Press
6251 Winthrop Avenue, Suite 2
Indianapolis, IN 46220
(317) 254-1221

ORDER FORM

To order copies of CopTales 2000, please complete this form:

Name _____

Address_____

City/State/Zip_____

Daytime Telephone (   ) _____

Please send me _____ copies of CopTales 2000 at $22.95 each
($18.95 plus $4.00 postage and handling) Indiana residents add 5% Sales Tax

I enclose a check for $_____, made payable to .38 Special Press.

☐ I would like to send copies to other addresses. I have included the information on the other side of this form.

Mail this order and your check to:
CopTales 2000
c/o .38 Special Press
6251 Winthrop Avenue, Suite 2
Indianapolis, IN 46220

ORDER FORM

To order copies of CopTales 2000, please complete this form:

Name _____

Address_____

City/State/Zip_____

Daytime Telephone (   ) _____

Please send me _____ copies of CopTales 2000 at $22.95 each
($18.95 plus $4.00 postage and handling) Indiana residents add 5% Sales Tax

I enclose a check for $_____, made payable to .38 Special Press.

☐ I would like to send copies to other addresses. I have included the information on the other side of this form.

Mail this order and your check to:
CopTales 2000
c/o .38 Special Press
6251 Winthrop Avenue, Suite 2
Indianapolis, IN 46220

Please send additional copies of CopTales 2000 to

Name _____

Address _____

City/State/Zip _____

Name _____

Address _____

City/State/Zip _____

Name _____

Address _____

City/State/Zip _____

☐ My check for these books is enclosed.

Please send additional copies of CopTales 2000 to

Name _____

Address _____

City/State/Zip _____

Name _____

Address _____

City/State/Zip _____

Name _____

Address _____

City/State/Zip _____

☐ My check for these books is enclosed.